bad dog's diary: Blake's progress

First published in hardback in the United Kingdom in 2008 by
Portico
10 Southcombe Street
London
W14 0RA

An imprint of Anova Books Company Ltd

This paperback edition published 2009

ISBN 9781906032753

A CIP catalogue record for this book is available from the British Library.

10 9 8 7 6 5 4 3 2 1

Printed and bound by WS Bookwell, Finland

This book can be ordered direct from the publisher at
www.anovabooks.com

Martin Howard

bad dog's diary: Blake's progress

Another year in the life of Blake:
lover ... father ... HERO

PORTICO

JANUARY

Thursday, January 1

A surreal but promising start to the year that began with the Owner*
reeling through the door about three hours before dawn, smelling
even worse than usual and howling like a dog. Not that he's ever
been what you'd call stylish, but on this occasion he'd abandoned his
fashion sense completely. He was wearing a pair of ragged trousers
and had a mouthful of plastic fangs as well as what appeared to be a
large amount of glue-on hair, like an all-over body wig. Behind him
was Samantha, his mate, who had grown a large pair of wings.
Unlike the idiot Owner she had complete control of her gangly
limbs, and didn't – for example – trip over my food bowl, lurch across
the kitchen, and end up sprawled across the basket I'd just vacated to
administer the licks and barks of a superbly executed 'welcome
home' routine. She also seemed just a touch impatient with him.

'Time for bed, Mr Wolf,' she barked.

'No' so fast,' said the Owner, putting his arm around me and
Coleridge the puppy, who began quietly humping while Ella
(Samantha's dog and my mate-for-life) sniffed at the weird hair that
covered him. 'As alpha male round here, I muss' commune with my
pack.'

Samantha sighed and left, while the Owner settled himself more
comfortably in my basket, apparently not minding that he was being
basted in the combined dribble of three dogs.

'As your glorious leader and provider of the daily tin of smelly
meaty things, I have to tell ya' I love youse guys,' the werewolf
slurred. 'You're my bess' frien's in the whole wide worl'.'

This was a pleasant surprise. Usually he spends most of his time
complaining about us. And when I say 'us' I mean 'me'.

* Although, strictly speaking, he is technically my 'Master' I prefer to
think of that term as an empty, old-fashioned honorific, like 'beadle'
or 'burgomaster', that should only be used on formal occasions.
'Owner' is more than good enough for everyday use. Some would
say even that unacceptably reinforces the servile nature of the
canine–human relationship, though in my opinion that's political
correctness gone mad. Besides, when servility was being handed out
I must have been at the back of the queue.

'Now, I know relayshons have not always been so good between man and beast in this houshehold. And I am by no means singlinging you out here, Blake, because Coleridge is mostly a little bastar' too. But it's a Happy New Year, and I wanchoo to know tha' isss all goin' to be different. I love my dogs. Gonna shout it from the washamacallits . . . pointy things on top of houses. Loofas? Roof tops . . . No, no, tha' doesn' mean you can put your tongue in my mouth Ella . . . Iss gonna be steak all the way this year, boys . . . and girl, sorry Ella.'

And then he passed out.

By the time Samantha came down carrying the telephone it was late morning. Coleridge – never the most continent of puppies – had not been able to contain himself and the Owner was now slumped across my bed with his head resting on Ella and his lower half in a pool of Coleridge's pee. The spotty puppy was chewing on the plastic fangs that he'd plucked from the Owner's slack and snoring mouth.

'No, he can't speak now I'm afraid,' Samantha was saying into the phone. 'Why's that? Well, I suppose because he's still dressed as a werewolf and lying unconscious in the dog's basket and a puddle of urine . . . Yes, I know. You don't have to tell me I should never have moved in . . . Yes, he is completely useless. Anyway, someone had better take care of *all* the animals. I'll tell him to phone his mother when he comes round, shall I? It will probably be next week sometime.'

For someone who made such big promises he failed to deliver spectacularly for the rest of the day, even after the application of some encouraging tongue and a wet nose as he woke up. A very unsatisfactory walk to the wasteland with Samantha and no sign yet of the promised steak, though to be fair the shops are all closed. I expect he'll get round to it tomorrow. Didn't see much of him for the rest of the day, but I celebrated the New Year in style by curling up with Ella in front of the fire and pressing my nose to my own sphincter then farting. Life just does not get any better.

Friday, January 2

Blake's Revised New Year Resolutions

1. While I have a quiet affection for the Owner and greatly admire his skilful handling of the tin opener, it is quite clear that as an alpha male he is deficient in certain departments. For example, in matters pertaining to hearing, smelling, biting, general alertness, and a primeval killer instinct he is sadly lacking. It's not his fault and I've found that if I don't expect much from Monkey Boy then I won't be disappointed, but as Samantha is expecting a small human it falls to the proud progeny of wolves to guard the den. Me, in fact.

2. Take a firm paw with Coleridge. As a Dalmatian–West Highland Scots terrier cross he's a little confused about his identity. After all, it's not the most comfortable mix for a dog. One half of his heritage is posh fashion accessory, the other is bred for vermin control. So far as I can tell, I'm a perfect blend of 64 separate breeds, so am in a good position to help him find his inner dog.

3. If sincere (and that promised steak has yet to materialise), the Owner's drunken offer of a clean slate in canine–human relations demands some kind of goodwill gesture in response. While admitting no previous fault or blame, I have identified the following areas where an alternative approach might be conducive to a more harmonious living environment:

   a. Stop knocking over cups of coffee, glasses of wine, etc. with tail.

   b. ~~Wait patiently to be fed. Do not trip him over, yelp, jump up at, whine, bark, paw at cupboard door, run round in excited circles, or otherwise be 'annoying'.~~ As if.

   c. ~~Wait patiently to be taken for walks. Do not trip him over, yelp, jump up at, whine, bark, run round in excited circles, snatch at the lead, or otherwise be 'annoying'.~~ No, I don't think that one will fly either.

   d. I've been really trying at the obedience recently, but I just don't have a natural talent for it. With a bit of extra effort though I'm sure I could get to at least a 50 per cent success rate.

   e. His obsession for 'fetch' borders on mania, but it may be time to start dropping the ball for him occasionally. It goes against my every political instinct, but frankly the dog hasn't been born whose principles couldn't be corrupted with a juicy chunk of fresh steak.

4. I have started scooting again, and though I'm only on one or two scoots a day I really should quit completely.
5. Though still rippling with muscle, I'm a mature dog now and being as bouncy as a bag of frogs is getting to be hard work. It's time to think about conserving those dynamite bursts of energy for when it really matters, such as lethal attacks on intruders or when the Owner is trying to put his shoes on for a walk.
6. No baths. No vets. No obedience classes. Definitely no postmen.

Saturday, January 3
Samantha was violently sick this morning, which according to Ella is something to do with her expecting a puppy. Rather than take us for a walk the Owner fussed around her for ages, and we had to make do with a run in the garden. Again.

I've often thought that humans are crazy, but willingly making a tiny human has got to be the most stupid idea I've ever heard. We used to have a perfectly happy den, but now it's 'baby this' and 'baby that' and we dogs have definitely slipped down the agenda. I wouldn't go so far as to say that we are being neglected, but there's been a noticeable drop in walks, and when you add into the mix the muttering over the tiniest bit of mud on the floor and unreasonable demands for silence the future looks bleak.

And when this new human arrives, what then? Your dog puppy is ready to leave home in about eight weeks or so, which in my opinion is about right. Human puppies on the other paw hang around for years, mostly making life a misery for everyone involved. I've heard stories about pulled tails, and worse. Not so much sleeping dogs being left to lie as sleeping dogs being poked in the eye.

Sunday, January 4
More vomiting from Ella's Mistress and again it's our walk that suffers. Coleridge is particularly upset as he's a connoisseur of previously digested food in all its forms and isn't allowed a sniff. Personally I think you have to draw the line somewhere. Although dogs only have a quarter of the amount of taste buds as humans, we shouldn't just go around slurping up any old vomit. Unless it's got some nice meaty chunks you can keep it.

Monday, January 5

Spent most of the day lying in front of the fire with my back legs splayed and head hanging off the sofa at an awkward angle. To the casual observer I may have appeared to be fast asleep, but actually it's a Zen thing. Reached a state of tranquillity that was deeply relaxing but did not affect my reaction time one whit. When the postman arrived I went from virtual coma to hurling myself at the door snarling and barking in 1.7 seconds. Good, but there's room for improvement.

Tuesday, January 6

At last the Owner and Samantha decided to take us to the park for a proper walk rather than taking it in turns to run us to the wasteland for a dump or just letting us run around the garden. While the Owner is the titular Top Dog of the park through right of combat with a pit bull called Razor, he's never shown any interest in actually ruling, being more your parasite kind of monarch. Consequently, the park dogs view me as some kind of unofficial power behind the throne, like an especially licky Grand Vizier, and I like to patrol regularly, making sure that all is well among the hoi polloi.

I haven't seen my second-in-command (and Coleridge's father) Scottie for a fortnight and was surprised to see the little Westie in the company of a cocker spaniel bitch. I was even more surprised that they were nuzzling each other, sniffing bums, and otherwise indulging in some outrageous public displays of affection. I've got nothing against being public with affection of course, but the local taxidermist has had his eye on Scottie for years while the spaniel appeared to be barely more than a puppy.

Intrigued, Ella and I trotted over to investigate.

After a polite round of stiff tails, sniffing, yelping and mock attacks I shuffled my eyebrows quizzically at Scottie and let my tongue loll suggestively. Shaking her head, Ella stepped up and asked if he was going to introduce us to his friend.

'Aye, right ye are. This is Ginger, one of mah bitches.' He looked at her. 'You'd better be runnin' along noo, hen.'

Ginger bounded away. '*One* of your bitches?' I barked.

'Whut? Whut? A dug's got needs.'

'Yes, and at your age they are a comfy basket, short walks, and food that isn't too chewy.'

'Well I think it's sweet,' Ella interjected as my lieutenant started growling. 'Scottie's got a lot to offer a younger dog. Or dogs. And he looks really smart in that little tartan coat.'

'Aye, that's right. Ah'm in the prime o' life and ah've a pedigree as long as yer tail . . .'

'As well as bad breath and trembly legs,' I continued.

'Och ye're jest jealous 'cos ah'm a bitch magnet. Ah can see where this is goin' an' ah've got another wee lassie tae meet so ah'll bid ye good day.'

And with that he trotted off, wheezy but haughty.

On the way to our small patch of territory – a clearing in the woods near the pond – Ella and I saw him again. When he said 'lassie' he was being more literal than I'd thought. This time he was with a beautiful and luxuriantly coated young collie. Exactly the kind of dog, in fact, that would look more at home rescuing little Billy from the well than having a small, elderly West Highland Scots terrier jumping arthritically at her hind quarters.

Wednesday, January 7

The Owner and Samantha were working in their office upstairs so I was on guard duty all day, which meant deep leg-twitching meditation on the sofa interspersed with enraged barking and trying to get out of the closed window.

'What exactly are you trying to achieve?' Ella asked after one episode of explosive violence brought muffled shouts of 'SHUT UP BLAKE!' from upstairs.

I told her about my mission as a keen and ever-vigilant guard dog, protector of the weak and vulnerable, nemesis of intruders.

'And plastic bags?' she asked. 'You are aware that that was just a plastic bag blowing against the window, right?'

'Plastic bags too,' I barked firmly. 'You never know where danger might lurk.'

'Good dog,' she sighed, getting comfortable on the rug again. 'You're getting as bad as Scottie.'

I'm beginning to think that the offer of steak was the drink talking. Today it was the usual tinned muck featuring unidentifiable meat by-product bulked out with the heavy use of breadcrumbs, served on a bed of teeth-breaking biscuits. If steak is not served soon then I will have to think again about my own concessions.

Thursday, January 8

After the now ritual throwing up, Samantha needed some fresh air so we got another walk in the park with both humans. They must have realised that they've been neglecting Coleridge's basic training recently. Neither of them are what I'd describe as expert dog handlers and Coleridge, for all his many great qualities, is not the sharpest fang in the jaw. Today it went something like, 'Sit, Coleridge. Sit. Sit. SIT! Aaaargh, will you SIT! Good boy, look, Sam, he's doing it. Quick, give him a treat. Oh no, he's just having a crap again. NO, don't sit now you stupid dog. Oh, hell . . . well, it's your turn to wash his bum.'

Friday, January 9

The average dog can recognise upwards of 150 human words; the most popular being 'sit', 'stay', 'walk' and all that rubbish. Of course, I am not the average dog, and if a human wants to grab my attention there's only one word that is guaranteed to do it every time. That word is 'steak'.

It started out as a normal day, just like any other. Eat, walk, sleep, psychological warfare with the postman, a little bit of Ella-sniffing, watching Coleridge chew his way through some old shoe and the back corner of the sofa. Fulfilling, but nothing out of the ordinary. And then it happened.

Towards the end of the afternoon, just before the evening constitutional to the wasteland, the Owner opened the freezer and shouted to Samantha, 'I'm just getting some steak out for tomorrow.'

I should have known better than to doubt him. He's a good Owner, brimming with the steak of human kindness.

As usual we were shut in the kitchen for the night. Just three dogs and a polystyrene dish of gently defrosting, meaty loveliness. I know he said tomorrow, but he can't seriously expect to leave temptation lying around like some kind of nasal torture. When the lights went off it was the work of a moment to get my paws up on the counter and brush it to the floor with my muzzle. Between me, Ella and Coleridge the clingfilm lasted less than five seconds. Four steaks. All beauties. Perfect examples of their type. One for each of us and we had a pleasant tussle over the last one. They were still a bit frozen in the middle, but a steak is not to be sniffed at in any condition. No, it is to be gulped down without

7

touching the sides. Anyway, plenty of time for it to thaw in my stomach.

Saturday, January 10

It seems that the steaks were not intended for us after all, but for 'guests'. If anyone deserves to be banished to the garden shed then in my humble opinion it should have been the human who broke a promise to man's most devoted and loyal friend in favour of mere 'guests'. I'd like to ask if 'guests' spend their every waking hour selflessly guarding the den? Do 'guests' provide endless companionship? Do 'guests' occasionally nuzzle the Owner's crotch? It seems to me that we dogs had earned that steak far more than they had.

However, it's difficult to convey all that with just your eyebrows and some yelping. I tried the easy-to-understand Eyes of Hurt Reproach, but amid the hysterical accusations I don't think he even noticed.

Sunday, January 11

We were let back in last night when the oh-so-special guests had left, after hours of huddling together for warmth in the garden shed. The Owner was in a far better mood, presumably having realised the error of his ways, though there was not a sniff of any leftover replacement steak. I'd like to have played the situation a bit cooler, and with shoulders as cold as mine were it wouldn't have been difficult, but one of the most frustrating things about being a dog is our vast capacity for forgiveness. When he let us out of the shed we were all over him like a furry wave of affection. I'm not proud of it but I admit that I both licked and nuzzled. Frankly, it's a tragedy that after thousands of years of selective breeding most dogs can't even sulk effectively. For the look of things I gave him an encore with the Eyes of Hurt Reproach, but when he patted me on the head and told me I was a 'funny dog' I couldn't stop myself thumping the tail on the kitchen floor and barking appreciatively. Pathetic.

I did have a quick scoot on the hall rug today when no one was watching, though. So did Ella. That'll teach him.

It was good to be back in the warm and I was in the mood for a spot of pampering, so spent most of the day licking my balls, which was pleasant even though I failed to get the desired shine on them.

Monday, January 12

Carried out my Top Dog obligations with quiet dignity. Mostly this means going round the park sniffing bums. It's the dog equivalent of smiling and waving. It sounds easy, but putting your nose anywhere near Denny the Flea's back passage requires a devotion to duty that few dogs could muster.

Tuesday, January 13

More vomiting turned into a nasty scene. Samantha left the bathroom door ajar and Coleridge crept in, then persistently tried to climb into the toilet bowl while Samantha was kneeling over it. She tried to push him away, but wasn't in much of a position to get rid of him so Ella, who errs on the side of 'ridiculously devoted' to her Mistress, became involved and a battle broke out in the bathroom. Although Ella was doing just fine, I'm not one to miss a good fight, plus 'Chivalry' is my middle name, so I launched myself at the ill-mannered little fuzzball. The final result was Ella, Coleridge and yours truly pushed out into the garden, Samantha dripping with puke. I've been banished from the house before for Crimes I Did Not Commit, but this time the Owner was particularly unpleasant about it.

You have to hand it to Coleridge, though, he's a plucky little guy. Even with Ella and I chewing his hindquarters and Samantha flailing at him while simultaneously throwing up, he still managed to lap up a few mouthfuls from the tiles, plus – as Samantha was quick to point out – one of her contact lenses which had apparently fallen out during the vomiting. When it comes to food I'm no slouch, but that puppy takes the biscuit. Frequently.

The tussle had us all worked up, so we spent the rest of the day fighting over an old chew toy in the garden, and chasing each other in and out of the pond. For some reason dinner was served alfresco, which is never pleasant in January and especially not when the service is so surly and the quality of the meal frankly abysmal. I would have sent it back to the kitchen if it hadn't already been halfway down my throat.

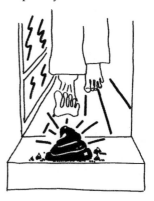

After dinner Coleridge took a crap on the kitchen step, which was discovered by the Owner as he finally emerged to call us in. It was a frosty night and though Coleridge's excrement had chilled it was still soft enough in the middle to make the Owner skid into the garbage.

Once again the Owner has proved that he's a harsh master. We spent the whole night locked in the shed.

Wednesday, January 14

Good government is another responsibility of my sort-of Top Dog status. As their leader it behoves me to settle small disputes such as the one that broke out between Rudy the Alsatian and Claude the boxer today over half a sandwich that Rudy had found on Claude's territory and eaten right in front of the boxer. Diplomatic efforts having failed, I resorted to joining in the fight that ensued.

Thursday, January 15

Met up with Constable in the park today. He's a big trophy-winning Old English sheepdog, star of several TV commercials, and appears to be made entirely of hair with a wet nose stuck on the front. Dumb as a bag of rocks, he's good company so long as the conversation stays away from anything that taxes his tiny brain – like existentialism, or cheese. I couldn't help wincing while sniffing at his beautifully coiffed coat. It was perfectly conditioned, blow-dried, and smelled of jojoba and walnut. All quite disgusting. An aversion to warm soapy water is as natural for a dog as a love of stagnant, muddy pools, preferably with a scum floating on top. The coat should be matted in places and give off a healthy odour, particularly when wet. It's a primary source of information about where we've been, what we've been eating, whether we're in good health, etc.

'Constable,' I remonstrated, 'you smell like you just stepped out of a salon.'

'Well, there's a big show soon and Mistress wants to make sure I'm in top condition.'

'And what's more important, winning prizes or obeying the call of the wild? We've been through this before, so before you answer try and remember you're a dog, not a beauty queen.'

'Arf, that's a difficult question. Is it winning prizes? I think the Mistress had a call from the wild once. Whoever was on the phone was really angry, but it turned out to be a wrong number . . .'

'No, Constable, it is important for your mental health that you indulge your animal instincts and not allow yourself to become exploited.'

'I don't think I've ever exploded, though I once had a bad sausage. The rug wasn't a pretty sight, I can tell –'

'Exploited, Constable. It means . . . look, just follow me and do what I do.'

There followed an enjoyable half-hour during which Ella and Coleridge joined us. Together we dashed through brambles and charged at ducks in the pond, raising great wakes of muddy water. And while all this fun was going on the Owner did star jumps and ran around in circles on the path. This speaks volumes about him.

When his Mistress called him, Constable was looking much more like a dog ought to. What I could see of his coat through the mud was now full of twigs and burrs, and he was panting like a traction engine. He smelled like a proper wet dog.

As the three of us wandered off to find the Owner and throw ourselves at his legs, we heard a high-pitched wail behind us.

'Noooo! Constable, my precious powder puff, what have you done!'

It was music to my ears.

Ella, Coleridge and I had to submit to the hose when we got back to the den, as well as more derogatory comments, but I consoled myself that it was all worth it for a job well done. Shaking myself over a newly painted wall in the hall also helped me forget the Owner's aggressive use of the scrubbing brush.

Friday, January 16

In disgrace. Coleridge's fault again. And the Owner has to accept some responsibility, too, for leaving the garbage bin in the kitchen full to overflowing. He should know all about Coleridge's insatiable appetite by now.

Even though he's only a small dog, the pup managed to bring the dustbin down after just a few leaps. As a past master of bin diving, I was quite impressed by his tenacity and technique. Once its contents were spread across the floor, there didn't seem much point in abstaining so Ella and I had a dignified nose through tins that had plenty to lick at, bones, vegetable peelings, plastic pots and wrappers, and all sorts of loveliness.

The Owner's attitude when he came down to investigate the noise was typical of his recent bad temper. Once again we have been banished to the garden shed.

Saturday, January 17
Having been reintroduced to the pleasures of the bin, I took a renewed interest in one in the park today. By climbing on a bench I could see a whole cheese and ham croissant, just sitting at the bottom. It's incredible that humans will pass this sort of thing by without a trace of interest. If the Owner cared to take a daily peek into the park bins he could probably slash his grocery bills in half at a stroke.

I strained to reach the croissant, but overstretched myself and fell in, head first. It took a full ten minutes of struggle to get out again at which point I found that I had an appreciative audience of six dogs and two female humans, one of whom was pointing one of those camera phones at me.

'That must be the most stupid dog I've ever seen,' one said to the other as I collected my tattered dignity and scrabbled out.

They can say what they like – that croissant was delicious.

Sunday, January 18
My therapy session with Constable has worked wonders. We were hardly through the park gates this morning when he swept past us barking, 'I'm off to roll in poo. Who's with me?'

Well, you'd have to be mad to refuse an invitation like that.

Monday, January 19
Due to the Owner's feeble sense of smell and pathetic powers of observation he didn't give us the scrubbing brush, hose and towel treatment yesterday, so I don't see how we can be held to blame now there's dried poo all over the carpet. If he just rubbed it in with his foot it would hardly show; the shouting, scrubbing, and Wrinkled Eyebrows of Stern Disapproval were totally uncalled for, as was banishment to the shed again.

Tuesday, January 20
Not a good day. The Owner and Samantha passed an evening talking about what was to be done with 'the dogs'. Ella and I lay on

the carpet, our eyes flicking from one human to the other. Coleridge, who doesn't understand human so well yet, jumped about in their laps and finally fell asleep on Samantha.

The conversation revolved around how unhygienic we were, the mess we made, our constant demands for attention, and how we might be dangerous to a small human. They are worried that they will not be able to cope with us and a baby and that we might inadvertently hurt it. Much was made of Coleridge's incontinence, his chewing and eating everything in sight, and my own constant jumping up and damaging things was examined in far too much detail. Ella – being of a naturally quiet and obedient disposition – came off relatively lightly, but even so Samantha is worried that having been her closest companion for so long she will not take to the baby. Ella whined at this and looked about ready to howl, and I wasn't acting when I made the Eyes of Wounded Betrayal at the Owner. He may not be perfect, but what does a dog care about that? I've got the DNA of most breeds swimming around in my genes and every single one of them has been bred to love him.

The Owner eventually noticed the looks I was giving him, leaned over and tickled me behind the ears.

'He may be a pain in the backside sometimes, but I swear if Blake was any more intelligent he could tell me what he was thinking.'

Yeah, well if *he* was more intelligent, *I* wouldn't need to. He should heed the words of John Steinbeck, who wrote, 'I've seen a look in dogs' eyes, a quickly vanishing look of amazed contempt, and I am convinced that basically dogs think humans are nuts.' Amazingly perceptive, John Steinbeck. For a human.

The evening ended with the Owner and Samantha agreeing that they would 'see how things go' after which there was a big stroke-fest, which is always welcome. Even so Ella and I went to our baskets chilled to the bone at the possibility that we will be ousted by the new human puppy.

Wednesday, January 21

Ella and I are on our best behaviour, which in practical terms meant Ella spent most of the day curled up at her Mistress's feet while I kept Coleridge away from Samantha during bouts of sickness and patrolled the house on constant alert for intruders. I can hear things four times as distant as the humans and in deference to their inadequate senses kept them constantly updated on the movements of other dogs, people, cars, etc., just in case any one of them was headed towards the den.

As it turned out, none of them were and all my dedication earned me was another afternoon in the shed.

Thursday, January 22

After my dustbin plunge there's a rumour going round the park that I'm a bit stupid. Scottie seems to think it was very funny, which in my view is treacherous behaviour for a good beta male, second-in-command. In other news, I upset the Owner by taking a dump outside the dog toilet, which he was obliged to pick up and carry four hundred yards. And he thinks he's the boss in this relationship?

Friday, January 23

Gave the postman an extra helping of menace – growling and teeth bared while trying to squeeze myself through the letterbox to tear him limb from limb is a forte of mine – but was shocked when he hit me hard on the nose with a wad of letters. Who would do such a thing to a poor defenceless creature? All postmen are evil. It's probably part of the job description. I bet in interviews senior postmen screen for remorseless criminal masterminds, probably through multiple-choice questionnaires.

While delivering letters you come across a perfectly friendly dog who just wants to play. Do you:

a. Give him a treat from a bag you carry for just such an eventuality
b. Drop to your knees and pet him
c. Viciously beat him about the muzzle with your letters then go home to torture some puppies

He probably owns a fluffy white cat with a diamond collar, too.

Saturday, January 24

More excellent guard work last night, which – again – went entirely unappreciated. My eternal vigilance and quick response may well have saved the day, but you'd think that the Owner wanted to be murdered in his own bed the way he carries on at me. My loud barking and growling should have brought him bounding down the stairs, armed to the teeth, and breathing grateful thanks to his brave and heroic dog as we faced the intruder side by side. Instead I was faced with a cursing vision of Hell in crumpled pyjamas.

Well, if he wants to wake up in the middle of the night to find himself at the mercy of serial-killing postmen that's just dandy with me. I settled back in my basket with a hhharmmphh of wounded disappointment.

Ella raised her head slightly and said, 'Plastic bag again.'

I did not dignify her observation with a response.

Sunday, January 25

Given the strained relations at the moment I decided to let the previous night's ingratitude pass and make a special effort, though it was with gritted teeth. The humans seemed oblivious to their close brush with a plastic bag that could just as easily have been a depraved, letter-wielding psychopath, and were more interested in the fact that Samantha didn't vomit today. To celebrate they took us for a long walk in the park. Ella and I trotted quietly along by their ankles and – Dog forgive me – I even let the Owner play 'fetch', though the tennis ball turned to ashes in my mouth.

After they had their own dinner the humans came across with a bone each and a big pile of meat, then there was stroking. I am a sucker for a scrap of affection and clambered into the Owner's lap to give him a thorough licking. Coleridge followed suit. It was all going very well until an excited bark in the Owner's ear almost split his eardrum.

Ella thinks they're being nice because they feel guilty about wanting to get rid of us.

Monday, January 26

Another upset in the den today when a sandwich fell off the table and into my mouth. I admit that its descent to the kitchen floor was to some extent assisted, but for Dog's sake, it's just a sandwich. The usual round of 'Bad dog, Blake, bad dog', but if you ask me the Owner needs to get some perspective. What exactly have humans done for the world – war, famine, pestilence,

environmental meltdown, that's what. And do I spend all day barking, 'Bad human! Naughty Owner?'

Tuesday, January 27

Scottie's at the bitches again. Today it was the turn of a mixed breed called Florence to experience the full weight of his charm followed by the full weight of his small body thrashing away at her haunches. I was intrigued to know the secret of his success and after careful observation believe that it's a combination of persistence and the small mercy that if he's behind her at least the bitch doesn't have to smell the full force of his breath.

Wednesday, January 28

We met Scottie and the two puppies Edina and Jock – Coleridge's brother and sister – at the wasteland this evening. There were more pressing matters to discuss than the Westie's sexual reawakening and while the youngsters ran off yapping excitedly I told him about the rapidly deteriorating canine–human relations in our den and how we were being constantly banished to the garden.

'Och, some dugs get all the luck,' was not the reply I had been expecting.

'This is serious, Scottie – it's cold out there and I miss the kitchen.'

'Yer problum is ye niver think. I wus left outside fer the night once, and it wus the best time I ever hud.' A wistful look crossed his hairy face. 'Bins everywhere, whole bagfuls o' leftovers oot the back o' restaurants. More cats than ye could chase, a full moon shinin' doon. Och, I could tell ye some tales aboot howlin'.'

'There's just the small difficulty of the fence, of course.'

'Whut's a fence tae a dug? The garden hasnae been built that a dug cannae escape frum.'

'But we might be split up and rehomed. What about the baby?'

'Whut aboot it? Plenty o' bairns ha' grown up aroond dugs. It's healthy for the wee 'uns. Bit o' dog mess niver hurt anyone.'

Thursday, January 29

Scottie could not have been more wrong yesterday. As previously noted Coleridge will eat anything, no matter how disgusting. Up to and including dog faeces, fresh and stale. I could smell it on his breath on the way home this evening, but didn't give it a second thought. After all, who hasn't experimented with a bit of poop?

All was well in the den this evening. Ella and I were even starting to relax after particularly full bowls of something that tasted almost like actual meat as well as pats and tummy tickles all round. And then Coleridge had to ruin it all by jumping into Samantha's lap and vomiting a stream of liquefied dog mess on her. Mostly Scottie's, if my nose did not deceive me.

There probably aren't that many humans who enjoy being drenched with the contents of a dog's stomach, especially when that includes semi-digested excrement, and it seems that Samantha isn't one of them. The stench made her vomit too and pretty soon she was swimming in the stuff. Ella and I made a discreet withdrawal and hid under the kitchen table, but it was to no avail. Even though neither of us would touch a turd these days, no matter how warm and curly, the Owner rounded all three of us up and we were dragged outside once more. All our good work over the last couple of days has come to naught and we're out here shivering again. And with the gate padlocked there's no way out into those bins Scottie was talking about.

When I think about giving up that tennis ball without putting up a fight I could puke too.

Friday, January 30

This morning the Owner sat on the step with a cup of coffee and gave us a speech. Many dog owners have observed that dogs are great listeners. (Making humans feel like they're a riveting orator is all part of the job, but this morning we didn't have to pretend to listen. After another night in the shed Ella was convinced that we were all going to be hauled straight off to the rescue centre, and I couldn't have been more hangdog if I was swinging from a gibbet.)

The Owner looked sombre. I had a pang of just how much I'd miss him and shuffled forwards on my bum to lick his hand.

'Blake, Ella,' he said (Coleridge, oblivious to the gravity of the situation, was chasing his tail around the garden). 'You are great dogs, and we love having you around, but we're going to have a baby in the house in about seven months and we can't go on having the three of you creating havoc.'

Ella whined and pressed her muzzle to the floor between his feet.

'Samantha and I have talked about it and until you can all prove yourselves trustworthy you'll be confined to the shed and the garden for most of the day.'

I looked up hopefully. This didn't sound like rescue-centre talk. If Scottie were right it could even be the start of a fantastic new night life.

'Don't worry,' the Owner continued, scratching my ears absently. 'I'll make you very comfortable, you just won't be allowed in the house so often. And you can make as much mess as you like out here.'

Saturday, January 31

The Owner spent the day fashioning a large flap in the shed door so that we could come and go as we please. Then he brought our baskets and bowls out along with some extra blankets. Although it wasn't the Ritz, by the time he'd finished it was cosy enough. Not 'sofa in front of the fire' cosy, but much better than a cell and the long wait for another human to take us home.

FEBRUARY

Sunday, February 1
I like to think I'm a dog with the kind of jaunty optimism that can always spot a silver lining and the new dog flap on the shed door is as much fun as a de-clawed cat. Scottie was so right. Ella, Coleridge and I took full advantage of our new pass to the outside world to hunt across the frosty expanse of the moonlit garden. There was howling, chasing of prey (I caught a stick, Coleridge brought down a daffodil bulb), and shouts of 'shut up' from many windows along the street. Coleridge and I have started a hole by the back fence. Freedom is just a foot away.

Even the bed in our new bijou den was warm when we eventually piled up on top of Ella like proper wolves. I'm thinking of turning feral, after all, what's ten thousand years of selective breeding against a genetic inheritance?

Monday, February 2
Due to the amount of complaints from neighbours this morning, the Owner has added a bolt to the dog flap. It is this kind of behaviour that makes me wish for bloody revolution. He'd think twice about restricting our freedom if there was a pack of angry dogs ready to hunt him down and chew on his intestines.

Tuesday, February 3
The new regime is harsh and our interaction with the humans is at a minimum. Apart from mealtimes, two walks, several times during the day when they come out to play with us, and a few hours in the evening when we are allowed to sit in front of the fire and be stroked, we barely see them. Rations are poor; just a small bowl of the usual filth and biscuits for breakfast, followed by a larger one later in the day and a handful of biscuits in the evening. They think they can buy our compliance with gifts of bones and doggie chocs – and to be fair that *does* seem to work, but only because we have been robbed of our canine dignity.

Ella spends much of her time whining by the back door and pawing at it to get in. I hate to see her reduced to this, but I'm trying to be strong, for her sake. Coleridge and I continue working on our tunnel, though we will need the cover of darkness if we are to execute a successful escape.

Wednesday, February 4

A proper run in the park today, but too late in the morning to see any of the dogs whose Owners leave the den to work. Scottie was there though, as his crumbly Master doesn't do much all day except totter around the park and drink tea with old Mrs Fortiss. He wasn't in a great mood.

'Whut's the point o' comin' doon tae the park at this time o' day? Not a sniff o' bum tae be had, an' young Trixie is comin' intae season an aw. I'm pantin' on a piece o' that tail.'

Scottie's always been something of a sexual adventurer, but it seems to be getting out of control lately. I thought I ought to say something.

'Trixie is a pedigree St Bernard, Scottie. Don't you think you should stick to bitches that are more your height? You don't want to be straining yourself at your age.'

'Dinnae talk foolish. I'm in prime fettle. And Trixie's a belter, she doesnae mind standing by a bench to let us hop on, if ye catch ma drift.' As I shook my head in an attempt to get rid of the mental image, Scottie looked around and continued in a small conspiratorial growl. 'Mind, I seem tae be fixated oan the bitches at the moment, ye ken. I cannae seem tae get enough o' thum.'

Light dawned. 'Oh, it's a sex addiction.'

'Och ay, well ye seem tae ken all aboot it, whut can I do? Not that I'm complainin', but tae be honest it's leavin' me nae time at all fae the aimless diggin'.'

I'm a talented dog in many ways, but my genius doesn't stretch to sex therapy and I told Scottie he'd have to work it out for himself.

'But be careful, I'd hate to see you get randy with the wrong bitch. Steer clear of Rottweilers if you want my advice.'

'Ye mean like yon Nancy? Wull, ah had her yisterday. Lovely anal glands, though.'

After dropping that surreal mental image Scottie wandered off to find his Owner (not before trying for a sniff at Ella's rear, though he got just a growl for his trouble).

Spent the rest of the day in the garden, jumping on my stick and barking at it. After the first four hours this was not so much fun as I originally thought.

Thursday, February 5

At the back of the shed is a pile of boxes left by the bad-tempered human who used to live in the house. The Owner hasn't even glanced at them, but with nothing else to do all night Coleridge and I began shredding them. I've laid off the chewing recently; like most pastimes it loses its appeal if you indulge too heavily and it usually ended up in shouting. Safe in the knowledge that the Owner wasn't likely to care about a few old boxes, I rediscovered the sport of pitting your wits and jaws against an inanimate object, the rush of pride in senseless destruction. By the time we'd finished Coleridge, Ella and I were muzzle-deep in torn cardboard and ripped magazines featuring pictures of cold-looking human females. With the exception of the Owner's leg, which has always exuded a powerful sensuality, I've never really understood

how humans can find one another attractive. Naked, they look just like those bald Chinese crested dogs, which are so freaky it's hard to imagine we share a common ancestor. What were the humans thinking when they created that lot? 'Look, I found a tiny bald wolf huddled in the back of a cave, let's breed from it. Who knows, we may succeed in creating a whole variety of dogs that can shiver and wear sweaters!'

Friday, February 6

It wasn't just magazines in those boxes. After the morning walk we were marched under guard to the garden, and as it was a cold, blustery day sought shelter in the shed. Beneath the pictures of naked humans Coleridge found a small box. Chewing and pawing at it, we found it contained a plastic tray, covered in foil. It was almost empty, but still had two little rhomboid treats inside. Coleridge snapped one up before I could get to it, but I used my superior weight to shoulder him aside and gobbled down the other.

It's hard to imagine that anyone would make treats that taste so disgusting, but a wolf takes sustenance wherever he can find it.

Everything was fine for about half an hour, and then I noticed that Coleridge had begun lazily humping a pile of sacks. At first I thought nothing of it. He's a young dog and full of vim. But after a few more minutes I felt a peculiar stirring in my own loins, and an overwhelming urge to mount my mate swept through me. I sniffed and pawed at Ella but she was sleeping and responded with a tired snarl. By now I looked like I had a giant prawn escaping from my lower abdomen. It was demanding attention. Licking just seemed to make matters worse, so I joined Coleridge at the sacks, which he was now pounding away at like Scottie at a dog show. This, too, failed to satisfy my ardour and my frenzied thoughts turned back to Ella.

I pawed at her, begging for some attention. Coleridge began running around in crazy circles humping at anything and everything: the chewed boxes, the lawnmower, me. I winced when he tried it on with the rake.

Ella opened her eyes on a scene of chaos. 'What's wrong with you two?' she yawned. 'Can't you go and jump on your stick?' Then she noticed that I was sporting an angry stick of my own. It had begun to feel like it was buzzing.

'Oh, I see,' Ella continued smoothly. 'Well you'll just have to wait for your Owner's leg to get home, I'm sleeping.'

'Please, mounting, please,' I whined. Without waiting for a reply I threw myself at her and began working away at her shoulder, my hips a blur.

She yelped and threw herself through the flap and into the garden. I gave chase. Coleridge bundled out soon after and made a beeline for the little stone gnome fishing in the pond.

Meanwhile I chased Ella round the garden until I finally cornered her by the kitchen door.

'Blake, what's wrong with you?'

'Can't help it. Little treats,' I panted.

In desperation Ella got a paw to the door and amazingly it swung open. She dashed inside with me in hot pursuit. Behind us I heard a splash as Coleridge's dalliance with the gnome toppled the both of them into the pond.

I caught up with Ella in the humans' bedroom. She had squeezed herself under the bed where there was no chance that I would be able to climb on top of her. As I stood looking desperately for an alternative Coleridge ran up behind me, covered in ooze and duckweed, his eyes wildly seeking a more compliant partner than the gnome.

At the same time we both spotted the large teddy bear that lay on the clean, white bed. With excited yaps we were on it in a second. Coleridge took the lower end and I had the head. We were pumping away in sheer blissful relief when the door opened and the screaming started.

'Blake, Coleridge, what the hell are you doing!?'

'No, they've got Mr Muffy. He belonged to my great-grandmother.'

'Look at the state of the bed!'

As one the humans lurched across the bedroom to grab us, but I was too far gone to stop now and Coleridge must have been in the same state. As their hands reached our collars a particularly frenzied burst of humping brought final release for the pair of us and both humans squealed with disgust as our lovemaking reached its natural conclusion.

Unfortunately, it wasn't the only thing that was at an end. My fierce grip on Mr Muffy had torn the ancient fabric and as the Owner dragged me off the bed his sticky head fell off and rolled to Samantha's feet.

Letting go of Coleridge to rescue the bear was a mistake. Like lightning he was across the room and humping the Owner's leg. Ordinarily I would have objected, but by now I was caught up in a fresh wave of lust. With the Owner frantically trying to pull Coleridge off I twisted like an eel and threw myself at the other leg, forcing the Owner to stagger across the room like a cowboy wearing writhing, furry chaps.

'I knew it!' Samantha snapped. 'Your dog is an out-of-control sex beast. And now he's teaching the puppy. Get them both out of here this minute.'

The Owner wrestled us yelping and bucking into the garden,

where he opened the shed door to throw us both in. A gust of wind caught the torn magazines and whipped them around his head in a blizzard. He gasped and ran into the garden trying to grab at the cyclone of naked humans, but most were already disappearing over the fence.

Eventually he gave up and herded Coleridge and I, still humping, back into the shed and locked the door.

No food tonight, but we were both too busy at the sacks to care. In the distance we could faintly hear the doorbell ring almost continuously, and human voices raised in anger. I wonder what the Owner's done now?

Saturday, February 7
The Owner came into the shed this morning looking pale and angry. Not feeling so good, I couldn't do much more than look at him guiltily with my tail between my legs. He collected up what remained of the shredded magazines and burned them carefully while talking nonstop to Coleridge and me in that disappointed tone he uses so often now.

Apparently old Miss Meddling next door had been taking tea with her 86-year-old sister when a large picture of 'Melanie' had pasted itself to the window beside them. Mrs Singh had been bringing her twins home from the shops when they were caught in the 'shower of filth' coming from our garden. Mr Lawson nearly burned his kitchen down when he caught sight of 'Stacey and Belle' fluttering against his window box.

However, when the Owner came across the chewed treat packet, he stopped, and for the first time he looked at Coleridge and me with a hint of sympathy, muttering, 'That stupid, dirty old man.' Then he put the box in his pocket and went inside.

Soon after, some food and a big bowl of water was put out for us. The Owner looked into our eyes, felt our noses and stroked us. I went for one last weak hump, but was pushed back firmly.

No sign of Ella all day.

Sunday, February 8
Ella was returned to the garden today, watched closely by the humans to make sure that Coleridge and I didn't immediately try

and force our attentions on her.

The slightly good news is that Ella heard the Owner explaining to Samantha that Coleridge and I had been drugged and has forgiven our behaviour. The extremely bad news is that there has been fresh talk about our future, and more specifically mine and Coleridge's future. The humans are thinking about putting an advert in the local newspaper to find us new homes.

Monday, February 9

Started the day in very low spirits. Only a few months ago the Owner and I had the den to ourselves. It wasn't perfect, there were moments of tension over such trivialities as hand-stitched Italian leather shoes, but for the most part we rubbed along fine. I had my place on the sofa and he had his. There was leftover takeaway food a couple of times a week. No one minded if you farted or spread a bit of dog hair around the place. Evenings were spent drooling into his lap and having my ears scratched while we watched TV. Then Coleridge came with Ella and Samantha and that was OK, too. The Owner was more distracted, but he still liked for me to sleep under his desk during the day and I enjoyed having a bigger pack. Now, there's no time for Blake. I have to twine around the Owner's legs whining for every ear scratch, and half the time all I get is a distracted 'Not now, Blake.'

When I was a puppy my dear old mum told me that owning a dog was a privilege for a human. Once we've given our loyalty then we never take it back, never complain, and are always on hand with a comforting lick or snuffle. All they have to do in return is treat us like a friend. But instead of being a valued member of the pack, I'm like a contestant on a reality TV show. Every day I'm up for eviction and after that who knows what. Another Owner? This one may be an idiot, but he's *my* idiot. I've put a lot of time and effort into training him, and for all that I might wish otherwise I do sort of love him. I don't want to be given away and I don't want to have to escape. I don't want to be far from my Owner.

A walk in the park this afternoon. Wandered listlessly, watching Ella and Coleridge chase imaginary rabbits, and stuck close to the Owner. He rubbed my chest and nuzzled the top of my head. I licked his ear. He sighed and gave me a hug. Then he bought a pastry from the coffee stand and shared it with me. Not bad. A bit stale, but the grin he gave me when I took it gently from his fingers made up for it. Went a bit over the top with gratitude, but he doesn't mind a bit of drool hanging off his face.

Tuesday, February 10
Felt better this morning after spending the night listening to rain beat down on the shed roof while sleeping nose to bum with Ella. She always knows how to cheer me up – breathing in the scent from her backside is always guaranteed to please.

Ella hopes that the chances are small of the Owner rehoming me and that once the baby arrives he will relax again. It's true he does smell more anxious recently, and is generally much more twitchy than he used to be. If he were a dog he'd spend all day pacing the kitchen floor and whining.

As if to confirm Ella's opinion, Coleridge and I were let back in the den for the first time since the Mr Muffy incident this evening. There was a moderate amount of ear scratching.

Later, when it came time for us to go back to the shed, Samantha noticed that the rain had turned to sleet and the temperature had dropped. She looked at the Owner and said, 'We can't make the dogs sleep outside in that.'

Bless her warm heart. We are all curled up on the sofa in front of the dying fire.

Wednesday, February 11
Another PR disaster in the park this morning, just as the hilarity over my bin adventure is dying down. The Owner was having one of his misguided 'fetch' sessions, which in practice meant me lying in the park chewing on the Frisbee and growling at anyone who tried to take it off me. Suddenly, I was aware of an aggressor. A light touch on the flank was all it took for me to spring into action, twisting and gripping the Frisbee thief with my teeth at something approaching light speed. Only then did I realise that I was chewing on my own tail. It was unfortunate that Scottie happened to be walking past at the very moment that I was fighting it into submission. I tried to pretend all was well, but too late.

'Careful noo, Blake!' the Westie barked. 'That's a dangerous miscreant ye have attached tae yer arse there.'

Thursday, February 12

Due to the recent soggy weather, work on the tunnel at the back of the garden went faster today, and by mid-afternoon a muddy Coleridge emerged in Miss Meddling's garden. It would be nice to say that he broke through with a flower perfectly perched on top of his head, but unfortunately he was just very, very muddy. I was able to get my head through, too. Freedom looked a bit disappointing. Very much like some rhododendron bushes in fact.

While Coleridge explored *terra incognita* Ella and I sat, panting, by the shallow escape route.

After half an hour he returned, growling happily and pulling what looked like some human underwear, though much bigger than any I'd ever seen before. Coleridge dragged his acquisition to the shed and into his bed where he set about chewing, and it was a while before we could distract him from the huge knickers. Finally, however, we managed to wheedle the story of his epic journey from him in little yaps and growls. Faced with an unobstructed path to liberty, the puppy had ventured no further than the cat flap on Miss Meddling's back door. Squeezing inside he ate the cat food, pausing only to throw it up and then eat it again, chased the cat upstairs, grabbed a memento of his visit from a basket, and returned.

Friday, February 13

Sent Coleridge on another exploratory mission yesterday evening. The short incursion was enough to gather the best possible intelligence: there is no gate from Miss Meddling's garden to the outside world. He ventured as far as the end of the road and returned with not a scrap of exotic food or any feline prisoners. It was a disappointment after what Scottie had told us; Ella and I had been expecting a Chinese food mountain at the very least. Neil Armstrong and Buzz Aldrin must have felt much the same after landing on the moon to find it was just a big dusty rock and not made of cheese teeming with little green men as advertised. Nevertheless, it was another historic moment. Now the only thing that prevents us from the romantic gypsy life of night-time vagabonds is the bolt on the shed, and knowing the Owner's patchy powers of recollection it won't be long before he leaves the flap to freedom open. In the meantime there is work to be done on the newly named Meddling Tunnel.

Saturday, February 14

Ran into Constable in the park today. Well, actually I nearly ran into him but recoiled pretty quickly when I smelled him. It takes a lot to disgust me, but the shaggy freak smelled like an explosion in a sewer. I swear that among the branches and brambles sticking out of his coat there was a rotting rabbit leg that even Coleridge wouldn't have touched. For some reason his Mistress was sitting on a bench looking very depressed.

Sunday, February 15

Word that I have been attacking my own tail has leaked out, thanks, no doubt, to that treacherous sex-fiend Scottie. On three separate occasions today park dogs went to sniff my behind, only to jump away barking, 'Whoah, sorry, Blake, thought your tail was going for my throat then.'

Monday, February 16

There has been no further mention of new homes, due to our exemplary behaviour I'm sure, though it's hard to be anything other than exemplary when half of the day is spent huddled in the shed for warmth and the other half is spent digging furiously. Coleridge went on another two expeditions today and came back with the upper set of a pair of dentures and a slipper. Already he has quite a collection of artefacts in his basket. Much more of this and he'll be able to open the Meddling Museum, though I doubt the turnstile will be spinning wildly for *that* exhibition.

Apparently the old cat-lover is always asleep in a chair with the television turned up loud and doesn't notice Coleridge running around with her belongings. He picked the false teeth right out of her lap and the slipper off her foot without waking her.

Tuesday, February 17

No sign of the Owner all day, but the light in the room he uses as his office is still on well after dark. When I think of him up there all alone without someone to keep his feet warm and perfume the air with the occasional waft of eau de dog's bum, I could whine in frustration.

Wednesday, February 18

Coleridge has added Miss Meddling's wig to his collection. It smelled of cat pee a little bit, but he has successfully masked that with his own urine, the clever little guy.

Thursday, February 19

Still no sign of the Owner. I'm beginning to wonder if I'll ever see his funny monkey face again. Samantha took us to the wasteland a couple of times and in the evening Scottie was there with the pups. As befits older animals we frolicked and chased each other in a dignified manner while Scottie's offspring tore around the field. Watching them, Scottie turned to Ella.

'Why is it a bonny lassie like yersel' dosnae huv any wee 'uns of yer ain?'

'I'd love some puppies, but the Mistress has always been very careful about keeping dogs away from me at those times of the year. You'd think Blake could find a way past her defences, but no. If I didn't know better I'd suspect he wasn't quite as cunning as he tells me.'

'Aye, yer no' wrong there, ah've met rubber bones wi' more upstairs than yon haggis. He wouldnae huv the sense tae lick his ain backside if it were on fire.'

I ignored the abuse. Ella wants to have puppies?

Friday, February 20

Ella wants to have puppies. Blake the father – proud sire, noble parent. I've often thought that it would be a crime not to pass these genes along, but with the den being so crowded and Samantha so tight with security when Ella's in season, I've stopped thinking about it.

'Well, you can stop thinking about it again,' Ella yawned as she curled up next to me. 'The Mistress won't let you near me and, even if you could manage it, she'd have kittens if I were to have puppies while she's having babies.'

I don't think Ella really comprehends the depth of my intellect and guile, and if the Owner is going to go around impregnating people then they do say that a dog comes to resemble its human . . .

Saturday, February 21

Most humans don't think that dogs have strong paternal feelings. As with so many things, they are to blame of course. They've taken over the feeding and training of puppies and consequently dogs don't get involved. However, the male wolf is an extremely paternal creature. Not only does it hunt and regurgitate food for its young, but it keeps them clean, guards them and takes an active role in socialising them and teaching them how to hunt. As I like to think of myself as more wolf than most of the domesticated pets around here – particularly now I have been cast out into the wildness of the back garden – I have been practising on Coleridge. His hunting is coming along marvellously. There's not many young wolves of his age who would return to the den having brought down a large brassiere.

Sunday, February 22

Samantha thinks the Owner is working too hard and has insisted that he get some fresh air. He was grumbling when he put his boots on, so I tried to cheer him up with the Crazy Anticipation of a Walk Dance. It was great to see him, but he must have been in a really bad mood because the dance didn't go down well at all.

A great run in the park, and a lot of the old pack were there: Scottie, Liquorice, Claude, Rudy and Dottie. Constable seems to have become very friendly with Denny the Flea and was scratching himself a lot. Leaving the humans to saunter with Coleridge on the retractable lead, we had a healthy run through the woods to the Eastern Park and back, with a short detour to herd a shouty human on roller blades into a waste bin. Denny found a dead squirrel, and shared it with Constable. Sometimes I can't help missing the old times in the park, when we were on a mission to save dogkind from the evil machinations of Razor the pit bull.

Ella's season is a week or two away by our calculations, but we also found some time to lope off to our clearing and practise, and still made it back to the Owner and Samantha not too long after they started whistling. This seemed to please the Owner; I got a rubbed chest and a treat without having to demand it.

Another nauseating dinner, but Samantha cooked a big supper for the humans and there was enough left to refill three dog bowls. The Owner appeared to have relaxed and fell asleep on the sofa, with a nice warm dog draped over him.

Factor in a refreshing three-hour afternoon snooze and this is about as good as life gets. So long as the black cloud of possible rehoming lifts, this den is a great environment to bring puppies into.

Monday, February 23

Filthy weather again. We were checked for cleanliness, but after that the humans turned a blind eye to us being in the den. I was taking advantage of the fire for a quiet bask when I heard the squeak of the front gate. An intruder.

I sounded the alarm in less than a second, paws up against the window baying at the human who dared approach the den. As the figure shuffled down the path I could see that it intended to make for the door. Twisting with lithe grace I was there first, my barks redoubled as the Owner ran down the stairs shouting, 'Blake, down. DOWN! Shut up, you stupid dog.'

Grabbing my collar, he opened the door. The old 'I've-got-a-vicious-dog-in-my-hand-and-I'll-set-him-on-you-without-blinking' routine was totally ruined by his continued shouting. 'Sorry, he's just very friendly, hang on one moment. Down, Blake, get down you great oaf. Sit.' If he had any style he would have shouted, 'Get away or I'll loose the dogs!'

Eventually I had to sit, but only because he was pressing down on my rump. Nothing could stop the ominous rumbling in the back of my throat, though.

The impudent intruder was Miss Meddling, though I wouldn't have recognised her if it hadn't been for the distinctive odour of cat, corned beef, cabbage and a peculiar musty smell that I couldn't quite put my nose on. She had crammed a hat down on her head but you could still see that she had no hair, and her top lip was all puckered up and rubbery. The Owner started in shock at this vision, recovered himself and straightened up, though keeping a firm grip on me.

'Miss Meddling. Look, if this is about those pictures, they weren't mine, they were left in the shed by –'

'Young man, you are a pedlar of shmut and shin.'

'Shin? Shin? Sin! But, it wasn't mine.'

She cut him off with a wave of her hand. 'I knowsh all about pervertsh like you.'

'I am *not* a pervert, Miss Meddling.'

'Sho you shay. Then how do exshplain me mishing shome pershonal itemsh?'

'Persho . . . Oh, personal items. And how can I help you with that?'

'I know your short, give 'em back.'

'But I'm six foot two, what are you talking about?'

'Your short, not you're short. The polishe won't lishen sho I've come to fashe you myshelf.'

'Miss Meddling, I really have no idea what you are talking about . . . Perhaps if you put in the other half of your teeth.'

She bent over and hissed at him. 'Sho, you'd shteal from an old lady and then laugh at her, would you? Where'sh my knickersh? Where'sh me bra? Where'sh me teef? Where'sh me hair?'

'What?'

'You dishgusht me. Knowing your kind, you'll be rubbing yourshelf with them all day. Rubbing, rubbing, rubbing, that'sh what you do, you pervertsh, ishn't it? Well, I'll catsh you rubbing shoon and then they'll throw away the key, you shee if they don't. Good day, shir!'

After poking the Owner in the chest the old woman hobbled off with me barking imperiously at her back. If he'd just let me rip her throat out the Owner could have saved himself an embarrassing scene.

As he shut the door, Samantha shouted from the top of the stairs, 'Who was that?'

'Miss Meddling. I think she's losing her mind. She seems to think I've stolen her underwear so that I can polish a shelf with them.'

'And have you?'

'Of course not. I'm far too busy to be stealing underwear.'

Tuesday, February 24

Back in the garden as the weather is brighter, which meant construction work forged ahead. I can now almost get my shoulders through the Meddling Tunnel and Coleridge can get in and out almost without ducking. Bless his heart, if he didn't snatch some more underwear today. That'll teach the old bag to come round here poking my Owner.

BLAKES CALENDER

FEBRUARY

1	2	3	4	5
6	7	8	9	10
11	12	13	14	15
♥ LOVE FEST ♥				
♥	♥	23	24	25
26	27	28	29	

Ella's season edges closer. She's urinating a lot to spread the scent around and even tried mounting me today, the little minx. Is it wrong to find that quite exciting?

Wednesday, February 25

I have been giving some thought to dodging Samantha while Ella is in season. The last time it happened they didn't live with us, but it seems certain that their exclusion tactics will hinge around keeping Ella in the den and Coleridge and I outside. What they don't know is that Ella can open the kitchen door with her paw, a skill that is the key plank of my counter-strategy.

In all we need two to three minutes of actual lovemaking and then anywhere between fifteen and forty-five minutes to tie together. (It's incredibly painful to be parted too early.) A diversion of some kind seems to be in order; I'm torn between making Coleridge set light to his tail in the fireplace or having him chew through one of the cables at the back of the Owner's computer. I will consult with Ella.

Thursday, February 26

'Or, we could just wait until they go out,' was Ella's idea.

Having given it further thought, although this plan lacks creative flair it does have some aspects to recommend it. Coleridge will be disappointed not to have the chance to be involved though – he likes to feel part of the team.

Friday, February 27

I'm through. At approximately ten minutes before dinnertime today I emerged triumphant into Miss Meddling's garden. There should have been a ceremony, but I couldn't think of anything and just licked my balls for a couple of seconds in quiet celebration.

Forging through the dense undergrowth I looked out on a strange, alien landscape littered with brightly coloured gnomes of various sizes. There was just time for a brief snuffle around before I heard the distant sound of the back door opening over the fence and the rattle of dinner bowls. Fortunately, our side of the Meddling Tunnel is also covered by bushes so I crawled back unseen; something tells me that the Owner would not be pleased by this jaunt into the territory of a known doorbell-botherer.

The path to freedom is clear and I can barely contain my excitement. All night to run around the park, a million bins to plunder, cats to chase. Ella and I will soon be sucking candlelit spaghetti around the back of an Italian restaurant while a jolly fat chef looks on indulgently.

Saturday, February 28

Ella's season is coming closer. Today in the wasteland Scottie would not leave her alone. Like a snake before a snake charmer he was totally hypnotised by Ella's bum. He didn't remain mesmerised for long, though. Within seconds he had hurled himself past me, barking, 'I cannae help mahsel', mah name is Scottie and ah am a sex addict.' I had to pull the little pest off of my mate by his ear. Coleridge made a play too, and fought so hard to get at her that he slipped out of his collar. The puppy is so much like his father it's frightening. Unluckily, it was Samantha who was on walking duty tonight, and she was quick to spot the rising male hysteria.

'Well Ella, we've seen this before, haven't we? When the dogs start behaving like they're at a pole-dancing club, it's time for you to stay indoors for a few weeks.'

Ella whined and I tried for a quick mount before paradise was taken from me, but Samantha is surprisingly strong. Still, they'll have to go shopping sometime, and Ella's been practising working the door handle.

And talking about practising, I got a brief go on the Owner's leg, but as usual he wasn't in the mood. Frankly, I think he has issues with sexual repression and could do with one or two of those little treats. The brief, cold encounter only left me more frustrated, so it was back to the pile of sacks.

MARCH

Sunday, March 1

Separate walk, as Ella is being kept away from the park. It's not fair, she's not even receptive yet, just smells fabulous. Samantha already seems to be especially watchful over her this season. Some dogs would be deterred, but I bark in the face of adversity and pee on the lamppost of danger. I am determined to have Ella or die in the attempt. Well, maybe not actually die, but I'm certainly prepared to risk the Rolled Up Newspaper.

In the meantime I met Constable, who was looking like his old, perfectly coiffed self again and trotting alongside his Mistress, who is roughly the size of three normal humans. I barked him over to join me for a run and he tried, but his Mistress had him and Barkly – another of Scottie's numerous children – on a short lead and easily pulled him back to heel.

'Sorry, Blake, Constable will not be playing today. He's been a very naughty boy. Dog dirt, fleas, mud . . . I don't know what's gotten into him lately.'

'Help me, Blake,' Constable whined pitifully. 'I'm being held against my will and given daily baths. Your Owner is Top Dog, can he set me free?'

I came closer, allowing his Mistress to give me a pat on the head, then walked along beside the trio, slightly miffed. 'Constable,' I barked with a touch of wounded pride, 'we don't need my Owner for a simple problem like this.'

'Oh,' he replied. 'I was hoping he would help. Or Scottie. No offence, but everyone knows you're a bit stupid.'

I looked at him in utter disbelief. My eyebrows took on a life of their own, passing through shock, reproach and anger in quick succession.

'You're very brave though,' the shaggy simpleton continued hastily.

'Say no more, Constable,' I barked with some hauteur. 'If you don't have confidence in your old pack leader liberating you, then we shall leave the matter there.'

'Thanks, Blake, then you'll ask Scottie to help?'

'I think you'll find Scottie, while a great help on one or two occasions, is past his best now. He's making a complete fool of himself at the moment and I think he may be going senile. Age catches up with all of us eventually.'

'Does it?' Constable replied, looking over his shoulder.

'Yes,' I barked firmly. 'You'd be much better off if you left your jam to me.'

'What jam? There's jam? Why do you get all the jam?'

I walked away slowly, shaking my head. If there's a brain inside all that fluff then it's the size of a dog biscuit. Still, it seems that some of the dogs around here could do with being reminded of my own awesome brainpower. We'll see how stupid my plans are when Constable is running free again.

No chance of getting to Ella, but we stared at each other through the kitchen door for a while and tried to nuzzle at the glass. Heart-wrenching stuff. At least it was until I remembered I had a bone to bury behind the shed.

Monday, March 2

It doesn't look like Scottie has his sexual problems under control, as he was making out with a French poodle today. I can't see the attraction myself, I've always thought that dog topiary leaves the victim looking like a member of a 70s funk band. Still, at least he's getting some. Ella's scent has me drooling. For a moment I even considered getting it on with Scottie myself, but a Top Dog has to have a certain authority that is hard to maintain if they are caught in flagrante with Rip Van Winkle.

Tuesday, March 3

Ella's season is in full flow; you can smell her from miles away and the humans are covered in a scent that enters your nose, takes you by the public parts and strokes them gently. I'd say I was a dribbling plaything of lust at the moment, but that would be an understatement. Frankly, if a black cat crossed my path right now I would be offering it dinner and a look at my fascinating collection of genitals. The Owner's leg has long exerted a fascination over me, but is now an object of frenzied desire. It's the way he teases with it, waving it about sexily in front of my very nose, only to act demure

36

when I try and take advantage of what he's so clearly offering. All I know is that if I can't have Ella then I must have that leg.

Coleridge is feeling the strain too, and has taken to humping Miss Meddling's knickers. I'm so distracted by the constant perfume of sex wafting from the den that I've followed suit on more than one occasion.

Wednesday, March 4

At last, the Owner forgot to bolt the flap tonight, and when all the lights in the den had gone out Coleridge and I nosed out of the shed. In the den we slept when the humans went to bed; it's a basic prerogative of being the alpha male that you get to set the day's schedule. After all, there's no point trying to bring down an elk if half the pack's dozing off. Out here in the wild (and I think a small, primitive shed can be considered 'the wild') however, we can stay up all night and sleep all day if we want to, like students.

Coleridge and I wandered at will, without a human constantly dragging us along shouting 'heel', and let our noses lead us to an alley at the back of a pizza restaurant. Even here we could still pick up the occasional tang of Ella and a lot of dogs in houses we passed were scratching at the door to get out. Even so, Ella a mile away could not compete with a pile of black plastic sacks that smelled appetising.*
We quickly clawed our way through one until it spilled its contents; a feast of hardly burned pizza, unfinished pizza, and only slightly spoiled ingredients. We gorged ourselves for what seemed like hours, spreading pizza goodness around, and then a door opened. Annoyed to have our meal interrupted we looked up to see a menacing figure.

'Oi, get out of there you filthy strays,' it shouted. 'Piss off.' Then it lashed out with its foot, catching Coleridge on the rump.

Faced with the option of fighting or fleeing, I considered for a split second and took the third option. Crazed with sexual frustration and the taste of freedom I threw myself on the only leg I'd seen for hours and let my haunches go wild.

'Aaaaaaargggh,' cried the figure. 'You dirty mutt, gerroffa me.' A fist smashed into the back of my head, but I was too lost in a

---

* Sexual frustration can put some dogs off their food, but luckily I've never found this to be a problem. In fact, my greatest fantasy would be Ella in season with a steak balanced on her head.

whirlwind of passion to care. The human obviously wasn't familiar with dogs; where the Owner would have had me off in a second, this one just shook his leg ineffectually, which spurred me on to even greater exertions. Coleridge yapped around us as the figure lurched backwards yelling, drawing attention from the kitchen behind him, and within moments a chorus of laughter.

It was all over too quickly, but there was no time to enjoy the blissful afterglow. As the human's fist descended again, I dodged and, with Coleridge close behind me, fled. Behind I could hear the human shouting abuse after us, and more laughter.

It was an excellent start to the night. As the moon shone down on us Coleridge and I made our way to the park, where we found rabbits. Real. Live. Bunnies. Obviously, they knew better than to venture out in the daytime when there were so many dogs around, but at this time of night they were everywhere, just sitting around nibbling grass and begging to be chased. The two of us obliged them for hours, making our way back to the den only as the sun was coming up. We arrived in time for another meal and an ear scratching.

'Oh, I forgot to lock you in last night,' the Owner said. 'But you've been very good boys. Maybe I don't need to bother with it any more.'

Sometimes I really do love him.

Thursday, March 5

Coleridge has been adopted. Mid-morning, he went back through the Meddling Tunnel intent on more burglary. I was following but stopped dead in the bushes when I heard the door open. Coleridge sat in surprise, looked up at the old woman and wagged his tail.

'Oh dear, a little lost doggie,' Miss Meddling purred at the thief. 'Let's see who you belong to, shall we?'

But of course, his collar had come off a few days previously, and as it is normally hidden by his coat the Owner hasn't noticed.

'Well, you must be a poor stray, let's see what we have for you to eat, shall we?'

I didn't see him for the rest of the day, but at dinnertime he squeezed out of the cat flap and came back through the Meddling Tunnel to eat, walk and gloat, then went back through to beg another bowl of food. She had fed him biscuits and cakes all day, and let him sleep on her lap in front of the fire. She calls him 'Bobby'. If she knew that 'Bobby' was a hardened knicker-thief then I bet she wouldn't be so ready to clutch the little viper to her bosom.

He hasn't returned and I'm too tired and depressed to go adventuring. Shivering in the shed alone, I miss Ella.

Friday, March 6

The treacherous puppy returned this morning for long enough to scoff his breakfast and come for a walk. He spent the night on a pillow in Miss Meddling's bedroom, while I almost froze to death in the shed with only several blankets and some large underpants to protect me from the winter chill. Now he's been over there for most of the day and the Owner hasn't spotted it. I guess because the few times he came out into the garden he was too intent on keeping Ella and me apart and me off his leg.

Saturday, March 7

The constant smell of Ella is driving me completely nuts, and whining by the kitchen door at her does no good at all. In high dudgeon I went for a snooze in the shed and tried to take my mind off sex, by giving some belated thought to Constable's problem. It will be a difficult bone to crack. His Mistress keeps a vice-like grip on that lead, though maybe an all-out assault from a pack of baying hounds would force her to drop it for long enough for him to make his escape.

I also offered some more fatherly advice to Coleridge on the subject of hunting. As every dog in the park knows, I am an expert at tracking down the discarded bun and half-eaten hamburger. It is skills like this that will be invaluable to him in later life.

Sunday, March 8

The Owner and Samantha went out today. My ears pricked at the sound of the front door opening and closing and I was by the back door before the car doors were slammed. Ella was already on the other side with her paw on the handle, panting and barking in anticipation. I tried with my paw, too, and stood on my hind legs with my front paws against the glass to try and force it open, but for once the Owner had locked the door and it wouldn't budge. Of all the low-down dirty tricks.

He must have noticed my paw prints against the glass because when he came back he gave me a stroke and said, 'Trying to get at Ella while we were out eh, Blake? You must think we're stupid.'

Well, yes. Yes, I do, but it seems that even apes have some primitive cunning. It's so unfair, I mean who's the superior species here? Put a monkey in the ring with a wolf and see who comes off best. Give them an opposable thumb and they think they're Lord Dog Almighty.

Ella's season has a week or so to go yet, and it will be a strange day indeed when I can't come up with a plan to outwit the idiot Owner.

Monday, March 9

Completely out of ideas. Stumped. Ella is taken for separate walks by Samantha and at all other times she is closely guarded behind the impregnable glass door. I have to admit that the humans have exhibited a hitherto unprecedented level of cleverness. For a while I considered enlisting Scottie's help, but Constable's words haunt me.

Tuesday, March 10

Coleridge has a new collar that says 'Bobby' courtesy of Miss Meddling and by making extensive use of the cat flap has perfected a system whereby he gets double rations, plus all the cake he can eat, a soft cushion indoors for the night, and is still free to run around with me all night if he's not too full to move. Fortunately for him, the Owner is very regular in his habits and we dogs don't need a clock to be able to time a human's movements to the minute. Coleridge always makes sure that he's around for the bowl of barely digestible offal and the subsequent walk and returns to the garden a couple of times a day when the Owner is known to take coffee breaks and throw a ball for us.

Wednesday, March 11

It must be the constant smell of Ella's season that is making it so difficult to think. It would be good to report that I had hatched an ingenious plan to outwit the humans, but instead I resorted to brute strength. When the Owner opened the door to deliver breakfast my nose was assaulted by the full flood of Ella's scent; all brain systems were immediately shut down save for an overpowering urge to get to her. I'm not a small dog, and the Owner was taken unawares. Shouldering him to one side as he bent with the bowls, I barrelled past and into the hallway where Ella was waiting for me. I was almost on her when the Owner came up behind and made a grab for my collar, shouting for Samantha's help, but I shook him off and Ella and I made for the lounge. Of course, the chances of getting away with a successful impregnation were zero, but such was our pheromone-induced passion that we no longer cared. Instead we scampered around, trying to make sweet love, foiled at every turn by the two humans. Furniture was overturned, ornaments were broken, tempers frayed. Ella even bared her teeth at Samantha.

It was all to no avail. Eventually the Owner grabbed my collar and lifted me, thrashing, into the garden. He shouted a lot. The door slammed and I was left alone, with only an overturned breakfast bowl and a tubby-looking Coleridge for company.

Thursday, March 12

The Owner is surly, Ella remains in the convent, and Coleridge now spends most of every day on a soft pillow, getting his tummy tickled and waggling his legs in the air. Lonely and despondent in the shed alone after dark, I pushed my way through the Meddling Tunnel to find some diversion.

Avoiding the pizza place seemed like a good idea, but I followed a promising scent to the back of a Chinese restaurant, only to find that they have an enormous bin on wheels. Every time I put my paws on it to grab a bag of leftovers it rolled away from me and I eventually gave up and trotted off to the park, where I chased rabbits alone.

The dog is basically a pack animal; he or she enjoys social interaction, and I now know that your average rabbit hasn't got a lot to offer in that department. They may be famed for promiscuity, but so far as I can tell if you're not another rabbit then they are surprisingly virtuous. In fact, running away at great speed seems to be just about all they're cut out for. It is highly likely that my genetic make-up contains greyhound, but apparently not enough to catch a bunny, so I found myself wandering the park alone, sniffing the urine markers left the previous day and wishing for some company.

And then it came to me, in a blaze of intellectual lightning. Constable wants to be able to run free of his Mistress, but no dog said that it had to be during daylight. For a dog, breaking out of a house in the night is as easy as jumping through a paper hoop. All you have to do is sit by the door whining and barking. Afraid of pee-soaked carpets the humans will always open the door and if you don't happen to be within earshot when they start calling you back, then too bad for them.

Armed with a plan to set Constable free and thus re-establish my own tactical genius I made my way back to the Meddling Tunnel in time for breakfast, a walk, and a well-deserved doze in the shed.

Friday, March 13

No walk to the park so I couldn't tell Constable of my breakthrough, but Scottie was at the wasteland this evening and I passed the plan on to him with strict instructions to tell the sheepdog it was all my idea. If I didn't know better I'd have said the little Westie was jealous; it must be hard on a pedigree old dog when he finds himself eclipsed by a younger, brighter mutt.

'So ye didnae think tae tell him tae pee up her leg, then?' he said, somewhat tetchily.

'What sort of plan is that?'

'Oldest trick in the tin, an' works iviry time, too. There's no' a human in the park that willnae drop the leash if ye pee on thum.'

'If you don't mind my saying, Scottie, that is the plan of a simpleton, completely lacking in finesse or intelligence. Mine is superior in every way.'

'Och, ah do mind ye sayin', ye big bag o' slobber. There's many a dug who owes his freedum tae the peein'-on-the-leg trick.'

There followed a polite exchange of views that led to Scottie walking away with his tail in the air, but I could tell that he wishes he'd thought of my plan. Peeing on a human's leg? How very vulgar.

Saturday, March 14

Ella's season is coming to an end, the smell is definitely more intense though she's still being kept in for observation. I barked a mournful poem of thwarted love at the stick and when that palled I found another and barked at both of them, then threw them around the garden with my teeth and tried to hump them. Frankly, they were no substitute for a warm furry backside. One of them even gave me quite a nasty scratch on the groin. Incensed, I made it suffer for its twiggy insolence.

Sunday, March 15

Spent most of the day asleep after a nocturnal prowl around the park. I was hoping that Scottie had gotten a message to Constable and the shaggy idiot might have made it to the park to congratulate me on my genius, but no such luck. Instead, I found a small knoll, which could easily have been a rocky outcrop with the application of some imagination, and howled for my lost love. If anyone had approached from just the right angle I would have been silhouetted against the full moon nicely, and my howl echoed off the shops and houses around the park. Any humans within earshot must have been shaking with terror.

Monday, March 16

The day started well when the Owner turned towards the park this morning instead of the wasteland. Eager to see how my plan had gone down with Constable I tugged at the lead a bit and didn't even try to make him stop so that I could pee on every lamppost and fire hydrant. Coleridge, being a stickler for his morning markings, was having none of that and sat back on his haunches and pulled in the opposite direction. It's a good job the pup isn't as strong as me or it's likely we would have ripped the Owner's arms right off. As it was we made very slow progress, with the human tugging at our leads and cursing. It was a relief when we finally got through the gates. Freed of my shackles, I bounded away to find Constable.

However, the first dog I came across was Scottie. I'm not one to hold grudges so ran up to him barking cheerfully and let him have a good sniff.

'Did you give Constable his instructions?' Not wanting to upset Scottie again I was casual and nonchalant.

'Whut? Oh aye, I gave the fluffbag instructions all right. Look, he's over there noo wi yon Mistress o' his.'

I could wait no longer to be showered with the sheepdog's praise and gratitude and ran towards Constable as fast as my legs would carry me, with Scottie behind.

Constable spotted us. Then, with a bark of welcome, he lifted his leg and urinated on his Mistress's leg.

My own legs ground to a halt beneath me as I watched, aghast. The large female human looked down and yelped, 'Constable!' In slow motion she took a step back, bent down to hold her dripping coat away from her leg, and *dropped Constable's lead*.

Scottie wheezed to a halt alongside me. 'And that is the peein'-up-the-leg trick in action,' he barked happily, as Constable sprinted away towards the pond, trailing his lead. 'Works iviry time, just like ah telt ye.'

Fighting down the urge to bite Scottie's perky little ear off, I stiffened my tail and, with it held aloft, jogged back to the Owner with icy dignity.

From a distance I could hear, 'Constable, get out of there. Right now. Constable, here, you naughty, naughty boy. No, not in the mud, Constable. Oh no, your lovely coat, no, don't shake it here, ahh, you bad dog. Bad dog!'

It sounded like fun, but I would rather have chewed my own leg off than join in.

Tuesday, March 17
Ella is back, thank Dog. Scrubbed and washed so that she no longer smells of her season, the humans wanted to give her a long run after her incarceration so we were all loaded into the car and taken to the forest outside of town for the day. As the car boot slammed I could hear a quavering voice in the distance shouting, 'Bobby, Bobby? Where are you, Bobby?'

'Bobby', who was missing his second breakfast, tried to leave, but was pushed firmly back inside the car. Ella curled up on the seat. 'Am I missing something?' she barked.

Where to start?

Wednesday, March 18
For the first time since the opening of the Meddling Tunnel we could finally take advantage of it as a pack. Even Coleridge left his soft pillow for the night, though it's now getting more difficult for him to get out of the cat flap. He really is very fat now, and moonlight runs are just what he needs.

Ella was keen to snuffle around the backs of restaurants first of all and as it was her first time out I led her towards the alley, only to find an elderly West Highland Scots terrier already emerging from it and walking in our direction.

Scottie.

'Hello, how did you get here?' Ella barked.

'Och, it wus easy. Ah jist whined by the door until ah got let oot for a wee wee, ye ken.'

My tail drooped.

'But that's *my* plan,' I growled.

'Aye, an' a viry good plan it is, worked a treat, ah must say.'

'But what about Constable?'

'Whut aboot Constable? He goat a nice roll in the mud, didnae he?'

'Yes, but he still thinks I'm stupid and you're the clever one.'

'Aye, well he might be ontae somethin' there. Anyway, we havnae goat time fer this. There's a sight ye need tae see reet noo. Follow me.'

I growled again, but Ella nudged me with her nose and barked, 'Come on, Blake, don't ruin my first night out.'

Scottie led us past the restaurants and deep into a labyrinth of alleys behind the high street. On either side was old fencing, a mixture of wire and old, rotten wood. There were no lights except a few left on in the buildings that backed on to the alley and I was becoming excited. Slipping through dark alleys in the middle of the night is what being in a pack of strays is all about. Finally, Scottie stopped beside a particularly decrepit fence. The smell here was awful. Dog excrement and urine, but not from a healthy dog, and with other smells that I couldn't place, but which made my nose quiver in sudden fear. Scottie gave a small yap, and from the other side of the fence came an answering bark. Weak, but delighted.

'Hello? Hello? Scottie, have you brought your friends?'

'Aye, hen,' barked Scottie sadly.

For a moment I thought he'd just brought us to meet one of his sexual conquests, but then the smell swept across my nose again. Scottie snuffled at a gap in the fence and I was just about able to get my head through.

On the other side was a small concrete yard. The smell here was almost overpowering, and quite disgusting. The smell of sickness and dirt and something dying slowly. In the corner was a small cage, made of wood and chicken wire. Inside, something stirred. It was a dog, but a dog like nothing I'd ever seen. Against skin that had lost almost all of its coat I could see welts and sores and ribs standing out. I could see the dog's every laboured breath. It – she – lay in a mound of her own filth, yet her tail was wagging a little and she tried to sit up, though her legs were thin and there was barely enough room.

'Hello,' she yapped happily. 'I can't see you, because my eyes don't work. But you're not Scottie, are you?'

Through my horror I managed to whine, 'No, I'm Blake. Scottie's friend.' I almost managed to make it sound normal. Almost.

'What's the matter, Blake?'

'I'm sorry, you just don't look very . . . well. I think you should be at the vet's.'

'What's a vet?'

'A human who will make you feel better.'

'Oh, I'm fine, though I'd kill for a biscuit. Master seems to have forgotten again. I'm Lolly, by the way. It's nice to meet you. I haven't smelled another dog in ages until Scottie found me tonight.'

'It's nice to meet you too, Lolly. I've got another friend here called Ella. She'd like to meet you as well.'

We stayed with Lolly for half the night, until she drifted off into sleep. And then we all went quietly back to our dens. Safely back, Ella whined for Lolly. So did I. For once Coleridge stayed in the shed.

How could any human treat a dog like that? And why?

Thursday, March 19

Back inside the den today. The kitchen has been scrubbed, Ella's bedding washed, and some vile chemical sprayed everywhere. It's supposed to smell like Alpine Meadow. I've never been to the Alps, but I'm betting the pleasantly mingled odour of edelweiss and pine doesn't strip the membrane right off your nose. Any lingering aroma of Ella's joyous season has disappeared without trace. I flopped on to my usual place on the sofa. Ella looked at me.

'Don't worry, Blake, there's always next time, and the Mistress must be planning to breed from me one day or she'd have had me spayed by now.'

That is true, though knowing my luck she'll want to breed Ella with a pedigree dog called Hunk or something and I won't get a look in. Now I've seen what humans are capable of I wouldn't trust them with a squeaky toy, let alone a dog's happiness.

Lolly's plight has had a profound impact on all of us and for once the house was silent as the three of us thought about the poor, starving dog.

Ella broke the silence. 'We'll have to rescue her.'

'Yes,' I agreed. 'But how?'

'We need a human. One who will treat her properly.'

'The Owner? He's not too bright, but he has got a heart like marrowbone jelly.'

'Possibly, but I can't see our humans adopting any more animals at the moment. I was thinking of someone close by who has recently taken in a "stray".'

We both turned to look at Coleridge. Of course. The Meddling woman may be as mad as a bundle of cats tied up round the middle, but her kindness to animals is proven, and if anyone needs a cushion in front of the fire it's Lolly.

'In the meantime, we need to organise some way of getting food to her.'

'Miss Meddling? But surely, she's got enough cake for a whole herd of old women.'

Ella sighed, 'Lolly, bonehead. Really, Blake, you are as dumb as a tennis ball. I sometimes wonder if you've been running with Constable too often.'

I am getting a little tired of dogs thinking I'm dim.

Friday, March 20

Gave the Owner some big love today. It's worth remembering that he doesn't actually starve us, however much I might question the quality of the fare on offer. And he doesn't beat us either, though the rocking on his heels, going red in the face and counting slowly to ten can be disconcerting. Anyway, prevention is better than a cure and shoving some affection in his face might help to maintain that status quo. Plus he's still acting stressed and it's a little-known but interesting fact that stroking a dog can lower human blood pressure. I am generous enough to selflessly offer my services, even if it means lying across his lap with my legs in the air and twisting with pleasure. It's undignified, but so long as *he's* happy.

Saturday, March 21

It's lucky for us that the Meddling Tunnel is open and that the Owner thinks we're all happily tucked up in the shed all night. We are perfectly positioned to mount emergency aid operations, though we got off to a bad start. Coleridge was supposed to steal some food from Miss Meddling that we could take to Lolly, but I don't think he really understood. The dark of night saw Ella and I waiting quietly by her cat flap for Coleridge to emerge with some liberated provisions. When he did finally show up, backwards out of the hole, he was dragging what smelled like another undergarment, though this was absolutely huge. If you took off the straps and toggles it would have made a nice doggie coat for a rhinoceros.

After the pup had taken his new swag to the heap in the shed, we switched seamlessly to Plan B. The forage at the alley was not good, but by ripping through the black plastic bags that had overflowed from the large wheeled bins, we assembled a slice of cold pizza, half a chicken breast in sauce, and a couple of spare ribs. These we took to the gap in the fence, which Coleridge could just about struggle through. A small hole in the chicken wire allowed Lolly to pull the food in, and while she ate we told her that we planned to take her to live with an old lady who was brimming with cake and cushions.

'Oh no,' she replied. 'I don't think I'd like that.'

'But you're sick and starving,' Ella woofed gently.

'I can't leave my Master. What would he do without me?'

No amount of barking would convince her and soon a light came on and a window opened.

'Shut your mouth, dog, or I'll come down there and break your teeth.'

Lolly cringed into the corner of her cage and would not stir again. I've often wished that humans had left off tinkering with wolves all those years ago, but never more so than now. Why spend thousands of years breeding a good and faithful companion just to treat them like this? If there is any justice in the world this human will be thrown to Lolly's distant cousins, and if no wolves can be found I'll happily stand in for them. Although I've never bitten before, I'd give my tail for a nip. Just one bite, straight to the jugular.

Sunday March 22

More relief work last night. Running around all night is leaving me so tired during the day that I could barely manage any craziness at all come walk time, but I just about mustered the energy to get my paws on the Owner's chest and do some high-pitched barking in his face. It's this kind of attention to detail that means he always knows I'm grateful for a walk.

Saw Scottie on the wasteland. His human had not been pleased about the night-time excursion, given that he had had to get dressed and spend two hours walking around town trying to find his dog. Further requests for a night pass had resulted in a quick trip to the gutter on a very short lead. I was able to set his mind at ease that we had been doing all we could for Lolly, but he is a dog of fierce principles and will not be happy until we have found a good home for her.

'That might not be quite as easy as you'd think.' I told him about her refusal to leave her Master.

'Aye, I wus afeared o' that. The puir wee bitch needs some re-educatin', an' if she willnae listen tae Ella then ah'll huv tae step in. It'll nae be easy getting' oot the den though.'

He looked pensive for a moment, with his little bearded head on one side, then he barked, 'Ah'll huv tae give it further thought.'

'You do that and I'll come up with a plan too,' I woofed kindly.

'Right, ye do that, Blake. Nuthin' personal, but ah willnae hold mah breath, eh?'

This was going too far. 'My plan got you out all right the other night,' I reminded him with a hint of chilliness.

'Aye, but it wus nothin' more than a one-hit wonder. Noo, this calls for the finely tuned wisdom o' an older heid.'

Am now officially fed up with the dogs around here.

Monday, March 23

A small spot of bother today. The Owner has suddenly taken to walking me on a lead in the park, as my grasp of the command 'heel' is deemed to have become shaky, and due to the lack of sleep, my head was a little fuzzy.* So I was chained to the Owner alongside

---

* I thought that we'd done with his ridiculous training regimes, but no. Apparently a transgression as small as trying to run down a cat while the Owner is drinking hot coffee will land a dog straight back in his walk-next-to-my-boot camp. He really should know better than to drink hot beverages while restraining a powerful beast such as myself.

Coleridge and not in the best of tempers when a duck whirred into the pond with a splash. I must admit, instinct did sort of take over at that point, and I did forget that the Owner was attached when I leaped at the duck. In my defence Coleridge was right alongside me when I hit the water. The trouble was, so was the Owner. As it turned out he was not in the mood for a swim, even though the water was not as cold as it could have been at this time of year.

Samantha's laughter did nothing to alleviate his mood when we got back to the den, and my whining, licky apology was not accepted. Fortunately he no longer resorts to the Rolled Up Newspaper, but the waiter service this evening reached such a nadir of surliness that I thought for a moment we might be in Paris.

On top of all that he broke my collar dragging me out of the pond. I was attached to that collar; it was a proper black, studded leather one and I've had it since I was a puppy. The Owner's a traditionalist when it comes to collars and I've always fancied it made me look a little like Freddie Mercury.

Tuesday, March 24

I seem to be thinking better now that I'm not being distracted by my hormones and had a brainwave to get Scottie out of the den at night. It is based on human psychology and personal experience, and is complex but infallible. All the hallmarks of a classic Blake manoeuvre.

Wednesday, March 25

Scottie was on the wasteland this evening so I strolled over with the relaxed nonchalance that is born of superiority and stuck my nose up his bum. After I'd had a good sniff (pleasant, but in my opinion Scottie needs to cut down on the carbohydrates), I rolled lazily in some decomposing leaves.

'Oh, by the way, Scottie, I have a plan that will have you running around at night as free as a rabbit.'

'Oh Dog, wull let's huv it then, though ye'll excuse me if ah dinnae start doin' the somersaults yet.'

I ignored the sarcasm. 'It's based on a close examination of human psychology and personal experience and is complex but infallible. All the hallmarks, in fact –'

'Och, jist get oan wi' it, wull ye?'

'I seem to remember you saying that your Owner has a shed in the garden?'

'Aye, whut of it?'

'And you are a terrier? Digging is part of your genetic programming?'

'Aye, ah could tunnel mah way tae Tibet if ah felt like it.'

'Well all you need to do is make a mess in the den on a nightly basis. Pee everywhere, leave a few stools around the place, some vomit if you have the stomach for it. Your Owner will have you out in the shed before you can say "Bad Dog". And after that it's just a quick dig to freedom.'

'Ye mean shit in the den? In the actual den? Like a puppy?'

'Yes, your Owner will just think you've lost control of your elderly bowels. Pee with abandon, do not stint on the stools.'

'Wuuuulll,' Scottie growled slowly. 'Ye can stick yer plan up a cat's arse. Mah elderly bowels indeed. As if ah could shit in the actual den!'

'But it'll work! Look at our Owners talking right now. It'll only take one mention of dog mess in the den and mine will be waffling about the advantages of a nice warm shed away from the shag pile. You'll be out like a shot, and Edina and Jock with you.'

'Aye, but yer so-called plan is basically poo. So ah think ah'll leave it thank ye verra much and stick tae the old "persistent-concentration-wreckin'-whinin'-by-the-door".'

'And meanwhile Lolly suffers?'

For a second he looked shaken. 'Aye, wull ah can surely get oot withoot losin' mah dignity.'

'Your dignity, Scottie?' I woofed quietly. 'You wear a tartan doggie coat. Last week I watched you mount a St Bernard with a flying leap from a park bench.'

His reply was lost on me as the Owner had sneaked up and grabbed me by the knotted rope that is currently serving as a collar.

Thursday, March 26

I was hoping for a visit to the park today, but the Owner now has a cold. It's one of those sicknesses that dogs can catch too, but of course we don't make such a massive fuss about it. Typically, the Owner pretends to have flu and will not venture more than half a mile from the den, shuffling and complaining all the while. Apparently it is my fault for dragging him into the pond, but even puppies know that's not how a virus works. I tried to communicate this to him with some extremely gymnastic eyebrow action, but he just thought I had wind.

Friday, March 27

A great haul from the restaurant bins last night. There's not much of an improvement in Lolly – looking at her makes me wonder how she could possibly still be alive – but she has started taking more of an interest in the strange dogs who bring her food. Unfortunately, she continues to refuse to listen to any talk of trading in her Master for a soft pillow and a plate of cake. We may have to dognap her for her own good. While Coleridge ferried scraps of food to her cage, Ella tried to reason with her and I set my jaws of steel to widening the gap in the fence.

Even though she has only met him for the one night, Lolly seems to believe that Scottie is some kind of canine Prince Charming, but then she is blind and was probably out of her mind with hunger at the time. Nevertheless, if she'll listen to any dog, it will be him, so now is not the time for him to be developing a sense of dignity.

After feeding Lolly and keeping her company for a while, the three of us followed the faint scent markings to Scottie's den to see how his plan was coming along. Inside we could hear him whining and pawing at the door, and Mr McCormick shouting, 'Will ye no' shut up Scottie, fer cryin' oot lood. Ye've ainly jest been oot fer a widdle noo go tae sleep ye silly begger.'

It doesn't look like 'persistent-concentration-wreckin'-whinin'-by-the-door' is such a winning strategy after all.

Saturday, March 28

We had another visit from Miss Meddling today, and I am sorry to say the Owner once again failed to take the opportunity to have me run the puppy-stealing home-wrecker off the premises.

The 'flu' has not yet cleared up and he has been wearing his dressing gown around the den and moaning constantly, so I think Samantha was glad to leave him at home when she went shopping. On her return he immediately dived into the shopping bags for pills and powders and then started to help his mate put the shopping away. Samantha was talking about how she had started stocking up on items for the baby, and I was pleased when he pulled a new collar out of a bag. Black and studded leather, exactly what I'd ordered. And a smart new chain lead too.

It was then that the doorbell rang. Samantha was standing on a chair to get to the high cupboards, so he reluctantly shuffled to the front door, pausing only to order me to shut up and push me into the lounge with his foot.

When he opened the door I stopped my enraged barking and switched to a low, ominous growling.

'Oh, it's you again, Miss Meddling. What can I do for you this time?'

There was a pause during which the old woman obviously looked over the items of shopping he was holding, then she said, 'A collar, chains, baby oil, and is that a bunch of carrots? How absolutely vile.'

The Owner sounded nonplussed, but was obviously trying to be friendly. He sounded a bit manic to me. 'I'm hoping I'll feel better with a few carrots inside me. They make your eyes sparkle, you know.'

'You're even more depraved than I thought. I have warned the police about you, you know.'

The Owner dropped the false cheeriness. 'Look, Miss Meddling, I'm dosed up to the eyeballs and just on my way to bed. What is it you want?'

'On drugs too, eh? I should have guessed. You perverts will stop at nothing to get your degraded thrills, will you? You're probably so high you have no idea what I'm talking about.'

'Miss Meddling, I honestly have no idea what you're talking about.'

'I knew it. I SAID, I KNEW IT,' she shouted. 'Now, where's my girdle?'

'Your . . .?'

'Girdle. I know you've stolen it, you beast.'

'What on earth would I be doing with your girdle?'

'RUBBING YOURSELF,' she shouted triumphantly. 'If you don't give it back I shall set my dog on you.'

'You have a dog?'

'Ah ha, then you don't deny it. Yes, I have a dog, so think about Bobby the next time you feel the urge to go rummaging in an old lady's washing basket.'

I could hear that tone in the Owner's voice. Any second now, I thought, he's going to start getting red in the face and clutching his own hair. 'There's no need to shout, Miss Meddling. Or to poke me. Can't you see I'm sick?'

'Sick is exactly the right word. Sick to the very soul.'

'Oh for fu–. For once and for all, Miss Meddling, I do not have your girdle. I do not have your underwear. I am *not* a pervert. If I *were* a pervert I would go to bed with a donkey rather than rub myself with your knickers. Is that clear?'

It was all going quite well, and I was rather proud of him. Very occasionally you see a glimpse of the chest-beating gorilla beneath that puny human exterior. Unfortunately he rather let himself down at the end.

'And now, if you'll excuse me, the medication is making me feel a little strange so I'm going to get into a nice, warm girdle . . . bath, I mean BATH.'

The door slammed loudly, and a few seconds later the lounge door opened. I ran out barking in time to see Samantha sitting in the kitchen doorway with tears running down her face. She was shaking and trying to eat her own fist. Displaying all the signs of a very upset human, in fact. After a quick glance, however, the Owner ignored her and walked stiffly up the stairs. I never imagined he could be so heartless towards the mother of his unborn child.

Samantha just about managed to stammer after him, 'You say you're not a pervert, but I see you're taking your sex paraphernalia with you,' and then she started howling.

Sunday, March 29

The Owner is still skulking upstairs, but Samantha took us for a walk in the park. She hasn't vomited for a while, but even so she smells really good at the moment, and I trailed behind her for a while insinuating my nose into whatever crevices became available, for which I got a Slapped Nose. It was late morning and most of the dogs had already been and gone, though Scottie was trotting alongside his Owner who was walking arm in arm with Mrs Fortiss.

Having little luck with the Samantha-sniffing I joined the party and told Scottie how Lolly had been asking for him. He replied stiffly that he was working on it and would be free soon. I barked that we'd heard how well his plan was going.

'Spyin' on me noo, are ye? Well ye can spy all ye like, ah will not be soilin' the carpet or peein' upon the foorniture. 'Tis fer puppies and old dugs whut dinnae ken any better.'

Monday, March 30

Ella thinks that Scottie is trying to prove himself young and virile despite his advancing years and that this explains his sex addiction as well as his aversion to doing anything that might make him seem infirm.

This is *deep* dominance psychology.

'So how do we make him stop?' I asked.

She thought for a while, then woofed, 'If he felt particularly youthful and dominant, perhaps the root cause of his objections would be removed.'

Clever thinking, though obviously it will take a certain amount of genius to weld Ella's insight into a workable scheme.

Tuesday, March 31

On the way out of the park gate today we saw an immaculately styled Constable being walked in by his Mistress, who was wearing fishing waders.

'Help me, Blake, the peein'-up-the-leg trick doesn't work any more. If I don't get some filth soon I'm going to go crazy.'

Hah, so *now* he wants my help. Blake the little bit dim but quite brave to the rescue, eh?

I didn't have the opportunity to pass on the den-defecation strategy, but an idea is forming, a big idea. An enormous plan to help Lolly. And the best thing is that once again the park dogs will have a common goal. Things have been getting sloppy recently, what the dogs need is something to bring them together, under the authority of a natural born leader of course. Forming a rescue and relief pack will help Lolly and put me back in charge where I can prove my mental abilities beyond doubt.

APRIL

Wednesday, April 1

The Owner finally got dressed and left his bed just in time to trip over Coleridge, who was sneaking out of the room designated for the baby. He shouldn't have been upstairs, and he definitely should not have been carrying a teddy bear in his mouth (he's developed a bit of a thing for soft bears since the Mr Muffy episode), but having the Owner fall over him was purely accidental. He most certainly did not deserve a proper Slap on the Nose, which made him yelp. Shouting about all dogs being a complete nuisance while bundling us all out into the garden was an enormous overreaction.

First the shed and the rehoming threat, then the slapping and shouting – the Owner is on a downward spiral. Soon it will be the chicken-wire cage with the occasional scrap pushed through by a charitable passing stray. Coleridge is all right of course, he just shimmied through the Meddling Tunnel and spent the rest of the day being stuffed full of cake and drinking tea out of a saucer.

Thursday, April 2

The day started with an apology, which was welcome if late. It made no difference of course – as I've observed, all dogs are a little bit Lolly at heart and I still would have snuffled, licked and made toothy grabs for the lead if he hadn't said sorry, but we all appreciated the gesture. Nevertheless, I hope that he hasn't started showing his true nature. The moment the chicken wire comes out I shall be forcing my way through Miss Meddling's cat flap and never coming out again.

While attempting to clip on three leads the Owner explained that he and Samantha are worried about money and he's nervous about the baby coming and doesn't know if he'll be a good father. The only real differences between dogs and babies as far as I can tell are that your human baby doesn't try and pull your arm off twice a day or hump your leg. Otherwise it's all the same: put food in one end and try and keep a safe distance from the other. What he *should* be asking himself is, is he a good dog owner?

Friday, April 3

Due to the inferior workings of human ears the Owner couldn't hear it, but when we walked to the park today a couple of old women I'd not seen before were talking about him. There was some discreet pointing, too.

'That's him, goes around on drugs stealing people's knickers, they say.'

'I heard he likes to bugger donkeys.'

'Well, I've been told stories that've put me off carrots for life.'

'Remember there was that time last year? They say he was running up and down the road with one of them vibratinors.'

'Yes, but that was some other man's.'

'So? What normal man runs up and down the road with another chap's vibratinor? That's weird that is.'

'You can tell just by looking at him, can't you. He's got "pervert" written all over his face.'

'It's his girlfriend I feel sorry for. Baby on the way too, they say. Not married of course.'

'And the dogs. If he'd bugger a donkey what must he be getting up to with those poor mutts.'

'Someone should tell the police.'

'Or those animal cruelty people.'

As I've often had cause to think, humans are crazy.

Saturday, April 4

My luck was in. The sun was shining, the Owner was up early and it seemed like every dog owner had beaten a path to the park. First stop Scottie.

'Hello, big dog, you're looking in peak condition today,' I woofed, just trying to warm him up.

'Are ye takin' the pish?'

'No, just saying that it's amazing how you seem to get younger and younger.'

'Ah'm nae stoppin' here, if ye're gaein' ta be funny,' he growled and wandered away to sniff at a golden retriever bitch.

That didn't go so well, so I tried my paw with Constable.

'Constable, I've got a plan that will have you rolling in poop by tonight if you can remember a few simple instructions.'

I told him of the whining-by-the-door ploy as it's quick and easy and will give him a taste for night-time freedom. It may take him some time to grasp the intricacies of the soiling-the-house plan. As it was I was pleasantly surprised by how easily he understood. I only had to explain it to him a dozen times or so.

'So I whine by the door until the Mistress opens it and then . . . whoosh?'

'That's right, whoosh. Then I'll meet you here.'

'Here, right.'

'Because?'

'Because there's a bitch in distress.'

'And?'

'And you're putting a pack together to rescue her.'

'Very good, Constable,' I barked proudly. 'Just remember, whine and whoosh.'

'Whine and whoosh, right.'

After that I felt I deserved a little break, so went for a scoot with Ella, after which the Owner started that irritating whistling. It would have been nice to spread the news of my new pack some more, but I've made a start, and breaking Constable out kills two cats with one bite. There's a dog who won't think I'm dim any more.

Sunday, April 5

Waited for Constable in the park, but no sign of him. Eventually, we gave up and went to find Lolly some food on our own. Another good haul, including a pork chop that I would have gobbled myself, except Ella stopped me with a growl. Lolly is still asking for Scottie, and I did my best to assure her that he would be coming soon. Those blind eyes of hers seem to see right through me, though.

'Are you sure, Blake? I miss Scottie, he's such a funny dog.'

'It's all right, Lolly,' I woofed. 'Nothing's going to stop Scottie coming to see you as soon as he can get out of his den.'

'Well tell him I wish he'd come soon. I can't wait to smell him again.'

I started to say that with breath like Scottie's I was surprised she couldn't smell him from here, but thought better of it.

'He'll be along soon,' I promised.

Monday, April 6

With all the night-time exercise I am looking sleek and fighting fit at the moment. In excellent shape to take command of a new pack, though I need to get the membership numbers up. The first dog I spotted today was Constable, on a lead as usual.

'Where were you the night before last?' I asked gruffly, falling in alongside him.

He looked at me with pity, the cheeky fuzzball, and said, 'I tried out your plan, but – and I'm sorry I have to say this Blake – it was absolutely useless. It was nice of you to try, but you're just not Scottie.'

I was shocked. How could such a simple strategy have gone awry? 'Why don't you take me through it, Constable, and we'll see if we can spot what went wrong.'

'Well, I did everything you said. I sat by the door, and whined and paced and tried to look as though I needed to relieve myself.'

So far so good. 'And then what?'

'The Mistress opened the door. I went through it with a whoosh and ran as fast as I could.'

'That all sounds fine, so what stopped you getting to the park?'

'Obviously I had to stop running when I got to the other end of the house. I turned round and ran back again, but by that time she had closed the door.'

I was puzzled for a moment and then light dawned. 'Constable. What side of the door were you on when you started whining?'

'Outside. Mistress always lets me out for ten minutes in the evening before bed.'

'Ahh, I think I can put my paw on the nub or crux of the problem. I think what went wrong, Constable, is that you are the most idiotic dog since Rex the Wonder Horse.'

Tuesday, April 7

Dog be praised, after receiving revised instructions, Constable made it to the park last night. He was there already when we arrived, though hardly recognisable. I was pleased to see that once again the elegantly coiffed Dr Jekyll had been replaced by the twiggy, muddy Mr Hyde. His silky, flowing coat was matted with faeces, dirt and more faeces. I'm sure I saw a family of rodents camping out in there, too.

'Rabbits,' he panted when he saw us. 'Lots of rabbits.'

It was obvious that he'd discovered the park's noctural denizens, as their droppings clung to his coat like baubles on a Christmas tree, and if I'm any judge of bad breath he'd eaten half a ton as well, along with some dead woodland creature.

Lolly awaited though. With a dog's life in the balance there was no time for more play. Constable proved an able helper, using his size to knock over dustbins and working through their maggoty contents with brisk efficiency to find scraps that we would never have considered. Those we rejected as too disgusting he happily ate himself.

The best-of-breed sheepdog, so used to being pampered, was more shocked than any of us at Lolly's plight and vowed instantly to join the relief pack. It seemed like a good moment to start instructing him on how to move his sleeping arrangements to the shed.

'Poo and pee will set you free, Constable. What will set you free?'

'Poo and pee,' he chorused.

I'm not sure he'll need to bother though, as I can't imagine that even his Mistress will have him in the house in that state. We went through the plan a few more times anyway, and then he barked that he had to go as he was competing in a dog show later that day and needed to be 'fresh'. He'll be lucky, the only way he's going to be fresh after tonight's outing is if he's shaved and dipped in detergent.

After he'd left Lolly looked up from her bed of urine and old excrement. 'I like your friend,' she said. 'He smells a bit though.'

Wednesday, April 8

Saw Scottie in the wasteland this evening and tried to slip in a few comments about how young and vigorous he's looking, but he thought I was 'bein' funny' again and made to walk away.

'Lolly really needs you, Scottie.' That made him stop.

'I'm assembling a pack of rescue workers, and we need you too. There will be a team assigned to rescue operations and another on food procurement duty.'

'Aye, wull ye can coont me in o' course.'

'But you're no use locked in the den.'

'I telt ye ah'm workin' on it.'

'Come on, Scottie, a little poo here and there, the occasional puddle. What does it matter to a dog of your legendary reputation?'

'Will ye no' stop talkin' aboot it? There wull be none o' that in *mah* den.'

'You're just being stubborn and stupid.'

He looked old and tired for a second. 'Aye, mebbee, but ah'm still no' goin' tae the toilet in the den.'

Thursday, April 9

The Owner had a visit from a policeman while Samantha was out today. My reaction time was excellent. I was at the door way ahead of the Owner and barking like a hound of hell.

'That's a good guard dog you've got there,' said the policeman approvingly as the Owner opened the door, struggling to restrain me. Then the policeman held out his hand for me to sniff. No intruder has ever done this before. I was taken aback, but smelled him suspiciously. He seemed bona fide so I downgraded from red to orange alert. At that moment Coleridge swept in from the kitchen. Knowing that the puppy only has two reactions to intruders – nip or hump – the Owner instantly let go of me and caught him, just before he reached the uniformed leg. I took the opportunity to jump up for a closer inspection, but the policeman instantly ordered 'down' in a tone I couldn't help but obey.

'Thanks, officer, Blake's just a bit friendly. What can I do for you? Nothing serious I hope.'

'I'm sure it's nothing, sir, but I've had repeated complaints about the owner of this house. Is that you, sir?'

'Yes. Complaints from someone by the name of Meddling?'

'Can't say that, sir. Seems that a certain party suspects you of stealing their undergarments.' The policeman's mouth twitched a little at this. 'But there are also allegations of illegal substances on the premises and animal abuse.'

I thought for a moment that the police must have heard that we're being forced to sleep in the shed, but the officer didn't seem to be taking the interview seriously. 'These dogs seem healthy enough, I must say,' he said, reaching down to stroke my head.*

---

* I'm not for a moment condoning intruders, but if they insist on coming to the den, then this is definitely the sort of behaviour that will see them leaving with the seat of their pants intact.

'Miss Meddling has gotten it into her head that I'm some kind of sexual predator. I'm not of course, and I'm not on drugs either, I just had a cold . . . well, it was more like flu really.'

'She said that you'd been throwing your dirty pictures at her.'

'Those weren't mine, and I didn't throw them, they blew over the fence accidentally . . .'

'Also told us that there's been a previous disturbance with a marital aid.'

'Again, that wasn't mine. It belonged to the man who used to live here. Lived here before we moved in, that is.'

The policeman held up a hand. 'It's no concern of mine what you do in the privacy of your own house, sir, so long as it's legal. Just a friendly bit of advice for now: keep it to yourself, sir.'

'But I'm not –'

'No one's saying you are. Not at present. We know how it is with the old ladies sometimes. They get lonely and forgetful about where they've put their knickers and there's the man over the fence who likes the "specialist" literature and . . . Well, I'm sure I don't have to draw you a picture.'

'Happens all the time, I expect.'

'Not all the time, sir, no. But we do take theft very seriously, so if you do come by any information about the lady's clothing, you'd do well to call us. And we'll be keeping abreast of the situation, of course. You never know where a major crime might be brewing.'

'No, I expect you don't.'

'What was that, sir?'

'I was just saying I'll keep my eyes open for Miss Meddling's knickers.'

'Ah ha ha ha. I think we'd all prefer it if you did exactly the opposite, sir. Well, I'll be off. I hope I won't be seeing you any time soon.'

Then he patted me on the head and walked away. The Owner had gone a bit red in the face, probably with jealousy. If he could give commands with that kind of authority the den would be a much quieter place.

Friday, April 10
A bad night. As is now routine Ella and I waited for the lights to go out at the top of the den and squeezed through the Meddling

Tunnel, where Coleridge joined us. Scavenging in the alley at the back of the High Street turned up nothing, every single black plastic bag had been put in one of those enormous bins and the lid closed. The Chinese restaurant had even fenced off its small yard to keep us out. Empty-mouthed we went to see Lolly, only to find her lying on her side unable to move.

'It's all my own fault,' she barked weakly. 'The Master let me out today and I shouldn't have tried to jump up. I was so pleased to see him, but I know he doesn't like it.'

He had kicked her hard in the ribs and then picked her up and thrown her back in the cage.

There was nothing we could do, not even offer her a few scraps to eat. Nevertheless she thanked us profusely for trying and, as we turned to go, woofed, 'Is Scottie coming?'

Saturday, April 11
Again, we could find no food for Lolly. Things are getting desperate. Ella and I had an emergency conference.

'We need more dogs looking out for food and Scottie to talk Lolly into escaping,' I barked. 'But how are we going to achieve it?'

'Let's start with the Scottie problem,' Ella replied. 'I've been thinking about it and I have an idea.'

I lay in the shed with my ears and tail wilting as Ella took me on a tour of Scottie's mind. She thinks that a sure-fire way of boosting his self-confidence would be for him to become Top Dog of the Lolly rescue pack. I pointed out the obvious flaw in the plan. They may think I'm dim, but every dog in the park acknowledges that if we had such a thing as a Top Dog it would be me. Ella lay down and put her nose to mine.

'Yes, I know.' She licked me softly. 'So you'll have to pick a fight with Scottie and let him win.'

Lose a fight to Scottie? I'd prefer to eat my own nose. I've worked tirelessly to achieve my status, and if I can't be seen to defend it from that old dodderer I may as well just paint 'lamppost' on my head and stand in a corner, or else bite my balls off, tie a little pink ribbon on my head and sit in a teapot. In a word, no.

'No,' I said, firmly.

'What would Churchill have done?' she asked. 'Or Napoleon?'

'No.'

'It would be the clever thing to do, appearing weak but all the time manipulating fortunes like a cat with a mouse.'

'No.'

Ella looked over patiently, and sighed. 'Someone's got to let go of their canine pride before Lolly dies.'

Sunday, April 12

I tried talking to Scottie again in the park today and although he looked wretched when I told him how bad Lolly was, he only muttered that his plan was sure to work soon and walked away when I begged him to reconsider.

Monday, April 13

We finally managed to scrape together a few mouthfuls of food from an overflowing bin further down our street and took it to Lolly. Ella and Coleridge ran away to see if they could find more and I volunteered to stay for company. There was a question I wanted to ask.

'Lolly?'

'Yes, Blake.'

'If someone asked you to give up your dignity to help another dog would you do it?'

She turned her blind eyes to face me through the wire of her tiny cage, and woofed very softly, 'What dignity?'

Tuesday, April 14

It is decided. I shall challenge Scottie to a fight at the earliest opportunity and throw it. Although I can hear thousands of ancestors baying their disapproval I am steadfast and resolute. Scottie may be the only dog who can save Lolly, and if I must become a laughing stock before the whole park then so be it. Bark as I might, Ella insists that a private scrap on the wasteland will not do. The fight must be witnessed by as many dogs as possible. It's enough to paralyse my tail permanently.

Fortunately, Scottie wasn't there today so I took the opportunity to have what could be a final saunter as nominal Top Dog, deigning to sniff the occasional bum and being generally noble and gracious. If anything it made me feel worse, so I twined myself around the Owner's legs looking for a scrap of comfort. Got a couple of pats and a 'Good Boy'.

Wednesday, April 15

No walks today, and the Owner noticed how much dog poo was lying around the garden, but it's not like we *made* him tread in it. He kicked up such a fuss I thought he was going to sew us all up at the back end for a moment, but what does he expect? The rubbish he puts in our bowls goes through us like a champion whippet, and a dog's got to keep his bowels in good condition.

Flicking all our mess over the fence with a trowel into Miss Meddling's garden was just juvenile in my opinion.

Thursday, April 16

Started warming up for the big fight today by allowing my stick to get the better of me with Ella coaching.

'That's it, Blake, loud barking. Good snarl. Circle it, circle it. Remember the stick is dangerous and cunning. Quickly now, jump on it, miss, and land on your back. Excellent work. Up on your hind legs, now drop, lunge and on your back in the submissive position. That's it. The stick is winning, Blake, you're doing very well.'

It wasn't that hard. If I'm honest it's always touch and go whether me or the stick is going to come out on top anyway.

Friday, April 17

It came as no great surprise to find that Constable did not win any prizes at the dog show. Although his Mistress had frantically tried to clean him and spent an hour blow-drying him, it must have been an impossible task. The judges found dried rabbit droppings beneath his collar, a nest of fleas hidden deep within his coat, and half a cold French fry lodged in his beard. Apparently, his breath nearly knocked one of them out and his coat was judged to have become 'dry and flyaway' through overwashing. For the first time since he was a puppy his Mistress came away with no rosette and no cup. She is distraught, but more determined than ever to get him back to peak show condition. He spent most of yesterday in a grooming parlour and is now under house arrest. Poo and pee has not set him free, it's just got him locked in the utility room with newspaper on the floor.

I only hope Scottie has more luck in forming a rescue pack.

Saturday, April 18

It is done. I am no longer the unofficial Top Dog, but a whipped and cringing cur. Yesterday's dog. If I were a wolf I would be licking my wounds and slinking away from the den to die alone in the snow.

I can't bring myself to think about it yet, but there is one tiny ray of light. Tonight we can tell Lolly that Scottie will be coming soon.

Sunday, April 19

Lolly was delighted with the news, but I haven't been this depressed since my dear old mum first told me about postmen. I expect my reward will be great in dog heaven, though. I deserve at least a kennel made of steak and the Owner to develop a love of having his leg humped.

Monday, April 20

In the interests of keeping a complete journal I should document my fight with Scottie. It has been two days and the pain and loss have receded slightly. I can now bring myself to write about it.

The day began with Samantha insisting that the Owner stop working and get some exercise. For once I hung back. There was no dancing, just a pleading look at the Owner. It was supposed to indicate that I wanted to stay in the den, but was instead taken as a sign that his flailing and shouting 'training' technique was finally paying off. The 'Good boy, Blake' as I was dragged out of the door was no consolation whatsoever.

Arriving at the park gate my worst fears were confirmed. I smelled that Scottie was in. He always leaves a little marker on the gatepost. So were a lot of other dogs, most of them chasing each other around the grass. Ella led me into the centre of the pack and gave me a woof of encouragement, then left. I couldn't bear to have her watch my downfall.

'Think of Churchill and Napoleon. Think of Lolly,' she barked over her shoulder.

I stiffened my tail, and walked up to Scottie who was romping arthritically with Ginger. As rehearsed with Ella, I was snarling, with drool dripping from my teeth in a very effective manner. Even in such trying circumstances I pay attention to detail.

'Hey, Scottie, you look stupid in that coat.' It wasn't a great start but picking a fight with your best friend and trusted lieutenant is not easy.

'De ye not like it?' he replied, spinning around to show it off. ''Tis verra fetchin' and warm as a lass's buttom.'

'I mean your Owner smells funny.'

'Aye, he does that. Ah'm thinkin' it's a glandular disorder, ye ken.'

It wasn't going so well, but then I had a flash of inspiration. Putting my front paws on Ginger's back, I made to mount her, barking, 'As Top Dog around here, I claim this bitch.'

Scottie looked shocked, his tail wagging very slowly. 'Tak' it easy, Blake, if Ella catches ye, she'll huv the balls oaf o' ye.'

'Ella? What's Ella got to do with it, I'm the Top Dog around here, aren't I?' And then I remembered the one thing that is guaranteed to send Scottie into a frenzy of rage. 'Aren't I, Laird Scotland McIvor of Strathpeffer?'

His full name did the trick; Scottie came at me like an enraged mop head.

Dismounting Ginger, I reared to my full height then, snarling, dropped and rolled, managing to present my neck to his teeth at exactly the right moment. It was actually quite a nifty little manoeuvre, not that I was very proud of it.

Scottie sank his teeth into me, and I yelped. He may need the attentions of a good dentist and hygienist, but teeth are teeth, and no one likes having a mouthful of them worrying the sensitive skin around the throat. My blood was rising now and it was all I could do to keep from tearing one of his ears off, but I reined in my temper and just windmilled my paws and twisted furiously beneath him. It must have looked ferocious but was about as effective as waving a ball of wool at a kitten.

Finally, he let go and barked, 'Had enough, ye big dumb mongrel?'

It was tempting to roll over there and then, but I had to make the fight look real so, thanking my rehearsals with Ella and the stick, began circling him, growling and trying to look as rabid as possible. Then I pounced, missing, but dipping my head just enough so that he could catch my ear, which he did and – I have to record – it really hurt quite a lot. I shook my head to try and dislodge my opponent, but he's tenacious is Scottie and he just swung around my head like he was on a fairground ride, with his little claws raking my muzzle whenever he passed close enough. Out of the corner of my eye I could see both of our Owners running over, mine shouting, 'Grab their back legs, grab their back legs!'

I ended it by rolling on my back and catching him on my chest, allowing him to get another grip on my throat, then I whined submission and it was all over. Scottie's Owner grabbed him while mine clipped the lead on me, scowling and shouting, 'Bad boy.'

I thought that Scottie's Owner might explode for a second, but after examining his dog and seeing him completely unharmed, he turned to mine and laughed, 'Did ye see the whuppin' mah wee Scottie gave yer brute then? It's a brave heart he's goat.'

Mine was less happy to see my ear bleeding and pointed this out to Mr McCormick.

'Och, 'tis ainly a scratch, and will serve tae teach the big haggis no' tae mess wi' mah Scottie.'

The Owner said nothing, but began pulling me away, shouting for Ella and Coleridge. The old human was still fussing over Scottie. 'Ye shouldnae be fightin', boy, but it did mah aild heart good tae see ye take hum doon like that. Ye showed hum, eh? There's plenty o' life in the aild dog yet.'

We passed through a crowd of dogs. Behind me Scottie began to yap triumphantly. The other dogs joined him in a chorus of barking.

Tuesday, April 21

Top Dog no more. Ousted from power. All the perks I used to enjoy – the quiet dominance of a stiff gait with a gently waving tail, the confident marking of territory, the cheery submission of other dogs – all gone. We were allowed in the den today and I hid under the Owner's desk, sunk in depression. After a while he slipped his shoes off and rested his feet on me. Normally I would have remonstrated, but being used as a footstool seemed somehow symbolic.

Wednesday, April 22

I am a Bad Dog for fighting in the park and we haven't returned so far, which is a blessing – I can't face seeing all those dogs again yet. On a lighter note, while I in no way condone the Owner's behaviour, it was satisfying to hear Miss Meddling discover the mess in her garden.

'Oh, Bobby,' she squealed. 'You've been doing your business all over the place, you naughty boy. I shall have to clear it all up. Goodness me, you've got a lot in you. No cake for you tonight.'

There was a pause for a moment, then, 'How on earth did you manage to get this one right in the gnome's wheelbarrow?'

Thursday, April 23

Back to the wasteland this evening and the good news is that Ella's subterfuge has worked, but at a greater price than I imagined. Who would have thought that beneath Scottie's mangy coat beats the heart of a born tyrant? We had scarcely swapped a tentative sniff and growl before he started issuing orders.

'Things huv been gettin' verra slapdash around here and with a puir wee dug tae rescue too, sae it's a good job ah'm noo Top Dog. Ah wull be headin' up the rescue team, an' Ella, ah'm putting you in charge o' supplies and provisions.'

'Yes, Scottie,' she barked obediently.

'What will I do?' I asked.

Scottie cocked his head and peered at me.'Och aye, Blake, ah've goat a special wee mission for ye, but ah'm keepin' it a secret for the noo.'

I did my very, very best to remain subservient, but just about managed politeness:'How will you head up the rescue team if you're stuck inside the den though, Scottie?'

'Ah've given that wee plan aboot shittin' oan the carpet and peein' oan the foorniture some thought, an' ah reckon that with some modifications it might just work aftir all.'

'Modifications? What modifications?'

Scottie looked haughty. 'Ah shall, in fact, be peein' oan the carpet and shittin' oan the foorniture.'

I growled. Scottie barely paused. 'And if ye tak that tone wi' me ah'll gi ye anothir good hidin'.'

Later I walked past the Owner, who was deep in conversation with Mr McCormick, just in time to hear him saying, '. . . so I cut a section out of the shed door and put some hinges on it like a sort of big cat flap. Now they're very comfortable in the shed and can come and go into the garden as they like. We've not had a single bit of dog mess in the house since.'

That's what he thinks. If he looked behind the sofa more frequently he'd find a little gift from Coleridge slowly fossilising.

Friday, April 24

A stroke of luck last night – after ripping open only four plastic bags along the street we found a whole piece of beef that had gone only slightly manky. A real feast for Lolly, and with a dog's powerful stomach acids it should be no problem for her to digest the smelly bits.

While she ripped at it hungrily, Ella asked how she'd come to be locked in a cage.

Between gulps she told us her story. 'Oh, I haven't always been in here. I used to live in the den with the Master and Mistress, but Mistress died. Master pined for her and then I stopped seeing so well and began to bump into things all the time. I broke so much that he put me out here, so it's my own fault really. That was a long time ago though.' She looked wistful for a moment. 'I was a beautiful dog then.'

We looked at the poor shivering bitch through the gap in the fence, all bones and bald patches of scabby skin. Without missing a heartbeat, Ella replied, 'You're still beautiful, Lolly. I'm not saying you couldn't use an afternoon in the grooming parlour, though.'

'Thank you, Ella. So, is Scottie coming soon?'

'Yes, and he's organising a pack to bring you food, and find you a new home where you can be beautiful again. That is if you want to.'

'I'm happy here, really, but it's nice of him to think of me. Is he an important dog, then?'

'Oh yes, Top Dog of the whole park.'

I winced at this, but Ella continued, 'And as well as being the strongest and fittest, he's also the wisest. All the dogs do what he tells them.'

'I knew he was important. You can tell just by smelling him, can't you? Some dogs have an aura about them.'

This was too much, she may be malnourished, but there's only so much a dog can take. With as much composure as I could muster I barked softly, 'Having smelled Scottie's "aura" hundreds of times I can confirm that it's composed mostly of flatulence and an unspecified but persistent dental problem.'

Lolly just yelped with laughter. 'Do you think Blake's a little jealous, Ella?'

'I think you might be right, Lolly, he's always wanted to be Top Dog.'

'I don't suppose there's any chance of that while Scottie's around?'

'No, in fact Scottie had to rip Blake's ear open just the other day for being too cheeky. He's fair, but he's firm.'

I could stand no more of this and trotted away with my tail held high to chase rabbits with Coleridge.

Saturday, April 25

Am still on frosty terms with my mate after her chat with Lolly yesterday. I can accept that by building up Scottie's reputation it will be more likely that Lolly will follow his advice, but did she have to be so gleeful about it? It wouldn't be so bad if the dogs in the park weren't being so disrespectful too. Our first day back and it seemed like all of them wanted some rough and tumble, just to test their strength against mine and see who might come off better in a real fight. Well, I may have lost a scrap to Scottie against my better judgement, but there's no way I was going to let a little pug like Hector or that weird mixed-breed Denny question my martial prowess. I sent Denny away with a flea in his ear (where it joined a prosperous community) and Hector with a bite mark on his rump, after which I got a lengthy talking-to from the Owner about fighting in the park again. I tried to feign interest, but he does drone on sometimes.

It's less than a week since I let Scottie become Top Dog, but I can already say that I am definitely not a Machiavellian, power-behind-the-throne kind of dog.

Sunday, April 26

Coleridge was nearly caught out today. The Owner brought dinner out a little early and Miss Meddling a little late. For a moment the puppy ran around the garden in wild circles and then joined Ella and I at the food bowls munching his way through his portion of horse's testicles and gravel like a food processor. Over the fence were shrill cries of 'Bobby, Booobbeeee. Dinnertime, darling. Where are you, you naughty boy?'

Back on our side of the fence the Owner looked down and said, 'Slow down for pity's sake, Coleridge.' Then he looked closer. 'Good God, you're getting fat, puppy. You're starting to look like a hairy basketball. We must be feeding you too much.'

Fortunately for the spotty little opportunist the Owner soon went back inside, and after giving the bowl a final lick, Coleridge ran across the garden to the Meddling Tunnel to assume his alter ego.

'Oh, there you are, Bobby,' Ella and I heard. 'What are you doing behind that bush? One of your great big toilets, I'll bet.' Miss Meddling seemed to think that the word 'toilet' was the peak of humour, and laughed as the sound of a spinning metal bowl signalled that Coleridge had finished his second dinner. The Owner's right though, if Coleridge gets much fatter his legs won't reach the ground any more, and that cat flap is getting tighter all the time.

Monday, April 27

More trouble in the park. This time it was Liquorice's turn to try and bring me down; he's probably still smarting about the bold, brilliant manoeuvre that brought him under my paw last year. It was only a bit of sparring really, all bark and no bite, but it's a good job the Owner didn't see. I definitely heard the word 'muzzle' two days ago.

This time it was Scottie who broke the fight up, jumping up and down to get our attention and yapping imperiously at us as if we were puppies. I started to tell him to go eat his own bumhole, but just about managed to bite back the words and busied myself with my nether regions instead. Meanwhile Scottie began barking orders at Liquorice.

'A'll huv none o' that nonsense in mah park, we huv a wee duggie in need o' help an' ah'm enlisting ye in mah crack rescue pack.'

'What do I have to do?' Liquorice barked back.

'Fer a start ye'll need tae be free o' the den of a night. Tell me, de ye huv a shed o' any description?'

'Yes, it's full of tools and the lawnmower.'

'Aye, well, ye can go hame and say hello tae yer new den. Ah want ye oaf yer comfy sofa and intae that shed toot suite. De ye understand?'

'Yes, Scottie, but how?'

And while I sat there gawping Scottie barked out the poo and pee plan exactly as I'd laid it out to him. Right in front of me. The nerve.

After Liquorice ran off at a whistle from his Owner, Scottie turned to me. 'Ah'm no' sayin' ye're a bad dug ye ken, Blake, but yer problum is ye didnae instil discipline. It's a good joab ah gie ye that seein'-to when ah did, the whole place is goin' tae the humans.'

'But Scottie –'

'Noo buts. Ye'll be interested tae know, Blake, there's a place open for mah number two. Ah've always said that wi' a bit o' discipline ye'd make a half-decent beta male, so mind whut ye do and you'll mebbee find yeself gaein' up in the park agin soon. How dae ye like that, eh?'

I sat staring, picturing ripping him to bloody shreds. Unconsciously, I was making small shuffling movements on my backside towards him, my jaws were gaping.

'Aye, I kent ye'd be excited. Ah'm no' promisin' anythin', like, but ye keep up the good work helpin' Ella tae feed Lolly and there might be a wee promotion in it for ye. Noo, ah huv tae go conscript a few more dugs. As ye were, soldier.'

Scottie wandered asthmatically away, muttering about discipline. At this point there were only two options open to me. I could relieve my frustration and anger by biting him in two, or give my balls a licking they'd never forget. Scottie escaped certain death, but it was a close-run thing.

'Why are you walking like that?' Ella asked on the way back to the den.

Tuesday, April 28

Coleridge spent most of the day over the fence and the Owner and Samantha stuck to the den, so Ella and I were left alone. As a guard dog, consigning me to the garden has taken away my whole purpose in life. I'm trying to make the most of it by assuming sentry duty as best I can out here, but there don't seem to be too many burglars around here intent on lawn theft, or the snatching away of gnomes. The sun was out, though, so the two of us made the most of the pond and chased each other around the garden before settling down for an afternoon nap to ensure that we would be alert for our hectic night schedule.

It would be nice to say that we dined on the choicest cuts of Aberdeen Angus washed down with a cheeky Spanish red, but the Owner must be feeling the financial pinch – it was the cheap brand again, the kind they sell out the back of the glue factory.

Wednesday, April 29

No park action for a couple of days, and Scottie's been absent from the wasteland. I wonder if the recruitment plan is working. It's not natural for a dog to defecate in the den. We're clean creatures and – as with so many things dog – this dates back to the time of wolves;

the further from the den the wolf took his or her twice-daily dump the less likely a puppy would happen upon it as a tasty snack, keeping internal parasites to a minimum and ensuring healthy stock.*

So long as any dog is walked regularly, healthy and well house-trained (here we touch upon Coleridge's little problem) there should be no reason whatsoever for it to do its business in the den. Scottie should be all right with Denny, who will probably revel in the chance to spread some dog dirt around, and I'm sure that Constable would answer the call of nature in his Mistress's handbag for half a pat, but the other dogs might be more of a problem. It's not as if you can decommission an entire evolutionary process in a couple of evenings.

Having said that, I'm all for soiling the garden at the moment. It's a dirty protest for forcing me out of the den.

Thursday, April 30

Arrived at Lolly's backyard this evening to find Scottie already sitting by her cage and woofing gently at her. When he saw my head emerge from the gap in the fence he turned his beady eyes on me.

'Whut time dae ye call this? Puir wee Lolly is starvin' here. I hope ye brung somethin' tasty is all.'

Coleridge scampered through my legs and dropped half a sandwich at Scottie's front paws. He sniffed at it. 'Salami, eh? Wull that will do fer a start, noo off ye go an' find a bit more. Ah want this wee dug stuffed tae the neck.'

For the remainder of the night, the tyrant had us running back and forth foraging for any tiny morsel. The choicest treats he fed himself through the wire to Lolly, but most was rejected. The majority of Coleridge's loot did not pass Scottie's stringent quality control, but then the puppy does have incredibly low standards of what constitutes a decent meal. Even so, half a decayed bird and a used nappy was stretching it.

---

* That's natural selection in action for you. Not quite sure how it worked with humans, whose monkey cousins actually throw the stuff at each other, but maybe there's something about the all-banana diet that kills worms.

MAY

Friday, May 1

Nearly snapped (literally) under the strain of following Scottie's orders, but Ella has been constantly at my shoulder with a nuzzle of encouragement, and I have to admit it was good to see the change in Lolly. She was overjoyed to see Scottie, sitting up almost alertly and trying to lick her sparse coat into the best condition possible. Although we were never around for long enough to hear what they were saying, the two dogs seemed to be having a long and gentle argument about the rights of dog and human responsibility. When it comes to philosophy Scottie knows his stuff. He can quote the classics: *How to Be Your Dog's Best Friend, Dog Care Made Simple, Love Your Dog.*

Saturday, May 2

Scottie was extra-officious in the wet wasteland this evening. Liquorice is on the verge of being banned from the house, and Barney the border collie has also been conscripted, without the trouble of having to escape from the den. He's been sleeping in a kennel outside for years and says he likes it. Weird. Must remind him of sleeping in barns and streaking around the peaks rounding up sheep I suppose. We asked about Scottie's own removal to the shed, but our questions were ignored.

Sunday, May 3

More rescue business with Scottie, or Genghis McKahn as I'm beginning to think of him.

'Noo ah'm in charge we seem tae be makin' some progress, an' first item o' business is a name fer the new pack.'

'How about S.C.O.O.T.,' I suggested, just off the paw.

'Aye, that's nice, what does it stand fer?'

'I don't know, I just liked the sound of it.'

'Ella, dae ye huv any sensible suggestions?'

'F.L.E.A. – the Free Lolly Efficiently Association?'

'Aye, no' bad. Better than Blake's pathetic effort, ah' gie ye that. But ah think we'll go wi' mah own idea.'

We looked at him expectantly.

'Canine Rescue And Protection.'

I thought about this for a moment. 'So as an acronym that would be . . .'

'Aye, C.R.A.P., whut of it?'

'Nothing, nothing. I like it, it's got a ring about it.'

'Yes, dogs will certainly know that C.R.A.P. means business,' Ella interjected.

'Wull that's settled, then,' said Scottie. 'We'll all be C.R.A.P. Noo, movin' doon the agenda; Blake, as ah mentioned, ah huv a wee joab fer ye.'

Unfortunately, he was cut short by his Owner, who wanted to get out of the rain. If the expression on Scottie's face was anything to go by though, this mission is not going to be a walk in the park.

Monday, May 4

The two humans went out for hours today, and when they returned the Owner sat on the back step in the sunshine looking at a scrap of paper with a small blob in the middle. He was grinning, so I chanced my muzzle for a bit of a scratch and instead got a ten-minute hug-and-stroke extravaganza, which Coleridge – on one of his increasingly rare daytime visits – was also quick to exploit. I hadn't realised quite how long it had been since I enjoyed a bonding session and might have become a tiny bit carried away. It seems that large dogs will *not* be worn across the shoulders this season. Drool, however, goes with anything.

Samantha joined us and had a more restrained session with Ella. I've noticed that the human female is starting to look a little bit Coleridge around the waist, but her coat is looking very glossy and the smell of her is delicious. Presumably, this means that the arrival of the human puppy is getting closer. Although nothing has been said on the subject of rehoming recently I am very aware that the possibility still remains. It's probably good that we are so active during the hours of darkness now. The humans must think they have the world's sleepiest dogs.

Tuesday, May 5

The humans' good mood seems to be holding, as we got double helpings of park, morning *and* afternoon, and let back in the den for a decent bit of guarding. That postman has obviously become too complacent recently. No whack on the nose with a bundle of letters this time, just a shriek of terror as I hit the door with my full weight and weeks of pent-up snarling and barking. His pitiful whining was music to my ears.

It would be nice to report double helpings of dinner, too, but apparently the good mood doesn't extend that far.

Wednesday, May 6

The Owner emerged from the den today for long enough to do some light gardening, which mainly involved flicking dog mess over the fence again. There was, however, some pruning of the rhododendron bush, during which there was a very tense moment as Coleridge emerged from the Meddling Tunnel. Fortunately it's thick and, well, bushy and Ella and I were distracting the human at the time by dancing around him – in Ella's case trying to force her favourite Frisbee on him – and our ploy worked, though of course he's never exactly Commander Keen when it comes to observation.

'Have you been sleeping behind the bush all that time, Coleridge?' was as close as he came to detection.

Thursday, May 7

Scottie has a little 'joab' for me, and it's smellier than Constable in a septic tank. I was in the wasteland this evening, having a quiet snuffle around, picking up the scent of the occasional hedgehog, chasing birds with Ella: the usual Thursday evening amble. Then Scottie arrived and dropped this enormous bit of flatulence that he has the cheek to call a plan.

''Tis like this, Blake,' he barked in his annoying voice of command. 'Once ah've talked Lolly intae findin' a new Owner, we'll need tae break her oot o' yon cage.'

I was interested in spite of myself; my middle name isn't 'Escapologist' but it may as well be.

'So we'll be wantin' a good set o' powerful jaws tae nash through.'

'Of course you can count on my mandibles of death, Scottie,' I woofed with just a note of pride. I knew it wouldn't be long until he needed my muscle.

'Not you, ye great puddin', I want ye tae inlist Razor for me.'

Immediately I went stiff all over. You could have put me in a taxidermist's window. Razor. My old nemesis. He nearly killed me twice and would have done so if it hadn't been for Scottie and Ella on the first occasion, and my Owner on the second. All right, the last time I'd seen him he'd been castrated, muzzled and pumped full of female hormones, but still, he's a pit bull. However docile he might seem, somewhere in there is the mind of a wrecking ball. He can't help it, he was bred to maul.

I recounted all this for Scottie's benefit, pointing out that though in no way was I afraid to sniff Razor out he is more than a little unhinged and therefore an unreliable accomplice in any breakout operation.

My objections may as well have been water off a shaking dog's coat.

'Aye, Blake, but when we come tae take Lolly ah'll want tae be in an' oot in seconds. If ah ken your style it'll be muckin' aboot fer half an oor makin' noise an' eventually liftin' a bit o' chicken wire ye couldnae fit a Chihuahua through.'

'But –'

'Aye, Razor's oor dug all right, he'll go through that cage like a crunchy treat.'

'But –'

'So ye'll see hum as soon as ye can? That's grand. And when he's in the C.RA.P. we'll see aboot that little promotion ah mentioned, eh?'

Oh, C.R.A.P.

Friday, May 8

Spent most of the day bored in the garden. It's a well-known fact that dogs not allowed access to the den and thus denied the right to guard will find other suitable employment for themselves. In my case this often involves running around in circles barking. It's not such skilled work of course, but it helps a dog feel useful. Also it relieves the mind from dwelling on 'wee joabs' that involve having to cajole a stick of dynamite in dog form into joining the pack of a small, elderly and scruffy West Highland Scots terrier. It did occur to me though that if and when I do meet Razor I should avoid touching on the part I played in the removal of his own parts.

Saturday, May 9

Ella and I were allowed into the den for the evening stroke and snooze on the sofa. Coleridge preferred his cushion at Miss Meddling's so after calling him for five minutes the Owner assumed he was gnawing a bone in the shed and gave up on him. The humans had taken a night off working, which they seem to do around the clock now, and were watching TV. Usually, I'll quite happily watch whatever's on for hours – it's amazing the way that screen hypnotises you – but I love it when they show dogs. It's a fantastic excuse to walk around howling and barking while pretending to look for the intruder. Of course I know it's just the TV, but I like to demonstrate that I take guarding seriously. It also means that the Owner, who knows the consequences by now, never watches any of those shows on how to train a dog, which is a nice additional bonus.

Tonight they had one of those 'amusing' stories at the end of the news. They call them 'human interest' but they're always about animals. Personally I think they should have some 'animal interest' stories with humans making idiots of themselves. They could start with my Owner.* I digress. This story was about a dog called Red who had learned how to open doors and had been filmed escaping from his cell at the local rescue centre then letting all the other dogs out so they could share a midnight feast. After eating everything in sight all the dogs went back to their cells, and Red closed the doors after them, leaving the staff scratching their heads until someone had the bright idea of checking the CCTV tapes.

An idea forms, and this time Scottie won't be hearing of it. He can stick with his time-consuming poo and pee while the Genius Blake, Blake the Liberator, releases all the dogs whose Owners trust in their faithful guards rather than a key. Then we shall see who is dim around here.

* On reflection he could have his own show.

Sunday, May 10

Barney joined us tonight for a C.R.A.P. night out. Scottie took his usual place by Lolly's cage to continue his campaign of persuasion while the rest of us brought a steady stream of food. I have to hand it to myself, my idea of forming a pack was a brilliant one. With Barney helping tear through the local black plastic bags every night, Lolly is going to be as fat as Coleridge in no time, particularly as he's been quietly stealing food around the neighbourhood at night for years and knows all the best places to hunt. The company is doing her good too. There's little you can do to a dog that's as torturous as leaving it all alone 24 hours of the day, and in a confined space is especially bad. Next to that, starving is almost easy.

Monday, May 11

The weather is getting warmer, which means that the Owner is coming out into the garden to spend time with us more often. Tried a little experiment in canine–human communication today by chasing my tail around the garden. As anyone who'd bothered to read even one dog behaviour book would know, this is a sign that I am bored and in need of stimulation; preferably the resumption of my guarding duties. The Owner, being a total ignoramus, just thinks it's cute.

Tuesday, May 12

Ella wonders if there might be better ways of making the two humans understand our needs, and talked about developing a new technique, called 'human whimpering'. Personally I think she's peeing up the wrong lamppost. The Owner wouldn't understand that a dog needed a toilet break if you gave him a gift-wrapped dump. I've been trying the eyebrow samba, which is about as obvious a means of communication as you can get, for as long as I can remember and for all the good it does me I may as well just have some embarrassing facial tics.

Wednesday, May 13

Molly is back. First Razor and now her, all my old adversaries are starting to crawl out of the litter tray at once. Ruthless dog trainer, one-time proprietor of Ruff & Tumble Dog Walking Services, the Owner's ex-mate and a psychotic supporter of testicle removal, Molly is every dog's worst nightmare.

The last we saw of her was only a couple of months ago when she was just about to leave the country for five years' 'helping' endangered species, so what she was doing walking into my garden and stroking me like we were old pals I have no idea. My initial thought was that she must have pushed all those poor animals over the edge into actual extinction (probably by castrating them all) and found herself twiddling her opposable thumbs, but the real reason – as she explained to the Owner and Samantha – was much, much more joyous. She'd been abroad a week before she was bitten by a venomous snake and nearly died. Fighting through and determined to return to the sharp end of animal welfare she then came within an inch of being trampled by a rhinoceros thought to be tranquillised. After that there was an episode with leeches, and finally she woke up in a tent with a scorpion tangled in her hair. Having been rushed to hospital again, she decided that the most endangered species in Africa was herself and got on the first bus back to civilisation. It's the snake I feel sorry for. It's probably still trying to get the taste out of its mouth.

I was so thrilled by her story I did the happy dog dance and put my feet on her shoulders so that I could 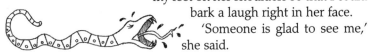 bark a laugh right in her face.

'Someone is glad to see me,' she said.

Thursday, May 14

Not a good day for the Owner. Flicking dog poo over the fence is all fun and games until someone loses an eye. In this case, Miss Meddling. She didn't *actually* lose an eye, unfortunately, but did catch a nice fresh stool across the back of the head while she was bending over to polish a gnome. The projectile poo pushed her new wig off and onto the head of the gnome, which ended up looking like that little-known eighth dwarf, Tranny. Coleridge saw it all.

It would be nice to say that the Owner bravely owned up and apologised, but as soon as he heard the squawk of surprise and horror he scuttled into the den, closing the door gently behind him. The doorbell rang all afternoon, but even though I know the humans were both in, they didn't answer it.

All this just goes to prove my theory that when a species starts flinging poo at each other it's very difficult to eradicate from the genetic code.

Friday, May 15
Nice long walk in the park this morning, during which I half-heartedly went over to the east side where Razor has a small piece of territory. He tends to keep himself to himself these days, but I smelled that he's passed through recently. If my nose is correct he's also no longer being fed the progesterone that keeps him effete, but docile. I made a mental note to tell Scottie that Razor is likely to be even more trouble than I thought.

Saturday, May 16
Samantha was making dinner with the door open and me lurking at her feet offering to dispose of any small ingredients of a Bolognese sauce that might be surplus to requirements. Luckily for the humans this meant I was on hand and ready to spring into action when I heard the squeak of the front gate. I went through the usual routine of making it quite plain that whoever approached wasn't wanted here, but calmed down when the Owner opened the door to that nice policeman. He is a natural dog person if ever I smelled one. This time he wasted no time with preamble.

'I have a complaint made against you, sir, that you did yesterday at 2.37 p.m. assault your neighbour by throwing faeces at her.'

I have to say the Owner played it remarkably cool. 'I'm sorry, officer, faeces did you say?'

'Yes, sir, care to tell me what you know about that?'

'Absolutely nothing I'm afraid. At 2.37 yesterday my partner and I would have been at the shops.'

'Your neighbour says that she came round to complain in person and that your car was in front of the house.'

'It was a nice day, we walked. Look, officer, this is bordering on harassment. Some ripped-up pages from magazines that belonged to the previous tenant got blown across the fence by accident. I didn't even know they were there. For the last time, I do not steal underwear or go around throwing dog shit at old ladies.'

'No one said it was *dog* faeces, sir.'

For a second I thought the Owner was going to crack, but he rallied dogfully.

'Are you telling me it was human faeces? How disgusting. The things that young people nowadays get up to.'

'As a matter of fact it *was* dog mess. Are you saying that was a lucky guess?' The policeman was taking notes in his book. It didn't look good for the Owner, so I gave the policeman a bit of a lick. No copper's above a bit of bribery.

The Owner shrugged. 'There are a lot of dogs around here, I just assumed.'

'Well it's very convenient that you're so good at *assuming*.'

The Owner started to protest, but the policeman held up a hand to stop him.

'Look sir, this situation with your neighbour seems to be getting out of hand. We have better things to do than investigating minor quarrels, but nevertheless, we do not tolerate citizens throwing crap at the elderly. Fortunately for you it is very difficult to fingerprint a dog turd, but if I hear of any further instances I will be questioning you at the station. Do I make myself clear?'

'Perfectly clear, officer.'

'Now, if you'll take my advice, sir, in spite of evidence to the contrary you seem to be a decent, sensible person, so I should try and make it up with the lady across the fence. Bunch of flowers, invite her in for a cup of tea, offer to help with her shopping, that kind of thing. You'd be amazed at the number of disagreements I've seen resolved over a cup of tea.'

'Tea, right. And some carrot cake? Maybe I can swipe her bra while she's distracted.'

The policeman glared at the Owner for a moment, then continued, 'If you do have her in for tea, sir, I would very much advise against serving carrot cake. The lady seems to have a bee in her bonnet when it comes to carrots.'

Sunday, May 17

The Owner seems preoccupied at the moment, and sat on the back step for about half an hour this afternoon vaguely rubbing my chest. I love this as it gives exactly the same sensation as mounting a bitch, which makes me wonder why he'll happily give *me* a sexual massage, but comes over all modest when it comes to a little friendly leg humping. In the circumstances I was happy to sit quietly and let him get on with it, with just the occasional low moan of pleasure and a small lick of appreciation that he wiped away without even remonstrating. However, for the record he is a tease, and it's no wonder that I sometimes try and take advantage.

Monday, May 18
Lolly duty last night and Liquorice joined the C.R.A.P. dogs milling around in the alley with food. She's now getting more food than ever, but not looking much better. If anything she's lost more of her coat. I'm no vet but it looks like the dreaded mange to me, which is common in malnourished dogs, but should be getting better with all the good food we've been giving her recently.

We were all trying to be quiet, but sneaky doesn't come easy to six dogs and a puppy so when a dog howled in the distance it was only natural for one or two of us to respond in kind.

Scottie barked for silence sharply, but the damage was already done. The upstairs window flew open and Lolly's torturer peered down to see a pack of strays looking up at him.

With a cry of 'Geerrrroffffoutofit,' he reached down and threw a boot at us. An actual boot. As if we were a bunch of cats.

We ran for it with Lolly barking, 'Come back tomorrow,' behind us. For once she didn't sound like a dog who cared too much about her Master.

Tuesday, May 19
Something's going on with the humans. Usually I'm completely on the ball when it comes to any changes in the routine, but the problem with being outside all the time is that you can't keep a watchful eye on them and they get up to all sorts of mischief. The first thing I noticed when we were let in for the stroke and TV session tonight was two suitcases in the hall. This means either extremely good news or extremely bad news. Scenario one is that we are all going to the beach together, which means Frisbee fun and jumping in and out of rock pools. Scenario two involves the kennel, which means sitting in a bare cell, howling the blues and counting the days while trying to figure out escape plans.

I snuffled around the cases, but they were giving nothing away, and neither were the humans.

Wednesday, May 20

Lots of activity in the den this morning, but none involving us, which was not a good sign. Who was to know how bad the day was going to get though? The humans have gone on holiday and left Molly in the den. All right, so she brought bones with her (good bones too, for me what looked like a whole cow's foreleg with chunks of meaty deliciousness still attached).

The Owner and Samantha left after a rushed departure, during which I got barely a stroke, let alone the sobbing farewells I deserve. Hardly had the front door slammed before Molly dropped the pretence that she was the dogs' friend. All afternoon it was 'sit' this, 'come' that, not to mention 'stay', 'down' and 'grovel in the dirt, dog scum'. Ella likes this as it gives her a chance to show off how obedient she is, and I'm a veteran of obedience school so put up with it for a while, mainly because there were treats on offer. Coleridge was very confused and just sat watching with his head cocked, though he did take all the treats he could get his mouth round. Apparently this was not the kind of response that Molly was looking for. Finally she stopped with a sigh, saying, 'Your master needs training more than you do,' and then dished out dinner. It was only the usual Canine Rescue And Protection, but I must admit Molly knows how to dish out a good dog-sized portion even if we did have to 'sit' one more time before service commenced. What she put in my bowl could have fed a pack of wolves for a week. After that it was a long walk in the park, though for Coleridge and I it was totally ruined by 'heel', then back to the den in time to curl up in front of the TV with Coleridge whining at the door to get to his second dinner over the fence. He had three trips to the gutter before he gave up trying. Come throwing-out time, Molly looked down at us all curled up on the sofa with her and announced that she knew dogs liked to be in the den and for this week only we would not have to sleep in the shed.

Despite the harsh disciplinarian regime this was a treat indeed, and one for which even Molly deserved some gratitude. I'm not the sort of dog that doesn't give thanks where it's due and was careful to let Molly know of every passing car, cat and plastic bag all night. A good guard dog is an alert guard dog as my old mother used to say.

Thursday, May 21

Heel training consists of walking away from a sit on a loose lead and staying within an imaginary perimeter beside the human. Should the dog break out of that perimeter, the human (let's call her Molly) turns sharply, gives the command heel again and continues to walk until the dog resumes its place, at which time it is showered with praise. Simple enough on paper, but in practice not quite so straightforward, especially when the dog being trained is my good self. Should the dog make an attempt for freedom, give it a small sharp tug they say, but remember to keep the lead slack at all other times. Ha! Nowhere does it mention what to do if the dog is straining at the lead like a kite in a gale. Ditto what to do if you make a sharp turn and the dog fails to come with you at all. Personally, I treated that imaginary perimeter as if it were mined and made it quite clear that lampposts were to be peed upon, other dogs sniffed at and sharp turns of very little consequence to me. Result: 1–0 to Blake.

Still, another very large dinner this evening and more sleeping inside, so again I let Molly know the den was in safe paws, which was nice of me considering her authoritarian attitude. You cannot choose what to guard, it's the act itself that is important.

Friday, May 22

Molly came down to breakfast a little late and looking slightly the worse for wear. Yesterday she made a bit of a show of pretending to be a dog lover when greeting us in the morning, but today Ella got a pat and all I got was a 'I'm starting to see why your master keeps you outside.'

Got a run in the park while Coleridge worked on some basics with Molly, then we got down to more work on my 'heel'.

Beaten again by my wily refusal to co-operate, Molly eventually unclipped the lead with a strained 'I've taught this in one afternoon a million times, Blake, I'm starting to think that you're incredibly stupid,' which stung. Obviously she hasn't considered that I just might have better things to do.

Back in the den Molly played with us all afternoon, though 'fetch' put a strain on things again. I'm pretty sure that the human is not allowed to actually prise the dog's jaws apart with their hands. Meanwhile, over the fence we could hear 'Bobbee, Bobbeeee. Where are you?' There was a tearful note in Miss Meddling's voice, but with Molly watching us all day and keeping us in all night, Coleridge hasn't been able to sneak over to his second home for days. Molly has also put him on a no-cake strict diet and he's starting to feel the strain.

Saturday, May 23
More 'heel'. I was so sick of it I actually gave in and walked in her stupid perimeter today. I've been showered with praise before, and it always goes down well, but this was something special. Chest rubbing, 'Good Boy', even some kissing, which the Owner hardly ever does and never with tongues like Molly, though in retrospect she may have just opened her mouth for another 'Good Boy' at the wrong time. Then she pulled out a great big treat, just for me. Crunchy on the outside with a soft, beef-flavoured centre.

Strangely, I can see myself getting the hang of this training thing quite quickly. I may have been slow to learn in the past, but I am a sucker for enormous treats. There was a small worry about the price of my principles but licking the crumbs from my muzzle seemed to dismiss them. Besides, I don't want anyone thinking I'm stupid, even if it is only Molly.

Sunday, May 24
With all the den sleeping, Ella, Coleridge and I have not been able to attend to C.R.A.P. for a couple of nights. As Scottie now has Barney and Liquorice to help we hadn't worried about it too much, but the despot caught up with us today during a brief interval in 'heel' practice and the munching of beefy goodness.

'Wher huv ye bin?' he demanded. 'Lolly needs feedin' and ye huv done nuthin' aboot Razor yet.'

We explained that we were being kept in the den for a short period, but that normal service would be resumed as soon as the Owner returned.

'Then why are ye no' pooin' and peein' yer way back intae the shed?'

'It's only for a few days, Scottie, by the time the poo and pee have set us free we'll be back in the shed anyway.'

'Rubbish, if ye do whut ah did ye'll be oot tonight.'

'So what did you do, Scottie?' I had forgotten that we still hadn't prised the story out of him.

'Och, it wus nothin'. Forgit ah said anythin'.'

He shuffled off quickly, looking about as embarrassed as a dog could be. He still took the time to bark back at me though, 'And dinnae forgit Razor. Ah want hum in the pack as soon as ye can.'

Monday, May 25

As we left the den on the way to the park today Molly noticed a piece of paper stapled to the lamppost. It read, 'LOST, small white dog with black spots. Answers to the name "Bobby". Reward to finder, contact Miss F. Meddling.'

'Oh, the poor little thing,' said Molly, looking down at a small white dog with black spots. 'We'll have to keep a lookout for him.'

Tuesday, May 26

Nice big breakfast today, followed by more treats in the park. I'm starting to think that Molly might not be as bad as I thought. So long as I humour her by staying in that perimeter she's very well behaved. Today I found myself flowing along beside her without even having to be on the lead; we were a slick act, professional standard. In fact, it was just like those sheepdog trials on the TV – one human and one dog in perfect tandem, the pinnacle of thousands of years of co-evolution. After 'heel' we did 'sit', 'down' and 'stay'. All as simple as a squeaky toy for a dog with a brain the size of mine. Molly is Very Pleased with my progress, and I am Very Pleased with the hugs, kind words and munchy treats. If she could teach the Owner a few basic tricks like this we might all get along better, but I'm probably asking too much of an old monkey.

The only shame was that with all the human–dog perfect tandem stuff I didn't manage the time to go and find Razor. Never mind.

Wednesday, May 27

The Owner and Samantha came back. All three of us were unstinting in our welcome home, which is traditional after an extended absence. There was a bit of a scuffle over who could give the most effusive treatment, with some quite unnecessary blocking and growling from Molly. She was actually crying over them and forced a huge present on Samantha. All a bit odd. I mean, I kind of missed them too, but wouldn't go so far as whining, and presents are totally out of the question, unless they want one of the old bones I've finished with. Coleridge left them another small gift behind the sofa when Molly was out though. Not sure it's something they'd want to put on the mantelpiece.

Being a keen observer, I couldn't help noticing that they were tanned and both wearing new rings. Apparently they are now married, which is an idiotic human ritual. For me the occasional romantic sniff and growling at any dog who tries it on with Ella is as much commitment as I can handle.

The response to our welcome was depressingly predictable. After a few minutes of grinning and patting and stroking we were chucked straight out in the garden, though Molly and I took a few moments to show off our impressive new skills. This left the Owner gaping in surprise, but if he thinks he's automatically getting the same treatment he can think again. It takes talent and an almost supernatural bond between human and dog to achieve that level of synchronicity.

Thursday, May 28

Coleridge spent his first night back with Meddling and didn't even emerge for C.R.A.P., so must have been busy eating cake and drinking out of the lavatory or whatever it is he does over there. Scottie was pleased to have us back though and once again we supplied an excellent haul for Lolly. She was glad to smell Ella as well and as the two of them wanted some bitch time, Scottie accompanied me on a forage run. For once he dropped the sergeant-major attitude and was almost his old self. I think he's really worried about Lolly. There's a little more flesh on her now, but her coat's not improving and what should be a wet, shiny nose is as dry and cracked as the Sahara.

'Ah think she's close tae leavin', Blake,' he confided in me. 'We need Razor as soon as ye can.'

I told him that I had information that led me to believe that Razor might be even more unpredictable than I had originally thought.

'Aye, and I ken it's no' an easy joab fer ye, but ye huv tae admit he's goat a powerful set o' jaws oan him.'

It's true. I can remember them almost breaking my neck.

'All right, Scottie,' I groaned. 'As soon as we get to the park, I'll be on his trail.'

'Good boy, Blake.'

Instinctively I started wagging my tail before I caught myself. Scottie wandered away with what I considered a smirk on his face.

Friday, May 29

It was a beautiful morning so the humans decided to take us for an early walk. My first opportunity to find Razor, and the stupid Owner wanted to spend the whole time practising bloody 'heel' while Samantha worked on Coleridge's training. Obviously, I kicked up a bit of a fuss, but it became painfully obvious that he'd be at it all day if I didn't co-operate a little. In the end I had to trot along by his leg for what felt like hours before he released me. Nice leg though, I love it when he wears shorts. Finally he stopped. Molly must have given him some lessons because there was a huge and very pleasant lovefest, with treats, after which I was at last allowed to run free.

I cut straight through the trees and over to the east where Razor is always to be found. Checking his territory with my bum in my throat, I found some markings that were all of twenty minutes old. If it hadn't been for the Owner and his pathetic control-freakery I would have caught him. All I could do though was leave a calling card of my own. Hopefully, he will smell that I've been there and come looking for me. Luckily, my urine has a very distinct character all its own – a unique bouquet with notes of lemon, elderflower, dried stick and tinned offal.

Saturday, May 30

Noticed today that all the posters offering a reward for the return of 'Bobby' had been taken down. Coleridge meanwhile is waddling about like a cat who's had the cream, several birds, some mice and a nice fish head on the side. If he balloons any more the Owner will have to use his lead to tether him to the ground, though I'm sure he'd be a hit at children's parties.

He must have been sleeping on his pillow like King Rex today as he had been gone for hours when the Owner came out into the garden and peered over the fence. Seeing Miss Meddling he quickly picked the few flowers that remain since we dug them all up and cleared his throat until we heard her say, 'Oh, it's you. Having a look to see what's on my washing line are you?'

The Owner replied politely, 'No, I thought you might like some flowers,' and shook his bunch of pansies at her.

'I know your type, first it's flowers then you'll have me tied to the bed for a spanking session.' As a response I thought this ungrateful and suspicious; after all, a bunch of pansies liberally soaked in dog urine is not something to be sniffed at.

'I'm honestly not a pervert, Miss Meddling. Your, erm, personal items are safe from me. In fact, I got married last week.'

'And not before time, too. It was unheard of in my day, unmarried women having babies. That's the trouble with you young people, it's all prawnography and sex and drugs, but what about the kiddies, eh?'

'Well, I promise you that there's none of that in our house. Except the sex of course.' The Owner ventured a laugh. It sounded false to me.

'Disgusting.'

'We *are* having a baby, Miss Meddling, they don't make themselves you know.'

'Well, there's no reason to go around boasting about it. And what about throwing dog mess at me?'

The Owner blushed and mumbled something about not knowing anything about that. Then he took a deep breath. 'Anyway, here's some flowers, and if you want any help with your shopping or someone to share a cup of tea with then please feel free to pop over.'

There was some more grumbling, but eventually she took the pansies. As the Owner walked back to the house, she shouted after him, 'These flowers smell funny.'

'And so do you, you barmy old battleaxe,' the Owner replied, but quietly. Even with my magnificent ears I barely heard him.

Sunday, May 31

Driven to urgent measures by Scottie's nagging and Lolly's deteriorating condition, daybreak found me barking beneath the Owner's window until his tousled head emerged. Then I ran around in excited circles. Again, he just didn't seem to get it, but behind him I heard Samantha's voice.

'Just take the idiot bloody dog for a run will you, I can't sleep.'

'If you're awake why don't *you* take him for a run,' was his terse response.

'Well, the reasons are threefold. First, I am a new bride and looking to my Prince Charming for an extra half-hour in bed. Second, I am pregnant and all the books say I should rest as much as I can. Third, if you don't shut him up I will punch you in the face.'

Samantha's not very good at mornings I've noticed. Nevertheless her arguments must have carried some weight because the Owner came out a few moments later with leads and bowls, just as Coleridge was struggling through the Meddling Tunnel.

With the Owner making a fool of himself with physical jerks the way was clear to the east, so I left Ella to play with Coleridge and ran over. Finding Razor wasn't difficult, he was sniffing around his territory, all alone though there were a few other dogs enjoying the early morning sunshine.

I slowed to a walk as I approached, barking in greeting. He sat and watched me, his stumpy little tail notable for not wagging at all. Not even a twitch.

'Blake.' It was a statement rather than a greeting.

'Razor,' I gruffed, trying to sound aloof yet conciliatory. Not easy in one short bark.

'Smelled your mark. What do you want?'

If he wanted to play it curt then two can play at that game, and I could feel my hackles rising. Not even the suggestion of a hello sniff. It was just rude. 'There's a bitch in distress. I've come to ask for your help.'

Razor sat, and began licking the place where his balls used to be. It was very pointed. 'No,' he growled.

'That's it, just "No"? Don't you want to know anything about her?'

'No.'

'She's being starved and beaten. She lives alone in a cage and has the most terrible mange I've ever seen.'

'No. I won't help you, or her.'

'Why not?'

Razor stopped licking his scar. 'Two reasons spring to mind,' he growled.

I felt a wince. All right, he was a very Bad Boy, but some things are sacrosanct. Nevertheless, I ploughed on. 'Come on, Razor, she's going to lose her life, at least you only lost your balls.'

I could see straight away that it was a mistake. He raised his head and I could see the old madness in his eyes and his jaws beginning to grind. He was salivating. I don't mind confessing, dear diary, that I peed just a little bit.

'I could tear you apart right now, Blake, if I wanted to. It was only trickery and humans that saved you last time. Go back to your own side of the park and keep away from this one.'

'All right,' I growled, backing away slowly. 'Have it your own way, but don't expect me to come running if they put you in a cage.'

'Any human who tried to put me in a cage would find themselves missing their hands,' he barked behind me.

I suppose I should be thankful. The old, intact Razor wouldn't have bothered with conversation at all, just tried to rip my windpipe out.

JUNE

Monday, June 1

Reported to Scottie last night. He thanked me for trying, but agreed that I may have been right about the pit bull. He looked dejected. Lolly was trying to be cheerful, but it was evident that she'd been kicked or beaten again. With no other plan to fall back on I renewed my attack on the fence. If I can make a hole big enough, my own jaws of steel should be more than a match for her cage.

Tuesday, June 2

Miss Meddling came over today and the Owner invited her in for tea. It was a shame that we were outside in the garden as I'd liked to have pinned her to the wall and barked her into submission or pulled her to the floor by grabbing an arm. All standard procedure for your guard dog, but do I ever get the chance to put these skills to use?

Ella and I sat by the door while Coleridge ran about in the garden. If she'd just looked out of the open kitchen window she'd have seen her precious Bobby running around in his natural habitat, but she was intent on glaring at the Owner as if he might bite. He gave her tea and made polite, if stilted, small talk. So far, so boring. Slowly, however, the conversation dwindled. In desperation the Owner asked her what her friends called her. Making it quite plain that the Owner should not count himself among her friends she replied that her name was Frances, but most people called her Fanny.

'Fanny Meddling, that's a nice . . .'

The Owner appeared to choke and turned to face the door. Through the glass we could see him go bright red. Tea was shooting out through his nose. Behind him, Miss Meddling got up and started hitting him on the back. It was a crazy scene, as is so often the case with humans.

Eventually, he turned back to face her, gasping, 'Thank you. Yes, some tea went down the wrong way.' He didn't seem quite right though and kept having smaller choking sessions.

After about five minutes of this Miss Meddling looked up at him and said primly, 'If you are quite recovered now I'm ready to go shopping.' The Owner almost choked again. 'Only you did offer, and I'm sure it won't take long.'

Nevertheless, he was an hour late with our dinner, and even more surly than usual. The light upstairs in the office was on for a very long time before we could go to C.R.A.P.

Wednesday, June 3

For a man supposedly enjoying a blissful honeymoon period the Owner acted like an ogre today. You'd have thought a dog had never knocked over a full dustbin before. It was an accident, too, though obviously Ella and I took advantage and had a look to see if there was anything that we could take to Lolly later. Once again he dished out slapped noses. It's only a short jump from there to the Rolled Up Newspaper, and then the cage and mange. If Molly knew he was treating us this way there would be trouble.

Thursday, June 4

Disaster. Another dog joined C.R.A.P. today and followed the markings from the park to Lolly's alley. The welcome when Denny arrived was just a shade too enthusiastic, though. First the window opened and then Lolly's Master charged out of the door, shouting obscenities and kicking out at Scottie, who was in his usual place by Lolly's cage. Scottie dodged the blow, but threw himself at the human's leg, snarling. Even his elderly teeth found no resistance in the thin pyjamas and he sank them into the human's flesh up to the gums. With a shout of sudden pain, the man grabbed Scottie by the scruff of the neck and tossed him over the fence, hard.

Scottie recovered quickly and would have gone back through the fence for another round if I had not blocked his way. With her nose, Ella shoved him down the alley, still barking in rage and frustration.

If Lolly's Master is on to us we'll need to act fast, there's no time to waste.

Friday, June 5

The Owner is like a cat with a new ball of wool; every time he sees me it's, 'Blake, heel.' I wouldn't mind so much, but I've even started dreaming about it, my paws twitching to keep up with that swinging foot and my head turning to look up into those cavernous nostrils. I have also discovered that you can have too much of a good thing. For so long an object of desire, familiarity with the leg is definitely breeding contempt.

Saturday, June 6

I was actually allowed five minutes to myself today for a snuffle round, and caught up with Constable, who is looking even more well groomed than usual. I haven't had an opportunity to put my Red-inspired plan into action yet, so was quick to catch up with him. He looked miserable.

Trying to appear unconcerned I asked him if his Mistress ever locked the back door at night.

'No,' he woofed. 'She thinks that with two dogs in the house and her dad's old shotgun under the bed, she's perfectly safe.'

'Well then,' I replied, 'today could be your lucky day.'

I told him about Red, and how the same tactics could be used if he were careful. It would all depend on the dexterity of his paws and the ability to cover his tracks by closing the door again.

'That's a brilliant plan, Blake. Is it one of Scottie's?'

'Not this time, Constable. What you have there is pure Blake genius.'

'Wow, who'd have thought you could be so clever. I suppose it's Red who gave you the idea, though.'

'Yes, but it takes a certain amount of clever lateral thinking to apply it to your situation.'

He seemed impressed, I suppose because any kind of thinking comes pretty hard to him, let alone the clever, lateral variety. I left him with one last thought.

'But don't get too dirty. The moment your Mistress comes down to discover you looking like Wheezy Fido the Vagrant Dog, your cover's blown.'

'All right, I won't get too dirty. I can roll around in poo though, right?'

I hesitated for a moment, but who am I to deny him one of life's great pleasures? 'OK then, but only a little bit. Mouse poo. Rabbit poo at most.'

He continued on with a spring in his step. The Owner whistled and without a thought I turned and streaked back to him. What made it so horrifying was that I was actually proud of myself. The very thought makes me shiver.

Sunday, June 7

The Lolly situation has worsened. Her Master has patched the fence with more chicken wire. We all took turns in trying to pull it away –

me, Ella, Barney, Liquorice, even Coleridge – but none of us could shift it. From the other side of the fence Lolly was completely silent save for a few low moans. Scottie is distraught.

He looked up at me, his eyes wide with fear and growled, 'We've got tae get her oot o' there. Whut are we goin' tae do, Blake? Whut can we do?'

Things could go very badly for Lolly. Now is not the time to worry about the park hierarchy. I tried to calm him, barking softly that we would find a way, but at that moment there was little we could do but woof encouragement to Lolly.

Monday, June 8

All day, Ella and I lay in the garden staring at each other and trying to think of some way of springing Lolly from her prison. Finally, as the light in the Owner's bedroom was turned off, Ella said that she had thought of something. With no time to discuss her plan we streaked off to Lolly's alley.

Scottie looked even more unhappy than yesterday, and before we'd even finished the round of bum-sniffing he barked, 'We've goat tae huv Razor, Blake. I cannae think o' any other way o' gettin' through yon wire.'

Quickly Ella barked, 'I agree we need to chase every Frisbee, but there might be another way, too.'

All heads turned to face her. She's usually a quiet dog, but when she has a thought, it's worth listening to.

She continued, 'It's based on the little-Johnny's-fallen-under-the-wheels-of-a-tractor principle. Most of us have humans who treat dogs kindly, so if they see what a state Lolly is in, they might alert the rescue humans. All we have to do is lead our Owners here.'

'Aye,' gruffed Scottie slowly, 'but they'll tak her tae one o' thum centres. 'Tis no' much better than where she is noo.'

'At least she'll be fed there,' replied Ella sharply. 'Have a vet to take care of her and won't be beaten.'

At that moment there came a weak barking from over the fence. 'Scottie? Is that you? Are you all right?'

'Aye, hen, ah'm fine, jest a couple o' scrapes.'

'I'm sorry the Master hurt you. It's all my fault for asking you to come and see me.'

'Dinnae worry yersel', Lolly, 'tis not your fault yon human's a brute.'

'He is a brute, isn't he? I think you've been right all along, Scottie. If he can hurt a dog like you then he shouldn't be allowed to have one.'

'So ye'll escape if we can get ye oot o' there?'

'Yes.'

Then it all went silent again and we couldn't rouse Lolly to bark any more.

'Right then, dugs o' C.R.A.P.,' Scottie sounded firm and determined. 'We huv a joab tae do. Any chance ye get, ye bring yer humans here. In the meantime iviry dug is tae go an' make friends wi' that damn Razor. Sniff his arse, play wi' hum, let hum hump ye if he's goat any hump left in hum. Just get hum here.'

Tuesday, June 9
Not a chance of putting either plan into effect today. Miss Meddling returned to demand the Owner serve as her taxi to the shops again, so no walk to the park. We were led to the wasteland on the lead and had no chance to run to Lolly's alley.

Wednesday, June 10
The Owner is 'catching up on work' so still no chance of whining and tugging at his sleeve until he follows us to Lolly's alley. I've often wondered about the veracity of the Lassie stories. It seems to me that farmers who are always falling down wells and under the wheels of a tractor are trying to work some insurance scam. Either that or they were hoping that Lassie would get fed up with the level of incompetence and take over the running of the farm. Your actual Wonder Dog is very versatile after all.

Thursday, June 11
The Owner's involuntary assistance of the elderly is obviously getting him down. Today, he had to drive even more of them to the shops then sat on the steps complaining while we ate, which was not very professional of him. A good waiter should glide into a jumping, exciting pack of dogs silently, lay down the bowls immediately and then glide away to let the dogs scoff in peace. Sitting around moaning just ruins whatever ambience might be available when you're eating minced tail, spleen and eyeball in a synthetic gravy.

Friday, June 12

Word seems to be getting around the local senior citizens that the Owner is running a free cab service. Today, a different old lady called, asking for a ride. For a second I felt the Owner's hand loosen on my collar, as if he were tempted to let me hound her off the premises, minus any parts of her anatomy or clothing that happened to come my way. I think asking him if he was 'that pervert that takes people to the shops', probably wasn't the most diplomatic of opening conversation gambits judging from the colour of his face. Nevertheless, he deposited me in the garden and fetched the car keys. It just goes to show that evolution is not all it's cracked up to be. Would a gorilla spend half the day following the elderly and infirm around the supermarket? No, he'd bounce her up and down on her head and then tear her arms off. By retaining their primitive instincts dogs have a much simpler existence that is much less stressful (the Owner serving as a textbook definition of stress by the time he returned – I was out in the garden at the time but I definitely heard him squeal when the old lady left, saying 'same time next week then, Mr Pervert?').

Saturday, June 13

No more old people today, but the Owner must have a lot of work on as there was still no trip to the park. In frustration I dug up a small tree that Samantha planted last week, and threw it around the garden. Coleridge heard the fun and came over for a tug of war. I was not to know that it was a symbolic commemorative wedding tree that was supposed to grow along with their love. It's a stupid idea anyway. If they want something to grow along with their love, my stomach could use some work. Chasing me around the garden with what little was left of the tree was not the act of a dog lover in my opinion, and the swearing is not going to improve relations with Miss Meddling. I heard several disapproving noises coming from over the fence.

Sunday, June 14

We have a new pet. His name is Crusty Bob and he is a tortoise, which is a small reptile looking something like a meat pie.

It happened like this. The Owner was behaving like a cat who's found its favourite pee place covered in pepper so Samantha ordered him to take us for a long walk today and we were all driven out on one of our rare trips to the countryside. The Owner nearly stepped on Crusty Bob as he got out of the car. After looking around to see if there were any humans who might have inadvertently dropped a tortoise, the Owner gave us a speech about humans abandoning their animals and deposited Bob on the front seat with some dandelion leaves while we went for our walk in the woods.

Back in the den, the tortoise caused a little bit of an argument. In Samantha's view they already have more animals than they can cope with. The Owner countered with it being inhumane to leave a tortoise by the side of the road to be run over.

'Anyway,' he continued. 'It's a tortoise, how much trouble can he be? It's not like it's going to be pulling up trees or getting into the bins. Besides, he's really cute.'

Samantha had to concede the point. 'Who would drive a tortoise out into the country to abandon?' she wondered. 'You could take it to the bottom of the garden and it wouldn't get back to the house until Christmas.'

Everything was quiet while she tickled Bob under his scaly chin, then she said, 'OK, you can keep the tortoise, but no more animals.'

Monday, June 15

The Owner spent a couple of hours in the garden with wood and chicken wire. For a while I thought the time had come for us to be jailed, and was ready to make a break for it under the rhododendron. However, it turned out to be a run for Crusty Bob. The poor little guy is caged like Lolly, though in fairness he doesn't seem to mind much. Ella and I barked at him for an hour or so, to encourage him to escape, but he just put his head back inside his crust. The Owner seems very much in love though and comes out to grin at Crusty Bob and sit in the garden with him on his knee, which is more than he does with me. Well, he can get his tortoise to do 'heel' with him.

Tuesday, June 16

At last, a chance to help C.R.A.P. We have been visiting Lolly at nights to bark support over the fence, but otherwise our opportunities have been limited over the past few days. However, today we made it to the park and were let off the lead. It is only a short run from there to Lolly's alley, so Ella and I skipped around the Owner and made darting runs for the gate, hoping he'd get the message that someone, somewhere needed his help. It is lucky that little Johnny was not wedged under a tractor. For all the Owner cared he would have stayed there until he rotted. At one point Ella and I made a break for the High Street, only to have the Owner chase us down shouting 'SIT!' and 'HEEL!' with Coleridge on the retractable lead. He had to stop to untangle the puppy from a shopping trolley, but even so we made it nowhere near the alley. I thought every human knew that the correct response in these situations was to kneel by the dog and say, 'What is it, boy? Someone in trouble? Just show me the way.'

Lassie never had this trouble. All she had to do was cock an eyebrow and she'd have a posse of humans equipped with ropes and pulleys follow her out to take her evening dump. Lassie never had to work with Monkey Boy though.

Wednesday, June 17

Caught up with Scottie in the wasteland this evening. He has been recruiting more dogs. Even those who haven't got a chance of getting out of the den at night have been conscripted. This afternoon there was a wave of dogs by the park gate, trying to lead their Owners to the alley. Not one of them had any success. None of the humans are responding to the Johnny's-under-the-tractor routine. Even Trixie only got so far as the newspaper stand, and she's a St Bernard. Just how stupid *are* humans? A bloody St Bernard is trying to lead them somewhere and it's still not enough of a hint. What do we have to do? Tie a barrel of brandy around her neck?

It seems my Owner isn't the only one who didn't watch the right movies as a child.

Thursday, June 18

It occurred to me that Crusty Bob's run offers good practice vis-à-vis breaking through the chicken wire and wood barrier, so I spent the afternoon gnawing and pulling at it. Never noted for his woodwork abilities, the Owner's handiwork parted to my gnashing jaws after only a couple of hours and I was able to release the little guy from his prison. He needed some help though and the Owner came out into the garden to find me carrying him to freedom in my mouth. To say he was cross would be an understatement. Eventually I had to slink into the shed to escape his withering stare, while he fixed the run.

Friday, June 19

Scottie has managed to forge a connection to Razor; a Chihuahua named Choo Choo. She is a tiny dog whose size belies her courage. Personally I would not have had the nerve to sit on Razor's small patch of territory day after day, wagging my tail and waiting for him to talk to me. However, there's something about a Chihuahua that not even a bulldozer like Razor can resist. It's probably something to do with the big eyes and the huge ears. Choo Choo has always reminded me of a character in one of the Owner's favourite movies. Yoda, I think he's called. Razor has no idea that she's an agent of C.R.A.P.

Saturday, June 20

Choo Choo reports that Razor's aggressive behaviour is due to feeling ostracised. A dog should have plenty of opportunity to play and mingle, even if it's only with humans. As Razor's Owner is out all day and the park dogs steer clear of him, Choo Choo believes that he is displaying the classic symptoms of separation anxiety.

Having gained his trust she is devoting her park time to playing with him every day. I watched with disbelief from afar as they chased each other around. He could swallow her without even biting. However, it looked like he was taking great care not to hurt her, and afterwards they lay on the grass together with the pricked ears of happiness. If I hadn't have seen it with my own eyes I would not have believed it.

Sunday, June 21

Spent most of the night on my belly gnawing away at the chicken wire covering the hole into Lolly's yard with Scottie yapping quiet support. She seemed a little better today and persistently interrupted my work by asking had I finished yet and why didn't I let Scottie have a go. Obviously the only way Scottie was getting through that wire was to be chopped into hexagonal strips, but I kept quiet with the kind of self-restraint that would have made a Trappist monk proud.

Monday, June 22

Constable is out. It is a triumph of paw over doorknob. I was still working on the chicken wire when he arrived at Lolly's backyard. He was covered in rubbish: predictable, I suppose.

Scottie was amazed, demanding, 'How did ye get oot?' then 'Whut's that smell?'

Ignoring the latter question, Constable replied, 'It was Blake's brilliant idea. After weeks of practice I can open the door all on my own.' He paused, then continued proudly, 'I can close it too,' as if he had mastered quantum physics. As we all sat and watched in stunned silence he said, 'Watch,' then put his paws on the fence, reached out and pushed down a little handle. A gate to Lolly's yard swung open.

The silence went on. And on.

Finally Scottie said stiffly, 'I think ye can stop chewin' that wire noo, Blake.'

Any dog will favour slipping through a hole at nose level rather than looking up for handles, of course, but this was a monumental oversight. Scottie looked around at his quiet troops seriously, and continued, 'We've been a bit stupit, but we'll say no more aboot it, eh?'

After that Lolly's yard was swamped with a carpet of quietly woofing dogs all eager for a sniff of her. Scottie sat near her head and whined softly, then got a grip on himself and began organising food-finding teams.

Tuesday, June 23

Early walk in the park today after the old yapping-under-the-window ploy, and the Owner seems to be getting bored with 'heel'. Fortunately for me he has Attention Deficit Disorder and the perseverance of a skittish fruit fly. As is usually the case when it's warm and sunny the park was full of humans and dogs, which gave us the chance to see some pals and observe Razor. We might be back into Lolly's yard, but it's a small victory; really we're just back at square one. As all the humans have so far condemned little Johnny to his fate, Razor is our next best option.

Choo Choo has persuaded a poodle called Fabienne to help in the pit bull's rehabilitation. As I watched, Razor put his paws and elbows on the ground and lifted his rump in the universal signal that a dog wants to play. I could hardly believe that this was the same dog that nearly disembowelled Scottie and me last year.

Lying on the grass next to me the Westie said, 'That wus a good plan tae get Constable oot – shame he wrecked it by gettin' filthy agin.'

'No, he should be all right,' I replied absently. 'I told him to take a dump on the kitchen floor when he got back and roll around in it. With some luck his Mistress will be so upset she won't notice the twigs and leaves.'

'Aye, that's no' a bad idea, Blake. Why did ye no' tell me aboot the door handle plan in the first place, though? We might o' had a dozen more dogs in the C.R.A.P. by noo.'

This was a time for the famous Blake diplomacy if ever I've smelled one. 'I wasn't sure it would work,' I barked after a few moments' thought.

'Och, that's all right then. Fer a moment there ah wondered if ye may huv wanted tae show silly old Laird Scotland McIvor of Strathpeffer that he's no' quite the Top Dug he thought he wus.'

My eyebrow twitched involuntarily. 'Never crossed my mind, Scottie,' I yipped.

'Aye, that's whut I thought. A loyal beta male like Blake wouldnae do a thing like that.'

'Beta?'

'That's whut ah said.'

I couldn't help it. My tail started beating a tattoo on the grass and I gave Scottie a huge, tongue-lolling grin. How quickly we dogs forget.

'Right, 'tis time we turned the pressure up oan Razor, dae ye no' think, number two?'

Wednesday, June 24

A good morning's work with the postman. You have to admire his persistence, but I soon had him scuttling back down the path again. The satisfaction of a job well done is a reward in itself of course, but some kind of praise from the Owner would not have gone amiss. Perhaps aggressively shouting, 'Shut up, Blake' is his way of saying thanks. Maybe I should give Ella's Human Whimpering a go.

After the postman I got a chance to swing into action again when a pair of humans came tottering down the path. By the time they actually arrived at the door my throat had almost given out. Crusty Bob would have sprinted to an easy victory over them. It was Miss Meddling again, this time arm in arm with a man who smells even stranger than she does. As I was jumping around like a dervish the Owner didn't see who it was until too late, but staggered back clutching at my collar when he opened the door.

'We'd like to go shopping, young man,' Miss Meddling barked.

'I'm sorry, but I've got a lot of work to get . . .'

'Only Mr Philpot has just had a hip replacement and needs some assistance.'

Mr Philpot nodded sagely, leaning on his stick, and added, 'That's a lovely dog you've got there . . . I remember when dogs was dogs.'

From the musty smell of him he probably remembered when dogs were wolves, or possibly even single-celled proto-organisms.

The look Miss Meddling gave the Owner could have pinned a jelly to the wall, and he's got much less backbone than a jelly. Grumbling under his breath he dragged me, still barking hoarsely, to the garden and fetched his car keys, calling to Samantha that he was going out.

That was the last we saw of him until dinnertime. He's been tense before, but never actually *gibbered* until now. I've long suspected that when evolution was taking place he was in the lavatory, and every day brings more evidence to support my hypothesis.

Thursday, June 25

No chance of any park today, the office light was on most of the night and Samantha's belly has been keeping pace with Coleridge's quite nicely.* Neither of them are very enthusiastic about walking at the moment, which means Ella and I had to shift for ourselves as best we could. In practice this meant relieving ourselves in some flowers and scooting around the shed. With a fair amount of excess energy to shift there was also some jumping up in the air while twisting and barking. All excellent practice for my 'welcome home' technique.

* It looks to me like she'll be giving birth to a litter of about eight, though Ella says that humans usually only have one at a time. If that's the case then her baby's already the size of a small car.

Ella and I also treated ourselves to a moonlit run around the park with Constable before going on C.R.A.P. duty. Tradition says that sleeping dogs should be left to lie, but up to now has been silent on the subject of ducks. I have, however, come up with a new phrase: it goes, 'Wake sleeping ducks up by bounding among them barking, it's brilliant fun.'

Friday, June 26

As barking under the window is working so well I gave it another try this morning and was soon rewarded when that head popped out again. Today's rant was on the subject of sleep deprivation. Feeling affectionate I tried a new and experimental combination of the Happy Walking Dance and Welcome Home, but overstretched myself and fell in the pond. Nevertheless, he seemed quite cheered at my display. Alerted by my barking Coleridge scrambled through the Meddling Tunnel while the Owner prepared our breakfasts and I warmed myself up for a walk with some simple yoga, the 'down dog' position followed by a 'salute to the base of the apple tree', which involves balancing on three legs and urinating.

With my mind always full of C.R.A.P. I charged over to the east side to see how Choo Choo and Fabienne's Razor therapy has been getting on. I caught him wriggling on his back while Choo Choo bounced around his head. Seeing me approach, he became instantly alert and even a little embarrassed.

'I wasn't being submissive. We were playing,' he barked.

'Is that so?' I replied. 'I've always thought Choo Choo might be half tiger. You wouldn't be the first pit bull she's chewed up and spat out.'

It would be a stretch to say he smiled, but there had been a slight raise in the temperature since my last visit. You'd need specialist scientific equipment to measure it though.

'I told you to stay away from here.'

'Yes, but it looked like you were having fun, so I was wondering if anyone could join in.' Walking slowly, as if I were approaching a cobra, I moved over and sniffed his muzzle. He growled at me but didn't move. If my eyes did not deceive me his tail trembled, just a tiny bit.

'You know, Razor, watching you play, I wonder if we didn't get off on the wrong paw.'

'Sniff me again and you won't have any paws to get off on.'

'Fair enough,' I woofed, backing away. 'Maybe tomorrow, then?'

'I'll help you save your friend the day I get my balls back, Blake.'

'That's OK, we've got Choo Choo now. A fearsome beast like her will tear through Lolly's cage like a charging rhinoceros.'

For a moment, I thought I might have overplayed it. Razor looked down at the Chihuahua and snarled, 'You're helping?' It sounded like he suspected he was being duped. Choo Choo rallied magnificently though.

Yawning, she yapped, 'Of course. What dog wouldn't? Can you imagine starving in a cage?'

Having started the conversation, I woofed 'Ciao, Choo Choo,' and left them to it. That little dog is a natural espionage agent. It would not surprise me if her collar was fitted with a small offensive device, maybe a tiny Rolled Up Newspaper.

Saturday, June 27

Reported to Scottie last night that Razor's softening a little. Despite myself I am quite enjoying being beta male. It's nice not to have the responsibility of Top Dog and I've always thought 'beta' is a dashing, romantic rank. Some of the most famous dogs in history have been betas – Cow Pat Charlie, Flatulent Patch and Duchess the Digging Diva to name just three. Betas always get a nickname: I wonder what mine will be when future generations howl about my mighty deeds. Something cool and edgy like Drooling Blake or Ripper would be nice. Appropriate too. I should start mentioning it to the C.R.A.P. dogs, just lightly drop a few suggestions into conversation now and again.

Sunday, June 28

A day of regurgitation after which the door to the den has been slammed shut again. All dogs eat grass and it's widely believed that this is another throwback to the days when your basic wolf would not waste a scrap of elk or moose. Out in the wild it's an unpredictable existence so they made the most of every meal. 'Eat fast, eat everything' is the wolf's motto, which is why they never found a scrap of grandma I expect. I digress. Eating everything includes the stomach, usually filled with semi-digested grass. I'm sure the first wolves spat it out in disgust, but over the years they developed a taste for it and even found that it added useful vitamins and roughage to their diet. Nowadays it's not so often you find a stomach lying around with your grass prepackaged, but we still like a nibble now and again. That's one theory anyway. Another is that we're just greedy bastards.

Either way a surfeit of the lush grass in the garden at the moment – which I'd like to point out the Owner has not cut in over a fortnight – tripped my sensitive vomit reflex while I was wandering around the den today. Four times. As it was such a nice day the Owner hadn't bothered to put any shoes on, and found each pile one after another.

Monday, June 29

Coleridge took an opportunity to try and lead the Owner to Lolly today. We were tied to a lamppost while the human bought a newspaper and when he returned Coleridge snatched the lead out of his hand and made a break for it down the High Street. He was doing quite well, too. We were in hot pursuit, but despite his swaying belly Coleridge maintained a comfortable lead and was well on the way to Lolly's alley. Unexpectedly, though, he stopped. His nose came up sniffing and his head swung sideways. Then he made a ninety-degree turn into a shop, emerging a few seconds later with a string of sausages in his mouth and a butcher chasing him. The latter was red-faced, waving a cleaver and wearing a striped apron.

I was very stern with the puppy after the Owner grabbed him and finished paying for the sausages. If he hadn't been so greedy we might have had Lolly free. Plus, of course, a puppy shouldn't be allowed to perpetrate such terrible clichés.

When we got home I noticed the Owner surreptitiously washing the sausages in the kitchen and this evening he had the cheek to serve them up to Samantha. The poor human is having his baby and the cheapskate is making her eat sausages that have been dragged along the pavement. By rights they should have been mine.

Tuesday, June 30

Razor is in. It was touch and go for a while, but he's agreed to help Lolly and escape from his den using the new Constable Method. It's lucky that his Owner doesn't lock the door* as I'm not sure how well Razor would have taken to the poo and pee plan.

* I've heard that Razor's Owner actively encourages burglars as it saves on his dog's food bill.

JULY

Wednesday, July 1

The pit bull came west today while we were having an early C.R.A.P. meeting. At his side Choo Choo walked proudly, nudging him with her nose occasionally. Fabienne brought up the rear. There was some tentative sniffing with tails held erect to show that while violence is being kept under control it's just a wag away, and after that Razor looked at me, barking, 'All right, I'll help your little dog friend. But just for Choo Choo. I still don't like you, genital thief.'

I glanced nervously at Scottie and shuffled in his direction.

'What?' Razor gruffed. 'Do you want my help or not?'

'Ah think whut Blake is tryin' tae tell ye is that he's no' Top Dug around here.'

'He's not? Who is then?' He looked expectantly at Claude the boxer.

'Ye've no' been keepin' up wi' the news huv ye, Razor?' Scottie was starting to sound irritated. 'Ah'm Top Dug noo.'

It was at least five minutes before Razor sat up again. I've never seen a dog writhe around on his back so happily or for so long. Finally Scottie stepped up to his head.

'Right, ye big haggis, ye're in the C.R.A.P. noo an' I dinnae stand fer that kindae insubordination. On yer feet an' listen up.'

I thought for a moment that Razor might snap him up, like an alligator raising its head from the water and snatching a baby gazelle from the shore, but to my surprise he sat to attention, still grinning with the whole of that gigantic mouth.

'Noo whut's yer problem wi' me bein' Top Dug, eh? Ye want tae challenge me?' In front of my goggling eyes, tiny, arthritic Scottie began growling. It actually looked as though he was going to attack Razor. Instinctively I felt my own muzzle begin to wrinkle. Scottie may be insane, but he is sort of alpha male at the moment, and a friend, too. However, I did begin a quick prayer to Dog.

Razor did not respond as I expected him to. Instead his grin widened to the point where it looked as though the top of his head might come off. 'No problem,' he said. 'I knew Blake wouldn't last as Top Dog, I just didn't think a stronger, fitter dog would come along so quickly.' With that Razor began writhing happily on his back again.

'Aye, well it didnae take much tae be honest.'

'You must tell me all about it. I want to hear every tiny detail,' Razor barked back.

'Och ye dinnae want tae know that,' Scottie yapped modestly. 'But ye be a good boy an' help us get wee Lolly oot o' her scrape an' ah'll tell ye all aboot it.'

At this point I was glad to hear the Owner whistling and for once felt inclined to obey him instantly.

Thursday, July 2

I've never liked pit bulls. In my view the world would be a slightly better place if the whole breed became extinct, with maybe one or two examples kept in zoos to illustrate the dangers of humans interfering with nature. However, I have to admit that having given C.R.A.P. his allegiance Razor didn't hang about. Dogs were only just arriving with morsels of food in their mouths when he trotted up ready for action and, under Scottie's direction, began work on the cage. Unfortunately, as is the way with pit bulls, he couldn't help snarling while chewing. In his tiny little brain he was probably taking down a juggernaut.

The growls and the noise of the cage being mangled alerted Lolly's Master. First the window opened and the loathsome human shouted, 'Right, I'll have you this time you little bastard,' then came the sound of footsteps from within. The rest of us evacuated into the alley, but Razor carried on with his work, completely unperturbed and ignoring Scottie's barks of, 'Away Razor, ye can do nuthin' noo.'

Then the back door opened and the human stormed out looking for a dog to kick. What he found seemed to come as a big surprise.

With scraps of wood, drool and a shred of chicken wire hanging from that ferocious mouth, Razor turned on the attacking human. He looked like a great white shark on little stubby legs.

With a cry of 'Oh, shit,' the human went into reverse. Reaching out a hand he picked up a brick and threw it at the pit bull, who was inching towards him. It caught Razor on his haunches, but the human may as well have thrown a fluffy toy at a charging rhino. Razor hurled himself forwards, arriving in time to find a door hastily slammed in his face.

Most dogs would have given up there, but the door just made Razor madder and he began trying to claw and bite his way through it.

Behind him Lolly was barking, 'No, just go. You'll get hurt.'

Sure enough, within a minute another window opened and a bucketful of water fell on the furious pit bull. The bucket followed. Then a mop, toilet brush, soap dish and shaving mug. It was only a matter of time before the toilet itself was hurled out. Without thinking, I launched myself through the gate. Bracing against the wall I butted Razor in his midriff and began slowly propelling him, still fighting, away from the door. Enraged, he turned on me and sank his teeth into my neck. There was a burst of pain and then Ella was there, biting his ear and pulling his head away, while Scottie danced in and out of a snarling ball of dogs barking commands. Lolly's Owner literally had C.R.A.P. on his own doorstep.

For a couple of seconds it was not looking good at all, then there was another deluge of water and a plastic bowl caught Razor just above one eye. It seemed to bring him back to reality. Shaking Ella and I off, he paused for one more snarl at the window above and walked out into the alley, with the rest of us scrambling behind him.

And that's why I don't like pit bulls. No sense, no off switch.

Friday, July 3

A sore neck, but otherwise no harm done. Razor punctured the skin in a few places, but not enough that the Owner noticed that I'd been wounded. Luckily, my collar seems to have absorbed most of the damage. Black, studded leather is not just about rock 'n' roll.

Operations last night were much more covert after the debacle of the evening before. Scottie told Razor to stay away for a few days and the two of us relayed food to Lolly's cage alone. I was first through the gate tonight and I had hardly sneaked over the threshold when my nose was assaulted by the magnificent odour of steak cooked just how I like it: raw. I've mentioned my love of a good juicy steak before, dear diary, but I don't think I can ever praise the loveliness of a chunk of dead cow enough. It is like music to my nose. Although I only have 2,000 taste buds, it makes each and every one of them howl like angels.

So I ate it. Without even thinking of poor, starving Lolly. Wolfed it down like the bad dog I am. Scottie was beside himself.

'Whut are ye doin', ye stupit mongrel? That'll keep Lolly goin' all night.'

I crawled on my belly across the yard, whining, 'I'm so sorry. It's just I can't resist . . .'

'It's OK,' said Lolly. 'Blake's done so much for me the least I can do is offer him a treat in return.'

Growling, Scottie ordered me out of the yard and on food-finding duty. I have never turned over so many bins so quickly. By jumping on some boxes I even made it over the fence into the back of the Chinese restaurant where I found a dish of spring rolls that had hardly been touched.

None of it was enough to mollify Scottie. With dawn coming and Lolly sitting in a pile of crumbs and dry faeces he was still furious. I deserve it.

Saturday, July 4

Passed a stool this morning, squatting and shuddering slightly with my tail held aloft – the usual polished performance. However, I was surprised to see that it was bright green. So green that had it been dark it would have been glowing like a poo made of pure Kryptonite. Remarkable. I felt quite proud. After all, it's not every dog that can manage psychedelic shit. Even the Owner was impressed, scratching my ears and asking, 'Blake, what have you been eating now?'

I'm not saying that life in the garden is dull, but when the high point of your day is a technicolour turd, it's time to think about taking up a hobby. Accordingly, I spent the afternoon barking at a steady stream of senior citizens who came to lean on the doorbell. The Owner seemed to have gone completely deaf though. I barked so much that I actually developed an irritating cough.

Felt a little bit ruff this evening. It could be I've been overdoing it with the late nights, or it could be the hideous 'meat' the Owner insists on feeding us. I'd give my hind leg for another steak right now.

Monday, July 6

Tuesday, July 7
Have been lying in a cell at the vet's for the past two days with a plastic mask over my nose and a tube under my skin. Starting to feel like I might live, but too weak to go on right now.

Wednesday, July 8
The Owner brought me back to the den this morning. A special bed has been made up for me in the den with newspaper all around. Twice I was led quietly around the garden then had a pill forced down my throat. It was a little lonely, but the TV has been left on for me all day. However, I can't muster much interest in *Teenage Pregnancies: DNA Results Special*.

Thursday, July 9
Feeling a bit better this morning, a miracle considering that I have been nearly poisoned to death. I should have known; that steak outside Lolly's Master's back door was extremely suspicious when Lolly was starving only a few feet away. It must have been meant for Razor I suppose, but what kind of human feeds rat poison to a dog, even one that's a bit loopy?

I remember feeling odd, but then very little. Just flashes. Ella barking under the Owner's window; being bundled in the car; bright lights and needles; the Owner crying. After that, nothing until I woke up in the cell with tubes running into me. I still can't breathe very well and feel as weak as a newborn pup, but it's nice that the Owner comes down and lets me lie with his head in his lap while he strokes me. That way I can snuffle his crotch without having to make too much of an effort. If I had died I wonder if he would have spent the rest of his life sitting on my grave pining for me. Probably.

Friday, July 10
The Owner is talking to me a lot at the moment and the drone of his voice is quite comforting in a soporific kind of way. He tells me that I have to take it very easy for the next couple of weeks. Apparently

rat poison makes your poo go green then attacks the blood and thins it dangerously. When he found me I was bleeding from the nose and backside and hardly breathing. I was lucky to get to the vet's just in time. A lesser dog might be put off steak for life and perhaps even think about taking up vegetarianism, but not me. When the Owner brought a pile in to help me 'get my strength back' it was down my throat before the bowl hit the ground.

The Owner still doesn't know about the Meddling Tunnel and thinks that I must have eaten something in the park or wasteland, thank Dog. When I'm fit again I have a message for Lolly's Master. A sharp, pointed message.

Saturday, July 11

It was a nice day and I was allowed out into the garden to play with Ella and Coleridge for a while. Samantha fell asleep on a sun lounger. I couldn't manage much more than walking round and round the perimeter with Ella nuzzling me, but it was fun watching Coleridge hump Samantha's pillow while she snored. Even the Owner had a chuckle and took a movie on his mobile phone (and I thought his sense of humour had been surgically removed when he found out he was going to be a father).

Ella says I'm not to worry about anything at the moment, even Lolly. However, she saw Scottie during a walk to the wasteland yesterday and he said how lucky it was that it was me that ate the steak. If we'd fed it to a dog in Lolly's condition she would have stood no chance at all. Not sure how lucky I feel right now. If Razor had eaten it, then that would be luck I could believe in.

Sunday, July 12

Spent most of the day sniffing and gnawing my own backside. It's still not feeling quite right, but this sort of intensive physical therapy should see it back to normal in no time.

Monday, July 13

The Meddling woman called again today. I managed to drag myself from the sofa and bark by the door, but it wasn't very convincing. A pathetic bit of guarding that would have frightened off a nervous plastic bag, at best. She wanted to go shopping again, but had caught the Owner at precisely the wrong time. He tried to be nice about it, but the trouble with old women is that they are the human equivalent of pit bulls.

'I'm sorry, Miss Meddling,' he began, running his fingers through his hair, 'but I've got a big presentation tomorrow, lots of work to get through, my dog's just been poisoned and my wife's not feeling well.'

'That's all right, young man, I only have a few things to buy.'

'You said that last time and we were at the supermarket for four hours. I'm sorry, but I just can't do it today.'

'So you'd leave an old lady with not a scrap of food in the house? Just half a stale Chelsea bun to feed her and her dog.'

The Owner was becoming a little irate. 'Miss Meddling, last week I ferried you and your friends to the shops three times. You bought enough food to feed the world's fattest army, and their dogs. And frankly I've got more important things to do than be called "Mr Pervert" in public all afternoon while discussing which brand of tea biscuit offers superior quality at an affordable price.'

Miss Meddling glared the kind of glare that makes charging bulls remember they left the kettle on, and I thought for a moment the Owner's resolve would crumble. But no, he stood firm. It's often the way with him. He's all marshmallow-soft, but with a core you could break your teeth on.

The response, when it finally came, was withering. 'Well, I wouldn't want to bother you, I can see now I was right all along. Lost in your own selfish needs and desires.'

'Miss Meddling, I have a baby on the way and a large mortgage to pay, I can't just keep taking afternoons off all the time.'

'That's what you say. More likely that you're watching people rub oil into each other's private parts on the interphone.'

The Owner looked stunned at this new attack. Meddling continued.

'Oh yes, don't look surprised. I may be old but I know all about this hemline prawn.'

'You mean online porn?'

'I see you know all about it too. Well, you enjoy your filth and I shall try and walk to the shops without breaking a leg. I won't bother you again.'

The Owner shut the door quickly, but I could still hear Miss Meddling shouting, 'I'm seventy-seven, you know,' as she walked down the path with the agility of a greyhound.

Tuesday, July 14

A close call with Coleridge today; it was fortunate that I was in the garden at the time and he's too fat to do much more than waddle. He'd just finished his first dinner when Meddling started calling for Bobby. There was the rattle of metal bowl on concrete – presumably Coleridge's half of a stale Chelsea bun.

Even with Samantha watching, the little hippo made a break for the tunnel. I got to the bush just in time to block him. He yapped at me furiously, but I danced to the left, Ella jumped to the right. I've never seen him so upset, like a tiny, round lioness parted from her cubs, but we managed to keep him from his cake until Samantha observed that I looked a lot better and went back inside the den.

Once we've got Lolly fixed up with Miss M I'm very much looking forward to blowing the whistle on the puppy's double life of gastronomy. Much more of this and he's going to explode.

Wednesday, July 15

Back to the park today. Scottie was the first to walk up with his tail between his legs.

'Ah'm sorry ah growled at ye fer eatin' yon steak,' he yipped.

I thought for a moment, and then confessed how ashamed I was at my greediness.

Scottie brightened. 'Och, wull it's a guid joab ye're sich a big porker, or Lolly's be deid. And it's guid tae see ye fully recovered. Noo, I reckon Razor's goat a few words he'd like tae get oaf his chest.'

Scottie trotted away and Razor approached, with his ears drooping and his head hung low. 'Scottie says I have to say sorry I bit you.'

This was a moment to be savoured.

'So you realise now that I was just trying to help, do you?'
'Yes, Blake.'
'And that sometimes "Mr Bitey" is not the way to solve a problem?'
'Yes, Blake.' His bark had dropped so low I could barely hear it.
'And that I took a poisoned steak meant for you?'
'Yes, Blake.'
'Which would mean I may have saved your life on two occasions

– three if you count my Owner not demanding you be put down after biting him?'

'Yes, Blake.'

'So, you won't be mentioning those testicles you used to have again, then?'

'No, Blake.'

All in all, a good day.

Thursday, July 16

It's been less than a fortnight since I was poisoned and officially I'm still in recovery. Nevertheless, my sofa and special food privileges have been revoked. My crime? Sniffing Samantha's bum. Nothing unusual, just an everyday part of being a dog; the Owner would be the first to complain if he didn't feel my nose wedged between his cheeks every so often.

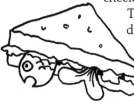

The fact that she was carrying a tray with iced drinks and sandwiches at the time was hardly my fault. I even gave her a hand clearing up the mess, as she's too large to bend over now. Tuna is a bit too 'catty' for me really, but I selflessly ate all of them.

Friday, July 17

Now that I'm well again, the Owner is taking a bit more interest. He still spends most of his time in that pokey room upstairs, but probably realises how close he came to being bereft. Obviously that little reality call has made him think about how utterly desolate he'd be without his faithful hound, so we've had walks to the park each morning and even a spot of light grooming today. A miracle.

Talking of the park, we were practising 'heel' again this morning (the Owner's interest is a double-edged sword) and I noticed Ginger approach Scottie with a determined look in her eye and a wiggle to her hindquarters that could mean only one thing. It was a surprise when Scottie ignored her. Could it be that he's getting too old even for humping?

Saturday, July 18

Another attempt to free Lolly last night and another failure. This time Razor had only just got his jaws around the cage when the window opened. With the lid of hair that covers his bald patch flapping crazily, Lolly's Master took aim and pulled the trigger of a small gun. Suddenly Razor yelped in pain. Laughing, the vicious human reloaded and took another shot at the pit bull who yelped again and began chasing his tail, trying to lick his wounds. There wasn't any blood, so it can't have been a very powerful weapon, and Razor has an enormous pain tolerance level, but even so he quickly had to give up under a hail of tiny little grey pellets. When he finally emerged it looked like he had been stung by a dozen wasps.

I just don't understand humans. This one will go to the trouble of buying a gun to keep dogs out of his yard, but won't lift a finger to look after the one he's already got in there. I'd happily lick the postman all day for the chance of just one small bite.

Sunday, July 19

I haven't seen Constable recently, so it was good to catch up with him during the morning promenade. Apparently, he's been letting himself out every night and hasn't been able to resist indulging his addiction to the old nose candy: poo. Any kind of poo will do; like most addicts he's an indiscriminate user and will roll in anything. To cover his tracks he's been coming home, quietly closing the door then dumping on the kitchen floor for one last roll. His mystified Mistress has been taking him to the grooming parlour almost daily, and, yesterday, a psychologist.

Constable's quite pleased to be in rehab, it's all the rage in celebrity circles apparently. The shrink explained to Constable's Mistress that to a dog scent is very important, and that constant shampooing lessens the dog's own smell. As a result the dog will try to replace the scent in the quickest way possible. *I've* always thought it was just a good way of letting other dogs know where you've been, and much easier than sending a postcard, but what do I know? I get shampooed about once a year on average, though if I've picked up a particularly strong whiff, the Owner will give me the hose and the broom held at arm's length. Even so, it's amazing how I can get my coat filthy again in under a minute.

In Constable's case it's just another example of aberrant human behaviour leading to a canine psychological disorder. If his Mistress weren't so obsessed with him being a show dog and TV star then he could be himself without the need for a stinky brown coat.

Monday, July 20

A C.R.A.P. night in every possible sense. We returned to Lolly's alley to bring her some food and found the hole in the fence mended and a chain on the gate. Not even Razor's teeth could make an impression.

We barked, but there was no reply from Lolly.

Tuesday, July 21

An emergency meeting of C.R.A.P. members present at the wasteland tonight, called by Scottie and consisting of him, me and Ella. He came straight to the point.

'It's been months since we foond Lolly. We've goat C.R.A.P. all over toon an' it husnae made much o' a difference. We need tae think strategically, there's somethin' we're missin'.'

Ella and I agreed, but what could we do? We had a sniff around to sharpen our faculties, then Ella woofed, 'I have an idea, but if it fails Blake and I will be out of C.R.A.P. for good.'

'Oot o' C.R.A.P.? Ye cannae be oot o' C.R.A.P. Ye an' Blake are pieces o' C.R.A.P. Vital pieces. A C.R.A.P. wi'oot the two o' ye there tae help wud be no C.R.A.P. at all. I'd be left wi' dugs like Constable an' they're . . . well, they're rubbish.'

Ella continued smoothly, 'But if we . . . Blake . . . succeeded there would be no reason for C.R.A.P.'

Scottie hesitated, then barked, 'Och ye're right, o' course, C.R.A.P. cannae last forivir. Whut's yer plan, Ella? I hope it calls fer iviry dug in toon tae answer the call o' C.R.A.P.'

'No, that might attract attention. This plan calls for a solitary dog, and his Owner. Blake will reveal the secret of the Meddling Tunnel, in one last chance to lead the human to Lolly.'

'Reveal the Meddling Tunnel?' I replied. 'But that's a crap idea.'

'Aye, Blake's right, 'tis an idea worthy o' C.R.A.P., Ella. Well done. But we huv tried tae lead yon humans before and it hasnae worked. Whut'll be different this time?'

'Blake will make sure his Owner gives chase by stealing something that he loves.'

'Whut, like his mate, ye mean? She's a wee bit oan the large side even fer Blake, especially noo.'

'I was thinking more of his mobile phone.'

By the time I finally got a word in edgeways it had all been settled. And it had all the potential of a plan that could go dreadfully wrong.

'So,' I barked wearily, 'the C.R.A.P. is going to hit the phone.'

Scottie looked at me strangely, and growled, 'Whut are ye talkin' aboot, Blake? Sometimes I ken ye're jest a wee bit dim.'

Wednesday, July 22

Not a good day. Ella and I are very worried about Lolly. Meanwhile, on Samantha's insistence the grumbling Owner took Coleridge to the vet's. Her actual words were, 'No dog should be that fat, he must have something wrong with him.'

Obviously there was nothing at all the matter. The Owner carried him out of the car, red-faced at the effort and shaking his head to Samantha. 'The vet says that we're massively overfeeding him, and giving him too many sweet treats. His teeth are going rotten, too.'

Crossing her arms, Samantha sounded annoyed: 'What have you been giving him?'

'Nothing that I don't feed Blake and Ella, and certainly not any sweets. I thought you must have done.'

'I don't give dogs sweets, it's bad for them. And if you haven't why is he so enormous?' It sounded like she wasn't convinced of the Owner's innocence.

The Owner set him down in the garden, just as Miss Meddling began calling 'Bobbee, Boobbeee,' over the fence. As the two humans went back into the den, still arguing about where Coleridge could be finding sweets, he was already halfway through the Meddling Tunnel.

Thursday, July 23

Coleridge is on a special diet the vet recommended. It consists mostly of boiled green beans. He is not impressed and tried for a share of mine and Ella's bowls until we menaced him away. I may not be Top Dog, but there are some things that you just do not tolerate. According to the vet the beans will help keep Coleridge in good condition while he loses weight, though he will become more flatulent than usual, which is good news for Miss Meddling. I was wondering what the combined aroma of lemon drizzle cake and green beans would smell like, and didn't have to wait long to find out. I would not recommend it as an air freshener.

Friday, July 24

The C.R.A.P. plan has been refined. This is how it goes. I steal the Owner's mobile phone, making sure he sees me, and dash through the Meddling Tunnel with it in my mouth. He will watch me emerge on the other side of the fence and race round the corner to find me already streaking up the road towards Lolly's alley. Making sure I ignore his commands (which is becoming strangely more difficult these days) I lead him directly to Lolly. When the Owner gets there I will dance around barking. We hope that Lolly is in a fit condition to answer me, thus attracting the Owner's attention. Once he looks over the fence and sees her, Ella believes his better nature will kick in and a rescue will soon be effected.

It's more complicated than I would have liked and hinges on the Owner's better nature, something I wouldn't be so quick to pin success on. Also it almost certainly involves a good telling-off for me, if not the actual Rolled Up Newspaper. Having given up being Top Dog, not to mention being bitten and poisoned, I just hope that Lolly's grateful when she's back to full health.

Saturday, July 25

All C.R.A.P. operations have ceased. Scottie visited Lolly's alley alone last night and barked the plan over the fence at her. She gave only a faint whine in response, but it will have to do. I am now on top alert, just waiting for him to leave the door open and his phone on the kitchen table. Ella and I prowled nervously, our nerves twanging with anticipation. Barking the stick into submission helped ease the tension, but not much.

Sunday, July 26

So close today. I was partaking of some more therapeutic stick intimidation when the Owner's phone rang in the kitchen. Instantly Ella and I were on the doorstep, our tails a frenzy of wagging.

'Oh yes, hello, Miss Meddling. What can I do for you?'

There was a pause.

'They are barking a lot today. Sorry, I'll try and shut them up.'

Then he pushed a button, and slipped the phone into his back pocket. Foiled.

He must have forgotten his promise to Miss Meddling because he did absolutely nothing to stop me barking. There must be a lot on his mind again.

Monday, July 27

The Owner was making coffee in the kitchen with the phone pinned to his ear when Samantha came in with a bag of shopping. The Owner ended his call and turned to help her, absently putting his phone on the edge of the table. Within seconds it was safely in my mouth.

'Blake, leave it,' Samantha shouted. As the Owner turned I was already through the door with it and running for the Meddling Tunnel. The human raced through the door, and I stopped. Something caught my eye. The side gate. It has never been attempted before, but seemed to offer a quick route to Lolly's without having to give away our secret pass to freedom. I turned, dodged the shouting Owner, sprinted up the garden and jumped, scrambled, was over. From there it was a short run and another hop over the front wall and I was on the road to Lolly's. Behind me I could hear Ella and Coleridge barking excitedly and the Owner shouting, 'Blake, sit. Blake, leave it. Blake, down.'

Steeling my mind to disobedience – once so easy, but now a struggle – I ran up the road with him in hot pursuit.

When the phone started ringing and buzzing I nearly dropped it in surprise, and had to tighten my grip. One of my teeth must have pressed a button because it stopped. Instead, a voice sounded in my mouth.

'Hello? Hello? It's Fanny Meddling here.'

Looking over my shoulder I could see that the Owner was still on my trail, but getting a little too close. I stepped up the pace a bit, beginning to pant from my exertions. The voice in my mouth spoke again.

'What's the matter with you, why are you breathing like that . . .?' There was a pause and then it started again, sounding disgusted, 'Oh, I see, you're one of those dirty phone callers. Sitting by the phone watching your prawn with your privates in your hand and waiting for an old woman to call.'

Meddling's voice was distracting, and beginning to annoy me, but I couldn't bark at her without dropping the phone so had to content myself with a low growl from the back of my throat while I ran.

'What's that? Growling at me now, eh? I knew I was right. You vile, filthy pervert.'

I tried to ignore the crone bleating away in my mouth as well as the Owner's shouting, but it was difficult. I was nearly there now though, across a road and into the alley I ran with the Owner following hard.

'You're slobbering, aren't you? Does your wife know you do this? She will when the police get there, you sordid man. I'll see you in prison for this.'

I was nearly there now, with Owner in tow.

'Well, I hope you've had your fun because you won't be getting any more for a very long time.'

Finally I could drop the phone by the fence, jumping back from that irritating voice and staying out of the Owner's reach as he arrived. I began barking as he bent to pick up the phone, panting from the running. Hearing a voice on the other end he put it to his ear and gasped, 'Hello?'

I couldn't make out any actual words but there was a torrent of tinny abuse from the phone. The Owner interrupted, saying, 'Oh, it's you again, Miss Meddling. You'll have to excuse me, I'm a bit out of breath right now. I'll call you back later.'

On the other side of the fence Lolly, roused by the commotion, also began barking weakly. The Owner's face was puzzled as he listened to Miss Meddling rant, but he turned and looked absently over the fence. His jaw dropped open and his knuckles whitened.

'I'm sorry, Miss Meddling, I really have to go now, I've just seen something absolutely disgusting.'

He snapped the phone off and put it in his pocket, my crime forgotten. Instead of shouting at me he was leaning over the fence, crooning at Lolly. 'Oh, you poor little thing. Who would do something like this to you? Oh, look at the state of you. Don't worry, we'll get you to the vet.'

In a bound that put my earlier effort in the shade he leaped over the fence. I heard him knocking on the back door. It was answered. The Owner spoke again, his voice angry.

'The dog. In the cage. You'll give it to me now.'

'Who are you? What are you doing in my yard? Get out of it.'

'Now. Or I'll call the police and every animal welfare group I can think of.'

'Yeah? And I'll have you arrested for trespass.'

'You'll hand the dog over right now or you can have me arrested for breaking your neck too.'

'It'll cost you.'

'What?'

'She's a valuable dog is Lolly. Pedigree. Not to mention the sentimental value.'

'You've got the cheek to stand there and tell me that a dog you've starved half to death has sentimental value?'

'Used to be my wife's.'

'Here's twenty. Now get her out of there.'

'Fifty.'

'There's a special place in hell for people like you.'

'Fifty.'

'There, now give her to me.'

There came the sounds from Lolly's cage and a yelp of pain as she was pulled out. Then the Owner's voice again.

'Is that a packet of rat poison?'

'Yeah, been having a plague of strays round here recently. I put some down in a bit of steak for 'em.'

I could hear the Owner sucking in his breath from the other side of the fence. 'You poisoned my dog, you bastard. I should break your legs,' he spat.

'I'll call the police.'

'You do that. They'll probably want to give you a smack as well.'

There was a pause and the fence rattled. Then the Owner continued, 'Umm, could you unlock the gate, please?'

He was doing so well, too.

Then he was out, with Lolly in his arms and me trotting at his side in the most perfect 'heel' I've ever achieved.

Tuesday, July 28

In all the fuss yesterday, the part I played in Lolly's discovery was completely forgotten. Not even a pat, let alone a decent meal. If I remember how the movies go, Lassie was always showered with praise and affection after leading the humans to the rescue. This is what you get for working with amateurs.

The Owner jogged home as quickly as he could while carrying Lolly and delivered her straight to the car, with Samantha looking over his shoulder with concern. Then he drove off to the vet's and didn't return for hours, without Lolly.

For a moment we thought it was too late and the vet had put her out of her misery. Samantha started sobbing when she saw him alone. However, it just seems that the vet wants to keep her for a few days. She needs a lot of treatment for malnutrition and mange. When she's stronger he's going to operate on her eyes and bring her sight back. Wonderful things humans, though in fairness I should point out that if dogs had been at the head of the queue when opposable thumbs were being handed out then we'd probably be cruising around distant galaxies by now, stopping every now and then to urinate on a new planet. Nevertheless, I made sure the Owner got a double portion of affection. From now on if he says 'heel', I'll bark, 'Which foot?'

Wednesday, July 29
Fortunately, the Owner also seems to have forgotten the small detail that someone nearly a mile away had poisoned me. It doesn't take a great detective to deduce that I must have an escape route from the garden. He may be a hero, but he's also reliably slow on the uptake and until the penny drops the Meddling Tunnel remains open for business. Coleridge is still flitting between humans, and the way was clear for Ella and me to enjoy a moonlight stroll.

They say that dogs resemble their Owners and it must be true. Monkey Boy's not the only one who can be forgetful. It had completely slipped my mind, for example, that Scottie and the rest of C.R.A.P. did not know of Lolly's liberation. Seeing Scottie walking out of the alley, his head bowed low in grief and followed by Claude, Constable, Razor and Liquorice reminded me. I bounded up to them full of cheer and vim.

'She's goan, Blake, Lolly's goan,' Scottie groaned.

'Yes, we know,' I barked.

'Well, ye dinnae huv tae sound so cheerful aboot it. The puir wee thing must o' died. We failed her. Puir Lolly, she's gone tae a better place noo.' He sat by the side of the road and began to howl. Well, sort of. Wolves howl. West Highland Scots terriers, however, make a sort of high-pitched keening sound, which always puts me in mind of a miniature banshee. It's unnerving. But I digress.

'Yes, she has. She's in –' Ella began to respond.

'Dug heaven. I ken that, Ella. The ainly dug ah ivir loved, an' noo she's goan forivir.'

'You love her?' I was surprised. She's not his usual type, but then

126

I suppose between Ginger and Trixie and the rest of the park bitches he hasn't really got a particular type. When I think about it they're actually a good match. She has mange, he has bad breath.

'Aye, I loved her. An' noo she's gone.'

'Yes, but only –' Ella began. Scottie interrupted.

'In boady. Aye, Ella. A spirit like hers will nivir truly die. It's kind o' ye tae say so.'

'That's not what she's trying to say, you daft haggis,' I barked.

'Whut? I'm grievin', Blake, 'tis no' the time tae be callin' me names.'

'Oh, for Dog's sake. Lolly's at the vet's. My Master took her there.' For once I thought I'd give him his full honorary title. He deserves it.

There was a pause while this sank in, and then C.R.A.P. exploded.

Thursday, July 30

The Owner brought Lolly back from the vet's today. She is still too weak to have the corrective eye surgery, but is looking healthier already. C.R.A.P. managed to keep her alive with scraps of food, but she is still painfully thin, though her various scabs are clearing up and her skin looks pinker and ready to grow a coat.

Friday, July 31

For the moment Lolly has my old sick bed in the den and the humans are bringing her out a few times a day for shaky walks in the garden. Having been confined to a cage for so long her muscles need building up. They also rub her with some vile-smelling ointment. The door was left open and Ella spent a lot of the day lying next to her nuzzling and woofing general comfort. When I went in she started shaking and tried to back away, so I left again quickly. Ella says that she's still disorientated after solitary confinement and her time at the vet's. She did however manage to bark, 'Thank you, Blake,' when I put my nose around the door later. It felt like I finally had my Lassie moment.

AUGUST

Saturday, August 1
A good day. Ella, Coleridge and I had a long walk in the park this morning and I am being treated like a hero. It's almost like being Top Dog again. Scottie keeps telling me that my services to C.R.A.P. deserve a medal, or at least one of those expensive chewy bones with the tasty centre. Even Razor offered a few words of congratulations. I am tempted to revise my opinion of him. Over the past month he's become a part of the park pack. His fondness for Choo Choo borders on infatuation, and it's a good job he's been neutered. When I imagine half pit bull half Chihuahua puppies, my brain starts to melt. What would they be? Chit bulls I suppose, or maybe Bihuahuas, though that sounds more like a modernist architectural style than a breed name.

Sunday, August 2
A very nice day with all the pack together. Samantha waddled out to the garden with trays of food. Crusty Bob stood on the table eating lettuce, while the rest of us dogs basked in the sunshine around the table. Lolly has relaxed a little and allowed herself to be slowly led out of the den, but stayed close to the Owner who fed her scraps when Samantha wasn't watching. After lunch, Samantha looked at him and sighed.

'We can't keep her, you know,' she told the Owner gently.

'Yes, but I couldn't just leave her there.'

'Of course not, and I love that you're so kind to animals, but we can't look after a baby, work and run a dog sanctuary all at the same time.'

The Owner dropped his hand to Lolly's ears and gave her a scratch. She lifted her head and licked his hand.

'OK, but let's give her a few weeks to recover before we move her on again.'

Samantha stroked her belly. 'Sure,' she replied. 'But you're going to be a very busy man about a month from now.'

'That's OK, I still have five minutes a day to myself, I'll just have to sacrifice them.'

Fortunately, Ella and I anticipated this eventuality. It is time to begin phase two of our plan. Coleridge must return to his rightful family and Miss Meddling acquire a new companion to share her cake with.

Monday, August 3

That nice policeman returned today. I like him more and more. He wasn't so liberal with the patting, etc., today, but still took time for a quick chest rub when the Owner answered the door. We dogs like a human with authority and he has it in spades. It's not all of them that can maintain a stern demeanour with a dog's nose poking into their bum, but he pulled it off magnificently.

'Hello officer, it's been months. We were starting to miss you,' the Owner began cheerfully.

The policeman's response was not so jolly. 'May I come in, sir?'

The Owner led him to the lounge, where Lolly was curled up in my old basket. She cowered when she smelled and heard a new human. The policeman dropped to his knees beside her, stroking her gently and making quiet noises. His charm won her over instantly and she shuffled her muzzle into his hands.

Turning to the Owner, he asked, 'What's the story here?'

'I spotted her in someone's backyard a few days ago. She was in a cage, covered with mange and almost dead from starvation, so I gave her owner some money and brought her home.'

'You didn't think to call the authorities?'

The Owner shrugged. 'No offence, officer, but I just wanted to get her out of there and to a vet as quickly as possible.'

'We can prosecute, sir. We take a very dim view of animal cruelty. Personally I'd lock him up in his own cage.'

'She's making a good recovery and I'll keep an eye on that idiot. If he gets another dog I'll be sure to let you know.'

'You do that, sir. In the meantime I have another complaint against you. A serious one.'

'Really? What am I now? Peeping Tom? Flasher?'

'It's no joking matter, sir. We have information that on the twenty-seventh of July at 3.37 p.m. you answered your telephone in an obscene and suggestive fashion. We have checked and the telephone records match.'

'That was Miss Meddling, right?'

The policeman nodded. The Owner continued, 'It was the day I found Lolly here. Blake . . .' he pointed at me, '. . . stole my phone off the table and ran with it to the yard where she was being kept.' He paused. 'You know, I haven't thought about it, but it's almost as if he was trying to lead me there. Like Lassie.'

'Leaving the dog out of it sir, can you tell me what was said on the telephone?'

'Well, Blake dropped it and she was already on the line. He must have accidentally answered a call I suppose. She was ranting about something, but I'm getting used to that and didn't pay much attention. I was a bit breathless having run after the dog, and then I saw Lolly here, so I told her I'd call back and hung up.'

The policeman checked his notebook. 'So you're telling me that the "heavy breathing, panting and slobbering" that Miss Meddling heard, was in fact your dog? Your very intelligent dog who answered the phone and led you to an animal in distress.'

I was glowing with pride by this point. 'Very intelligent' sounds absolutely right. And they called me dim.

'Doesn't sound very likely, does it, sir?'

'Well, it's the truth. My wife will tell you, but she's out at an antenatal class. The baby's due in a few weeks.'

The policeman snapped his notebook closed. 'Can I be honest, sir?' He didn't wait for a reply. 'You're an enigma to me. I've interviewed a few sex pests in my time and you don't seem like one.'

'Well, that's because –' The policeman held up his hand for silence.

'Nice home, kind to animals, wife with a baby on the way. I'd hate to see you lose all that just because you can't control yourself.'

'But, I –'

'Yes, I know, the Wonder Dog did it. I'm afraid I must ask you to accompany me to the station for an official interview. You're not under arrest, but we may issue you with a caution and inform the telephone company.'

'Look, I just told you . . .'

'Now's as good a time as any if you'd like to get a jacket, sir.'

'This can't be happening, I've never made a dirty phone call in my life. Not even a crank one.'

'We'll talk about it at the station, shall we?'

While the Owner was fetching his jacket from upstairs, Coleridge ran through the open back door.

'Hullo, Bobby,' the policeman said. 'What are you doing over here?'

By the time the Owner had come back he was back out in the garden.

Tuesday, August 4

Very little walk action today, and not a sniff of a stroke. The Owner is behaving like a Doberman at the vet's, just because the police gave him an informal warning. Samantha has been to the police station to corroborate his story, but the police are refusing to believe that I am the villain they're looking for. I tried to give the Owner a bit of affection for taking the rap, but climbing into his lap didn't seem to help. Dinner service was even ruder than usual.

None of this bothers me as I am an officially approved, police-appointed Wonder Dog. A Wonder Dog outranks a mere Top Dog in the same way that a general outranks a private, so Scottie will be upset, but he'll just have to show his teeth and bear it. Obviously it will become my beta nickname, 'Blake the Wonder Dog', and I'll have to have my own theme tune. Something upbeat and anthemic in D major I think. It should be uplifting but noble. Something a tail can wag along to.

Wednesday, August 5

Lolly is getting better by the day and now follows the Owner around as if he were made of steak. Wherever he goes she's next to him, always with some part of her touching him. This is common for blind dogs, they adopt a human to become their guide and like to be in constant contact. Mostly, though, the adoptee isn't quite so clumsy and doesn't keep tripping over their dog. If he had any sense he would buy himself a little harness and lead that Lolly could carry in her teeth, but human ingenuity doesn't seem to stretch this far. He seems very taken with her, too, and is always leaning down to scratch behind her ears and murmur sweet nothings.

If any other dog started usurping the Owner in this way there would be fur flying by now, but my jealousy is tempered with optimism. Having Lolly rubbing along next to him all day seems to satisfy all his 'heel' needs and he hasn't given the dreaded command for days. Plus, of course, us Wonder Dogs take such things in our stride. Not for me the growling and pushing of a jealous dog. No, I merely contented myself with jumping in his lap when it became available and letting off a dignified fart.

Thursday, August 6

Another landmark on Lolly's road to recovery; today she came out and ate with the rest of us in the garden. As usual the menu was limited and getting the waiter's attention next to impossible. I could have died with embarrassment when the kitchen skipped the hors d'oeuvre and the entrée and went straight to a main course that was below standard in terms of both quality and presentation. Lolly didn't seem to mind though, but I suppose when you've been through what she has the eyelids and testicles in jelly are the pinnacle of fine dining.

Friday, August 7

With no C.R.A.P. duties to attend to, Ella, Coleridge and I are free to roam the park at night with our erstwhile colleagues. Like a Roman Emperor, Scottie has organised a week of games and contests in celebration of C.R.A.P.'s triumph. I am the guest of honour. Tonight there were gladiatorial competitions in which the fiercest and strongest dogs pitted their martial prowess against sticks (Razor was declared champion after going through an entire bough like a wood-chipper). Ella competed well in the 500-metre Bunny Dash, and I won my laurels in the Duck Frightening event. Constable romped home in the All-star Poo Roll, though to be fair he and Denny were the only competitors.

Saturday, August 8

A long walk in the park today and Lolly accompanied us for the first time. There is now the faintest black fuzz on her skin, and she appears to be growing a coat made from Velcro as she was stuck to the Owner's leg throughout. She did though manage to tear herself away when she sniffed Scottie and the reunion was a sight to bring a lump to my bowels. There was the first gentle muzzle-sniffing, with both of them whining softly in joy, and then they continued to sniff each other all over as if they could never get enough. Even the Owner seemed quite touched at the gentle way they greeted each other. If dogs could weep like humans I would have done so when Scottie reared up and mounted her. It was a magical moment and one completely wrecked by my oaf of an Owner, who wouldn't know romance if it peed in his shoes.

Sunday, August 9

Another relaxing afternoon in the garden with all the pack turned into a drama when Samantha suddenly dropped her forkful of food and yelled, 'Aaaah, contraction!'

The Owner was instantly on his feet and grabbing at his hair, trying to carry her to the car while collecting bags, finding keys and generally running round in circles shouting directions at himself. All of which he totally ignored, I should add. I don't know why I'm supposed to obey when he can't even listen to his own instruction to 'calm down'.

Obviously, I got caught up in the general excitement, and Lolly tripped him up several times. Ella meanwhile snuffled at her Mistress who seemed to be getting stressed out.

'Sit,' she commanded eventually, and instantly every backside in the garden hit the floor, including the Owner's.

'It was only one, just stop all this nonsense.'

The Owner did not seem convinced and throughout the rest of the afternoon asked 'Is it coming?' about six times a minute, while Samantha sighed and stroked her enormous belly.

Having seen him 'sit' at her command, I'm wondering if I haven't completely misjudged the power structure in the pack.

Monday, August 10

Constable has lost another show. It was the Poo Roll that did for him. Despite some furious washing and brushing on Saturday morning, he came nowhere near the champion's podium and apparently his Mistress lost her temper when one of the judges told her she may as well have dragged in a stool on a string.

On the plus side, she seems to have resigned herself to the inevitable and for the first time in months Constable was allowed off the lead in the park. He celebrated in his usual fashion, of course. Although his Mistress winced, not a word was said while she applied a brush to the worst areas.

Tuesday, August 11

Samantha had more contractions last night. They came to nothing again, but the Owner was a bag of nerves all day. Every time we go out for a walk he phones her every two minutes and keeps biting his nails. Being so finely tuned to his moods, it's making me pretty jumpy too. So jumpy, in fact, that I managed to lick his forehead from a standing start. Impressive.

Wednesday, August 12

I recounted the story of how I rescued Lolly again to an audience of admirers in the park. Ella reminded me that the Owner had played a part too, but I don't think his role was sufficient to dwell upon. The leading and barking were the vital factors, after that the human just did what he was supposed to do.

All dogs naturally love being the centre of attention so Lolly and I are like dogs with brontosaurus-sized bones at the moment. I wonder if some sort of parade is in order? A twenty-one cocked-leg salute, maybe?

Thursday, August 13

Ella and I have formed a plan to introduce Miss Meddling to Lolly while separating her from Coleridge and I would say it's masterful if the word 'master' didn't have such unfortunate connotations. Over the past few months we have gathered enough intelligence on the elderly human to play her like a dog-sized violin. If we poo in her garden she will think the Owner is throwing it over the fence again. Loud barking during her afternoon nap-time is guaranteed to have her complaining at the door.

With Lolly constantly at the Owner's side when Meddling comes a-calling it is inevitable that they will meet and, having a soft elderly heart beneath that crone-like exterior, Meddling will instantly fall in love. If we can make sure that Coleridge is in the den at the same time, so much the better.

Friday, August 14

I've had a new tune buzzing around my head for a few days now. It goes something like this:

Who should you whistle for, when things go astray?

Blaaaaake, the Wonder Dog!
Bounding to the rescue with a hip-hip-hurray,
Blaaaaake, the Wonder Dog!

Then there's a twiddly howl solo, then the chorus:

Who's that . . .
Saving the sick?
Blake!
Guarding the apes?
Blake!
Eating the steak?
Blake!
Licking his balls?
It's . . . Blake, Blake, Blake, Blake, Blake, Blake, BLAKE!
He's Blaaaaake, the Wonder Dog!

It's a work in progress, but combines a dignified modesty with a noble message, plus it's so catchy I keep growling it under my breath. Ella keeps looking at me quizzically, but I need another verse and a crescendo before the debut performance.

Saturday, August 15

Ella and I put stage one of the Lolly–Meddling Unification Programme into action last night by leaving a couple of prize-winning stools close to Meddling's back door where she couldn't fail to miss them. I've always been exceptional when it comes to my ablutions, but my own was worthy of the *Guinness Book of Records*. It could easily have accommodated a small- to medium-sized winter sports resort at the peak.

We followed this up with some afternoon howling and barking. Well, I say we, but it was mostly me as I couldn't contain myself from breaking into a couple of choruses from the new theme tune. Ella was so impressed that she sat and stared at me with her mouth hanging open and her tongue unfurled.

Afterwards she asked what I was singing and I told her about my official police promotion to Wonder Dog and the necessity of a theme tune. I asked if she liked it and she replied that it says a lot about me, which is absolutely what I was aiming for. I wonder if it could be released as a single? It would almost certainly go to number one, though Ella thinks it has 'number two' written all over it.

Sunday, August 16

More pooing last night followed by some howling. Today Ella joined in on my theme tune though she kept getting the words wrong.*

It didn't take long for the plan to have the desired affect. By mid-afternoon there was a telltale squeaking of the front gate and I streaked through the open back door to bark at the old woman before she could get her finger to the bell.

Unfortunately, it was Samantha who opened the door. The Owner stayed upstairs, with Lolly. Coleridge was nowhere to be seen.

Miss Meddling seemed taken aback to have a very large Samantha to deal with rather than the Owner, though it could have been my expert groin-sniffing that caused her to take a step back.

'Hello, Miss Meddling,' Samantha said pleasantly, and allowed my questing nose to carry on its exploration. 'I've been wanting to talk to you for a while.'

'So long as it's not dirty talk like your nasty husband.'

Samantha sighed.

'It really was the dog on the phone, you know.'

'Dogs answering the phone! I wasn't born yesterday.'

Samantha muttered something under her breath, about not being born in the last millennium, but I didn't quite catch it. Louder, she continued, 'After all the shopping trips my husband's taken you on I would have hoped that you'd think better of him.'

'I did my best, no one can say that I didn't give him a chance.' Meddling leaned closer to Samantha, 'But where's me underwear, eh? The police never solved it.' She crossed her arms with a look of triumph on her face.

'Just because you've mislaid your knickers, it doesn't mean he took them. He's a very kind man.'

'I see he's got you fooled. You want to get a divorce, young lady, before he drags you down into his pit of depravity.'

* I told her it's not, 'Who should you shout at when things go astray?' or 'You might get tuppence if you put him on eBay,' but she seems to have a problem remembering. If I didn't know better I might have thought my mate-for-life wasn't taking my Wonder Dog status seriously. Still, she'll learn the words soon enough when they're etched into the base of a life-size bronze statue.

Samantha was getting angry, like a bitch protecting her puppy. An elderly couple in the street passed to watch.

'Oh just, fu– . . . forget it. You're a mean-spirited woman. My husband's spent half his life ferrying you and your friends to the shops over the past few months. Did you know that he has to work until three in the morning to make up the time? Did you know I've had to take a bus to the doctor because you've been dragging him around the supermarket for hours on end?'

At that moment, the Owner came down the stairs, Lolly at his side. He put his arm around Samantha, and said, 'It's OK, Sam, no need to get upset. What can we do for you today, Miss Meddling?'

'You've been throwing mess in my garden and your dogs are too noisy. I'll have the police on you again.'

The Owner tried a few conciliatory words, but Samantha interrupted him.

'Police, police, police. That's all you ever think of, isn't it? Don't you think they've got better things to do than worry about your petty complaints?'

'I don't call pinching an old lady's knickers petty.'

Samantha breathed deeply. 'For the last time, my husband has NOT stolen your underwear. Just go away, Miss Meddling.'

And then she leaned against the door frame and doubled over. 'Oww ow owww. Contraction. Big one.'

Meddling was left standing at the doorway. After a couple of moments she noticed that I was edging towards her growling softly and walked quickly away with me pursuing her off the grounds. All in a day's work for a Wonder Dog.

Monday, August 17
The Owner and Samantha returned from hospital late last night. No baby, late dinner and a very quick walk. No apology from Meddling today either, not even a short note to enquire whether the cute little dog needs a home.

Tuesday, August 18
At last the doorbell rang again today. We thought it must be Miss Meddling returning to offer Lolly the cushion and cake of luxury; Ella and I bounced through from the garden just in time to see the Owner open the door to a different elderly woman.

'Umm, hi Mrs ahh . . .'

'Ramsay, Delia Ramsay,' said the old woman with a grin. She reached down and scratched my ears. I decided to let her live.

'Yes, we went shopping a few times, didn't we?'

'That's right, Mr P. I heard old Fanny Meddling was stirring up a bit of trouble for you, so thought I'd pop round with a couple of things, show you we're not all ungrateful old beggars.' She handed over a bag and a package tied up in brown paper.

'Umm, thank you, Mrs Ramsay, that's very nice of you.'

'Call me Delia, dear. Now that one's for the baby, it's a pullover I knitted myself. I made it white because I didn't know whether you're having a boy or a girl. The other one's a little present for you. I know you'll appreciate them. They used to be my husband's.'

'Thank you. Doesn't he want them any more?'

'Oh, I shouldn't think so, dear, what with his being dead and everything.'

'I'm so sorry.'

'Don't be – at my age it's nice to have a decent night's sleep. He was a lot like you that way.'

The Owner spluttered more thanks and the old woman had another grin. Then with a final pat on the head (for me, not the Owner) she wobbled back down the path. At the gate she stopped and turned. 'Oh, by the way, Mr P, if you had a couple of minutes tomorrow I'd be so grateful if you could run me into town for a few things.'

The Owner shuffled, and went a bit red, but finally squeaked, 'Of course, Delia.'

In the kitchen Samantha held up a white pullover that looked like it would fit a full-grown orang-utan, if it had three arms, while the Owner unwrapped his package.

'It's very sweet of her,' Samantha began, 'but I don't think the baby's been born that would fit this, though maybe to a family of very large flu viruses . . .'

The Owner groaned as his own gift slipped through his fingers and onto the floor.

More magazines, like the ones we found in the shed with the naked human bitches in, but not

138

quite like them. These ones had titles like *Sexy and Seventy*, *Wriggly and Wrinkly* and *Senior Vixen*.

That afternoon, while Samantha cackled, the Owner had another small fire.

Wednesday, August 19

The Owner departed the den with a car full of senior citizens and a scowl. He phoned every five minutes until Samantha lost her temper and shouted, 'No, it's not coming. If it starts coming, I think I'll be able to remember your telephone number.'

Thursday, August 20

Lolly is now a changed dog. Her coat is growing sleekly black, her nose is wet and shiny and she's a little less shy, though she still likes to have the Owner close, except when Scottie's around. She's quickly become part of the pack, but I hadn't realised how much she was taking in until we met up with her beau in the wasteland this evening.

Scottie was barking about the cares and responsibilities of being a Top Dog; trying to impress her even though she's already smitten. He's like a puppy meeting his first bitch in season at the moment.

'I'm really lucky to have met such important dogs,' Lolly barked.

'Och, 'tis no' that important bein' Top Dug,' Scottie yapped back, swelling with pride. ''Tis more of an administrative role these days, ye ken.'

'You don't need to be so modest about it, Scottie,' she barked affectionately. 'Blake's very proud of being a Wonder Dog.'

In reply, Scottie made a noise I've never heard from a dog before. A kind of half-choke, half-growl. He finally managed to bark, 'Blake's a whut?'

'A Wonder Dog. You must know that. He has his own theme tune, Ella taught it to me. It's very good.'

Scottie had meanwhile started running around in tight little circles, pausing every couple of seconds to squirm around on his back.

'A theme tune, ye say. Och, ah cannae wait tae hear this. Ella, please sing it for us.'

I was definitely getting the impression that Scottie was less impressed than he should have been at being in the presence of an actual, fully certified Wonder Dog. As Ella was preparing to howl my anthem the Owner called us over. He doesn't like being away from the den for more than ten minutes at the moment.

'Bye, Scottie, see you tomorrow,' Lolly barked.

'Aye, bye, hen. Bye, Ella, Coleridge, Wonder Dug.'

Again, as we were leaving he seemed to be spending a disproportionate amount of time writhing on his back.

Friday, August 21

More contractions. It's becoming a bit of a den ritual now. Samantha yells, the Owner runs around pulling at his hair while we dogs get in his way. Then they drive off to the hospital to return a few hours later without a baby. A lot of fuss and nonsense if you ask me. What Samantha wants to do is find herself a nice warm, quiet spot – in a box in a cupboard, perhaps – and lick herself until the baby comes out. The Owner doesn't even need to know about it until it's all over. Then – if he's feeling particularly paternal, and really it's optional – he could put down a nice bit of fresh straw.

Sometimes I wonder how humans got where they are now. Probably they cheated at evolution.

Saturday, August 22

Molly came over to see how Samantha was and ended up taking us all for a walk. As the Owner has been finding recently, that's not as easy as it once was. Four dogs on leads are a pawful, particularly when one of them is Coleridge, who is Teflon-coated when it comes to even the most simple instructions. Nevertheless, Molly is a professional-level dog walker, and once we got to the park it was a relief to have a proper run instead of the Owner's nail-biting ten-minute forays to the wasteland.

Scottie was there, and after greeting Lolly with his usual blissful adoration, turned to me and said, 'If it isnae the Wonder Dug. Help me, Wonder Dug, ah'm trapped in a cave an' the roof hus fallen doon.'

With aloof coolness I ignored him and left him and Lolly to woo while Ella and I got down to some wonder scooting in the clearing by the pond.

I was sniffing around a bin a little later when he rambled over.

'Och, Blake, the very Wonder Dug ah've bin lookin' fer. Noo, dinnae run away, ah'm ainly jestin'.'

I stopped and gave his bum a sniff, though keeping my tail stiff with disapproval.

'Ah've bin wantin' tae run somethin' by ye.'

'What's that?' I barked.

'Wull, ah cannae help thinkin' there may be one last joab fer C.R.A.P.'

'But Lolly's free now, what else is there to do?'

'Aye, Lolly's free, thanks tae ye, but there's somethin' playin' oan mah mind.'

'Well?'

'Yon human goat away far too easy. De ye noat think he deserves some punishment?'

'Revenge, you mean?'

'Aye, revenge.'

I thought about it for a moment. 'There was that poisoning incident, too,' I barked. 'We shouldn't forget that.'

'And puir Razor goat shot at. Whut kind o' human would shoot a defenceless wee duggie like Razor?'

My tail began waving. 'What exactly did you have in mind, Scottie?'

'Somethin' he'll no forgit in a hurry. Somethin' classic. Somethin' C.R.A.P.'

'I'll have a think,' I barked. Molly was calling and I turned to go.

'Aye, ye do that. Oh, and Blake?'

I stopped and turned. 'Yes.'

'Gis a woof o' ye theme tune.'

Sunday, August 23

A quick walk in the park today and Constable raced past me singing the new theme tune. Ella must have taught him it. Unfortunately she still seems to be having trouble with the words. I only caught a snatch but I've told her dozens of times it's not, 'Who's that stuck in the bin?' or 'Who's that humping a leg?' Still, it's catching on and when they get the words right it'll be a pleasure to hear around the park.

Monday, August 24

Now there's no necessity for feeding Lolly I've taken to having a rummage through promising bins on my own account. It's amazing what humans will throw away – last night's haul included a plateful of very good stew and a whole chicken carcass. It's well known that chicken bones are dangerous for dogs, but I just couldn't resist. I crunched them up very small and so far it doesn't feel as though my stomach lining's been pierced, so I'm wondering if the whole chicken bone thing hasn't been blown out of proportion.

The point is that while munching I found myself wondering if I shouldn't take Scottie a little, which led me to ask myself 'Why?' Now that Lolly has been sprung – in no small part due to my own efforts – the need for Scottie to be Top Dog is a big fat zero. As a title it pales in comparison to Wonder Dog, but it would be nice to have the whole set. Would Napoleon have been content with being Emperor of France with the rest of Europe ripe for the plucking? I think not.

Tuesday, August 25

Just me and Ella in the garden today. Lolly remains glued to the Owner's feet and Coleridge can still just about manage to squeeze himself through the cat flap and onto Meddling's lap. Tentatively, I brought up the subject of deposing Scottie and taking my rightful place at the head of the park pack. She wasn't that interested though.

'You might find you'll be concerned with other things within a few days,' she woofed quietly. 'Have you had a sniff recently?'

Obediently, I sauntered round to her back end and breathed her in. It was very, very faint, but unmistakable. Her season is coming around again. It's too early yet, but we practised behind the shed all afternoon anyway.

Wednesday, August 26

I was having a quiet sniff around the pond this morning when I caught the strains of the theme tune coming through the trees. I went to investigate and as I drew closer to the source it became apparent that the words had been mangled once again. Instead of a paeon to my general Wonder Dogginess, they had been bastardised almost out of recognition, into something (in my opinion) quite sinister:

> Who's that, edible cruchy little treat?
> It's Blaaaake the dunder head,
> Impossible to bite because he's fast on his feet,
> It's Blaaaake the dunder head.

Rounding a bush I found Razor and Choo Choo rolling around on their backs. Razor spotted me and yelped, 'Morning, Blake, have you forgotten your cape and underpants today?'

For a moment I considered showing him what being a Wonder Dog means, but I realised that I could see so far down his throat there was almost daylight at the other end and decided that being a Wonder Dog meant having a sense of humour. He'll be singing a different song when they start making TV shows about my exploits. I hope so anyway. The theme tune is not catching on quite as I hoped.

Thursday, August 27

My brain is already being melted by the chemical methyl p-hydroxybenzoate. Even though Ella is still days away from her full season the smell of her has completely lobotomised me. I should be forming plans to disguise her condition from the humans, but anything more complex than 'sniff, hump, sniff' is completely beyond me already.

Friday, August 28

I tried my hardest to resist, I really did, but once again I am passion's plaything, a mindless drooling puppet of desire. The Owner came out for a coffee this morning and Ella put her paws in his lap to say hello. All I could see was her cute little tail waving at me and that smell weaving its spell across the garden, taunting me with lust, calling to my loins without bothering to check in with my brain first.

I was on her in seconds, my hindquarters a blur.

Unfortunately, the Owner insists on buying cheap garden furniture, which is obviously not tested to withstand high-velocity sexual relations. The deckchair collapsed beneath the yelling Owner, who was soaked in hot coffee.

Of course, I wasn't going to let a small thing like a thrashing monkey stop me and with Ella standing on his chest I continued for all I was worth. As I might have mentioned, my mental faculties were somewhat impaired, but on the edge of hearing I heard Meddling's voice from over the fence say, 'Disgusting.' Then the back door was flung open and Samantha was there, my collar in her hand, pulling me away at the vital moment.

Ella is locked up indoors again, I am alone with my memories, a stick, and the blues.

Saturday, August 29

The Owner is now forced to give four walks a day. Two with myself, Lolly and Coleridge, two with Ella at times of the day judged to be safe from prospective suitors. He failed to take into account the former dogs of C.R.A.P. though, all of whom still have a night pass and all of whom had exactly the same reaction to Ella's scent as myself. The Owner was swamped on the wasteland by a baying pack of sex-crazed dogs. Against such numbers his options were limited and he was reduced to carrying Ella home in his arms while trying to shake humping animals from his legs.

Sunday, August 30

All heroes have an Achilles heel and it looks like my own personal Kryptonite is the smell of Ella's backside. My famous mental powers have deserted me, and my movement is restricted to a spasmodic thrusting of the pelvis.

Monday, August 31

My head cleared a little during our own walk today and I thought I'd take the opportunity to have a few words with Scottie about the park hierarchy, with a view to taking up my old position. Nothing so vulgar as an actual challenge, but perhaps a quiet confession about throwing the fight, which we could have a chuckle over, followed by a discussion about how the transference of power will be best effected.

Accordingly, I attempted to corner him in the wasteland, but Lolly was glued to him. I didn't want to embarrass him so asked if she could leave us alone for a few moments. She walked a few steps, but got so frightened at being without a guide that Scottie had to lead her back to the Owner, gently calming her as he went.

Finally he returned, still looking over his shoulder to make sure that Lolly was all right, and barked, 'Whut's this all aboot?'

'It's about your being Top Dog.'

'Aye? Whut of it?'

Looking at him carefully watching his mate as she snaked around the Owner's legs, my planned address died in my throat. 'Well, you mentioned revenge. And as Top Dog I wondered what you had in mind.'

'A verra guid question, Blake, an' yer right noat tae want tae talk aboot it in front o' Lolly. Huv ye had any thoughts o' yer oan yet?'

'No,' I barked truthfully. It's been impossible to think about anything other than Ella's bum for the past few days.

'Wull, ah've nae been so lazy mahsel'.'

I restrained a terse response and instead barked, 'So what's the plan, Scottie?'

'Nothin' short o' rippin' the arse oot o' yon human's troosers will satisfy me. Ah'll see the color o' his underpants.'

'But Scottie,' I remonstrated, 'that's so clichéd. Just imagine if he wears spotty shorts underneath.'

'Ah prefer tae think it's traditional,' Scottie barked back. 'Iviryone kens the bad human gets the bum torn oot and chased up a tree.'

'Oh, Scottie. Surely not chased up a tree?'

'Aye, the tree, Blake. 'Tis the proper punishment. The stealin' o' sausages will nae suffice fer his crimes. The chewin' o' valuables would be but a slap oan the paw. The rippin' o' the troosers an' the chasin' intae a tree is the harshest o' penalties an' nuthin' else wull dae.'

Leaving aside the fact that it has all the originality of a bone-shaped chew toy, as a plan this has the makings of a one-way trip to the dangerous-dogs pound. I had imagined something more subtle, like mining his front path with poo and digging his front garden up.

SEPTEMBER

Tuesday, September 1
Spent the day whining at Ella through the kitchen door again and making the Eyes of Immense Pleading at the Owner whenever he came out into the garden. Usually the eyes can be relied upon to thaw even the iciest of hearts and have served me well in matters of leftover Chinese food and stroking, but today the Owner just played with my ears and gave me a talk about Responsible Dog Ownership. Apparently this means that he, as a human, has been awarded complete control over my sex life. I must have been asleep when that bit of legislation was passed.

Wednesday, September 2
It finally happened. Coleridge has been rumbled. The Owner was picking up poo from behind the shed and straightened in time to catch sight of the puppy* wriggling through Miss Meddling's cat flap carrying a pork chop in his mouth. He gasped and shouted Coleridge's name, but the not-so-little puppy completely ignored him, as usual.

Gabbling about Meddling and the police the Owner rushed out of the side gate and appeared ten minutes later carrying the struggling Coleridge under his arm. Then he inspected the bottom of the fence until he discovered the Meddling Tunnel. For so long our gateway to the outside world and all its riches of food and rabbits, it's now filled in and impassable. It was the passing of an era, a sad day for dogkind. At least it would have been if I didn't know I could clear the side gate at will.

Thursday, September 3
Coleridge sulked on the lawn with his head between his paws as his life of cake, cat food and endless biscuits faded away. He has begun digging out the Meddling Tunnel again, but the Owner filled it in well and he barely managed to scrape a hole a rat could shoulder its

---

* I say puppy, but he's a year old now. Fortunately for his cat-flap adventures he takes after his wee dad rather than his Dalmatian mum. Still, it's probably a good job they've come to an end. One more cookie and he might have ripped the door out of its frame.

way through before we were locked in the shed for the night.

Friday, September 4
Coleridge remained in the shed while the Owner went shopping and Miss Meddling called for her Bobby. Shortly after she had given up the Owner returned with a roll of chicken wire, which was nailed to the bottom of the fence, preventing any more digging. He seemed very proud of his handiwork, and dragged a singularly uninterested Samantha out to inspect it.

'At least now we know why he's been getting so fat,' she said. 'He must have been stealing from Miss Meddling for months.'

Saturday, September 5
Ella and I have been mulling on our humans' lack of deductive powers. Curiously, neither of them have made the intellectual leap from 'stealing' and 'Miss Meddling' to 'knickers' and 'girdle', so Coleridge's stash is still mouldering undiscovered in the corner of the shed. I suppose they've got a lot weighing on their minds at the moment, and in Samantha's case a lot weighing on her pelvis, too. When it finally appears this baby could easily be larger than the average human. If the Owner's genes are anything to go by I'm thinking that by age five it could be climbing tall buildings and swatting planes out of the sky.

Sunday, September 6
Samantha started having contractions again soon after the morning walk. It's now become routine of course, and through the eternally closed kitchen door I could hear the Owner swing into action with polished ease. Falling down the stairs, swearing, tripping over Lolly and rushing about aimlessly are now second nature to him. However, Samantha finally managed to get him under control and into the car.

I thought it would be another false alarm, but a few hours later Molly arrived. And bless her sweet human heart if she didn't immediately open the kitchen door for Ella. I may in the past have expressed disapproval for Molly, but it was a passing thing. A whim. On reflection I am quite prepared to overlook her political views regarding the removal of testicles in light of the enormous service she has done Ella and me. And talking about services, what bliss! Ella is in full season and with Molly sitting fretfully by the phone with Lolly at her feet there was nothing to disturb us but Coleridge yapping about. We mated, we tied together for what felt like hours, and then we did it all over again. All the while I had a triumphant song running through my head:

> Who's that sexy canine-ophile?
> Blaaaaake, the Wonder Dog!
> He's got class, he's got doggy style . . .
> Blaaaaake, the Wonder Dog!
> Who's that . . .
> Mounting Ella?
> Blake!
> Humping her bum?
> Blake!
> Barking with joy?
> Blake!
> Making some pups?
> It's . . . Blake, Blake, Blake, Blake, Blake, Blake, BLAKE!
> He's Blaaaaake, the Humping Wonder Dog!

Monday, September 7

The Owner returned early this morning looking exhausted. He is the father of a small human, of the female variety. No sooner was he through the door than Molly threw herself at him, shouting in delight. In response he looked over her shoulder at Ella and me straining to get past to give him a welcome home and screamed.

'How long have those two been together?'

'What?' Molly replied. I suppose it's not the usual way to accept congratulations.

'Blake and Ella?'

'Oh they're fine, though I'm afraid I was very naughty and let them sleep in the house last night.'

'Together?'

'Yes, of course.'

'And you didn't notice him humping her like a dervish?'

'There was some noise, but I thought it was Blake guarding . . .' She stopped. 'Oh no, she's not in season, is she?'

'Yes! And you're supposed to be a bloody dog handler.'

'Well no one told me and I was worried about Samantha . . . I didn't see them actually mating.'

The Owner seemed to be having some sort of seizure. 'Oh damn, oh damn. We'll just have to hope that Blake's love of my leg is exclusive.' He turned on Molly and waved a finger under her nose. 'You're not to tell Sam about this.'

'OK,' Molly replied, 'but won't she guess when Ella, you know, gives birth.'

'We don't know she's pregnant, it's possible she isn't. And if she is then you're taking some of the puppies.'

Molly smiled and reached down to Lolly. 'Actually, I've been getting quite fond of this one.'

Tuesday, September 8

Samantha and the tiny human came home today, but went straight upstairs and only Ella and Lolly were briefly introduced to 'Charlotte', as they are calling the baby. It's a pretty name, but not so pretty as Droolah, which would have been my preference. No one asked me, of course, or offered a formal meeting with this new denizen of the den, and I'm still stuck out in the garden with Coleridge as the Owner attempts to maintain the fiction that Ella's chastity has not been broached. I did what any dog would have done and sulked on the lawn with my nose between my front paws. This achieved absolutely nothing, so eventually I went round the back of the shed for a solitary scoot.

Meanwhile the Owner is walking about aimlessly with a glazed smile on his face and bags under his eyes. Whenever he comes to see us, I keep catching wafts of a new smell, like a kind of dusty sunlight. It's highly addictive.

Wednesday, September 9

Impossible to get a decent nap today with Meddling shouting, 'Bobbeeeee! Bobbeeeee!' every two minutes. Clearly she's a little deaf, otherwise she would have heard Coleridge yapping and throwing himself at the fence in an effort to feed his cake habit. The puppy spent the rest of the day running around in circles and panting on his back: classic withdrawal symptoms. Grass and the couple of daffodil bulbs that he managed to dig up are apparently no substitute for a constant supply of lemon drizzle cake and chocolate éclairs.

He swears that he's wasting away to nothing, but to me he still looks like the offspring of an opera singer and a beach ball.

Thursday, September 10

I've noticed before that the Owner is not what you might call eagle-eyed, but today we walked straight past another 'Lost Dog' poster with a photograph of Coleridge on it without even a glance. Sleep deprivation could be making him even less alert than usual I suppose. His eye bags look like two tortoises.

It was a good likeness, though. Coleridge was lying on a frilly cushion with an empty plate in front of him and crumbs scattered around.

Friday, September 11

At last Coleridge and I were introduced to Charlotte, who was brought out into the garden to meet us. We were allowed a snuffle and she smells like a little slice of dog heaven. She's so tiny and defenceless that all my guarding instincts kicked in at once. The entire time she was outside I lay beside her pram and carefully checked the credentials of anyone who came close. To be honest, it was touch and go whether I let the Owner get past security. He's a bit too clumsy to be allowed to hold such a fragile creature, but as a soon-to-be-father myself fellow feeling got the better of me, though I watched him very closely.

I am determined to gain entrance to the den again. I cannot allow the tiny human to go unguarded all night. While the sight of the Owner in the middle of the night might frighten off the majority of burglars or psychotic postmen, rumpled pyjamas and bloodshot eyes are not as effective as a jaw full of needle-sharp death. A Wonder Dog needs to be on constant alert.

Saturday, September 12

A visit from Molly, who even after the welcome of a lifetime almost totally ignored me except for a few pats and an (admittedly handsome) treat. She spent a long time in the den with Samantha then told the Owner to get some rest while she took the three of us for a walk in the park. Even Coleridge seems to be getting the hang of her funny little Gestapo ways now and didn't pull too much on the lead, but Molly didn't even notice; she was totally pre-occupied with Lolly, who is a 'heel' obsessive's dream come true. Without a single command or twitch on the lead she sticks to the human ankle like a dog-shaped barnacle.

I would have thought that a dog so badly treated by a human would be cautious about giving her affection elsewhere, but Lolly seems to have limitless stores of it for every visiting policeman or dog-botherer. I asked her about it as we sauntered off in search of Scottie.

'Blake,' she said. 'When you've spent a year starving in a cage alone it's easy to appreciate anyone who'll give you a stroke and a kind word.'

Sunday, September 13

Lolly made a good point yesterday. Perhaps I should show the Owner how much I appreciate him a little more often. A wet tongue to the face should do the trick. I've put it on my To Do list, but he'll have to wait. I have a busy schedule, though I can let him have a face-licking after I've finished with my own nether regions. It would be easier if he didn't have his hands full of baby so often now. Or nappies. Nappies suddenly feature largely in our lives; Coleridge is eager to get his teeth into one.

Monday, September 14

With the humans out all day showing Charlotte off to friends and family, Ella and Lolly still stuck inside the den, and the Meddling Tunnel closed for good, there was little for Coleridge and me to do except fight over our old friend Mr Stick all afternoon. With Coleridge being absent for so long I've neglected my mentoring duties and it was good to see the little lard bucket working up a pant and barking defiance at our twiggy foe.

His hunting skills were really coming along when a loud 'Bobby' disturbed us. That Meddling woman's head was bobbing up and down over the fence. Coleridge responded by trying to jump over it, an impossible task for one so small and tubby.

Within minutes the doorbell was ringing and when there was no answer the old woman tried the side gate, which is padlocked. Foiled, she resorted to alternatively calling endearments to her little Bobby and listing the Owner's shortcomings, which took some time.

Tuesday, September 15

The Owner was barely out of bed this morning before the doorbell was ringing again. I did my best to guard by growling at the back door and I could see Ella and Lolly at his ankles. Through all the barking I could hear voices. Meddling's affronted squawk, the policeman's calming low voice, and the Owner's own familiar grumpy morning growl.

'So now I'm being accused of kidnapping a dog? I've heard it all now. Sexual perversion, underwear theft, dirty phone calls and now dog rustling?'

The policeman spoke again in a quiet tone that I didn't quite catch. It was soothing though. Mellifluous, that's the word. Behind him Meddling was shouting, 'Put the handcuffs on him, drag him off to the dungeons, he likes that sort of thing.'

Then the Owner shouted again, 'I've got a new baby in the house and you want to come tramping through to inspect my dogs? I've had it up to here with you, Miss Meddling, and you, officer. If you haven't got a warrant you can bugg– . . . go away.'

The mellifluous tone came again drowned by the squawking, and after a few minutes the Owner responded, 'All right, if it will get you out of my life, but be quiet and I want you gone in two minutes.'

The little party came through the house to be met by one of my most effusive and professional welcomes yet. I really do like that policeman, and it would have taken more than the Owner shouting 'Down, Blake' for me not to show it. He got the double-twist, yapping face-lick. Not easy for even the most athletic dog, but I pulled it off with polished ease. Meddling got the paws on the shoulders, face-bark treatment, which I've been longing to do for ages. I even managed to pee on the front of her skirt before the Owner pulled me off, though I sensed some reluctance and he was grinning during his apology.

'There,' he said eventually. 'Happy now?'

'Where's my Bobby? I know you've got him here somewhere.'

'I don't have a dog called Bobby.'

I looked around. It appeared that Coleridge was bright enough to realise that there was a Bad Boy storm of gigantic proportions brewing and had made his escape. There was no sign of him but a gently swaying flap in the shed door.

The policeman interrupted. 'Small, white, black spots. I've seen him over here myself.'

'You mean Coleridge? He must be in his bed. In the shed.'

The group of humans walked up the path to the shed just as a nose came around the door. The Owner hadn't shut it properly and Ella was pawing her way through. The shed door was swung open.

Meddling shouted 'Bobby', the Owner shouted 'Coleridge', I barked 'Hallelujah' and climbed on top of Ella once more.

The humans were all too distracted to notice the happily mating dogs behind them. Meddling dived into the shed to rescue Bobby with a speed that belied her advanced years and instead came up holding a large expanse of material, gasping, 'Me knickers! I knew all along you stole them, you nasty, sniffing, knicker thief.'

The Owner looked stunned, but reflexively reached down to stop Coleridge, who was trying to slide out the door. 'What?' was the only word he could manage.

Meddling had bent over and come up with more items. 'Me bra, me girdle, more knickers . . .' she cried with each new discovery. Standing up she displayed her trophies, and demanded triumphantly, 'Officer, arrest this man! He's been caught red-handed.'

The policeman, however, merely winced at the sight of her 'personal items'. They had never been the shade of bluey-whiteness advertised on detergent commercials, but after months of being humped and gently mouldering in the corner of the shed they would now defy the most effective stain buster. Soaking in sulphuric acid may help, but only at the cost of totally dissolving them.

He took a pair of knickers from Meddling and held them up gingerly. 'Ma'am,' he said stiffly. 'I think even the most degraded pervert would think twice before sniffing these.'

'How dare you,' she shouted, snatching them back. 'I just have a slight bladder weakness, but that's best cotton that is. And if he's not been sniffing them why are they in his shed? And what about Bobby?'

The policeman meanwhile stepped forward into the shed and picked up the top half of a pair of dentures and a slipper, both of which had clearly been dog chewed. Looking at them closely, he said smoothly, 'I'm not Sherlock Holmes of course, but another explanation does suggest itself, ma'am.' Turning to the Owner he said, 'You call the dog Coleridge, sir? May I ask how long you've had Coleridge?'

'Almost a year, since he was a tiny puppy.' He paused for a moment, then went a little paler than usual. 'Oh no, that tunnel. He's been going through and stealing Miss Meddling's, umm, items.'

At that moment I couldn't help barking in delight at my own sexual adventure. The kitchen door opened, Samantha appeared in her robe, carrying Charlotte, and shouted 'Ella!' then 'Blake!' and the humans on the lawn turned to look at the two of us, caught in flagrante.

'There!' screamed Meddling. 'That's proof, that is. All dogs are like their owners. Everyone knows that. Give me my Bobby you disgusting brute before you turn him into a sex maniac too.'

The Owner was only too willing to release Coleridge as he raced down the garden to separate us. Lolly – keen for the security of his ankles – tripped him up on the way. Even Meddling winced when he hit the wall. Samantha marched down the garden, thrust Charlotte at Miss Meddling then marched back to where I was now tied to Ella and tried to pull me off by the collar. It hurt. A lot. I howled and so did Ella.

Looking bemused and rubbing his head the Owner sat up and said, 'Don't bother, Sam, it's too late for that.'

'What are you talking about?'

'They were at it like rabbits while you were in the hospital.'

'No. I told you specifically to let Molly know . . .'

'You were in labour. I forgot!' Events had obviously taken their toll on the Owner. His face was changing colour and he was getting that 'I'm fed up' tone in his voice.

The policeman interrupted with a polite cough. 'If we could just get this small matter settled we'll leave you and your dogs to it.' He turned to Miss Meddling, who was now cooing into Charlotte's face. 'So it would appear that the dog Coleridge does not belong to you, Miss Meddling, but *has* been stealing from you. You are at liberty to press charges for negligence, of course, but as no one has been hurt if the gentleman has taken steps to block the dog's access the judge would probably just ask him to reimburse you the cost of the items.'

She looked up and her face hardened. 'He's my Bobby, he's got a collar and everything.'

The policeman leaned down and checked. 'It's true, sir, his collar does say "Bobby".'

The Owner shrugged. 'I just clip the lead on, I don't check it every day. She must have changed it.'

'He never had a collar on when I found him,' Meddling protested.

'Then he must have broken it. If you knew anything about dogs you'd know it happens occasionally.' The Owner pointed at me, still joined at the groin to Ella. 'You see here Blake modelling the black leather number you were so eager to believe was part of my pervert gear.'

'But –'

'No buts, Miss Meddling. Coleridge is my dog.'

'But –'

'I'll happily pay for your underwear and teeth and I'm very sorry for the inconvenience, but the fence has now been sealed so he won't be stealing from you again.'

'But he's *my* Bobby.' Miss Meddling had that quaver in her voice that humans get when they are upset.

'Coleridge, Miss Meddling. Now if you'll excuse us.'

Miss Meddling tried appealing to the policeman again, who was now busy stroking Lolly, but he just shrugged and said that as far as he was concerned the Owner had acted responsibly and there was nothing more to be done. Then he added, 'And in light of this I'm prepared to believe that the gentleman was telling the truth about Wonder Dog here answering the phone by accident.'

Samantha took Charlotte from Meddling's arms and the policeman escorted the old woman off the premises with a bag containing the exhibits from Coleridge's museum. As the front door slammed on her, she was still protesting.

Wednesday, September 16

Lolly is smitten with the policeman and for once I can't fault her on her taste. Having said that, we dogs are an affectionate species, but Lolly takes the biscuit, she's even been seen to sniff Meddling in a friendly manner. When I pointed this out to her she reminded me that I've been known to hump the furniture when the humans aren't looking, but that's completely different. It's not like I treat the sofa with respect or love, it's merely a sex object to me.

Thursday, September 17

It's too early to tell for sure, but Ella thinks she is pregnant. I am like a dog with six tails, but our parental joy is strained by the atmosphere in the den. With a reproachful look on her face Samantha keeps asking the Owner how he could have forgotten something so important as keeping us apart. He maintains that there is nothing so effective as clearing a human male's mind of any rational thought than knowing that a baby is due any moment. He seems sincere and I would be inclined to believe him if I thought he had a rational mind to begin with. Samantha tends to agree.

Friday, September 18

I would have thought that Miss Meddling would stay away from the den after the ferocious face-whuffing and skirt-wetting she received the other day, but she was back again. Obviously, I would have loved to give the old woman another dose of Blake, and Coleridge was desperate to get at the old cake dispenser, but we were dragged into the kitchen before the door was even open. Nevertheless, the following conversation was clearly audible to my ultra-sensitive ears.

'Miss Meddling. What is it?'

'I, err . . . That is, I was wondering if I could have my Bobby back? He's such a lovely little dog.'

This description doesn't tally with my own understanding of Coleridge, but as I've observed so many times, humans *are* crazy.

The Owner paused, then said, 'I don't want to seem cruel, but we're attached to him too, and I'm not so sure you're a good dog owner. I assume it was you that was feeding him cakes and sweets?'

'Well, he likes them so much.'

'But the size of him! It's not healthy for a dog to be that fat.'

'You could show me what I should feed him, and visit whenever you like.'

'I don't know, Miss Meddling. You've not exactly been kind to us this year, but it is true we have too many dogs. I'll have to speak with Samantha about it.'

Did he say 'too many dogs'? Is there such a thing? Surely he's not thinking about rehoming again. I thought he'd forgotten about that months ago.

Saturday, September 19

On my best behaviour after the mention of rehoming. I didn't leave the Owner's side all day. No matter how hard he tested me by pushing me away and snarling at me, I made sure he knew I was watching over his and Charlotte's safety at all times, and that of a piece of apple pie he had left on the coffee table. I watched over it quite carefully for all of fifteen seconds, then I decided that I could guard it better if it was in my stomach. No thief is going to find that pie now.

Sunday, September 20

All day in the garden again, just when the den so clearly needs guarding by a dog with my expertise. If I could just have an opportunity to remind them how effective a deterrent I am against every type of intruder there would be no more rehoming talk. I don't like to criticise my mate, but between you and me, dear diary, Ella's laissez faire attitude towards plastic bags indicates a less than serious attitude towards the serious task of guarding. Lolly, of course, is excused all duties on account of her limitation in the senses department. Being able to see the trespasser is, after all, a vital component of the job.

Monday, September 21

Charlotte cried almost all night and even from the shed we could hear it. Nevertheless the Owner stirred himself to take us for a rare walk to the park today, which was heroic of him even if he wasn't very energetic. In fact, we ended up having a very long run after he fell asleep on a bench. I wouldn't say he's looking terrible at the moment but a tramp put some newspaper over him and left some money by his head.

Tuesday, September 22

Meddling had found a box to stand on and spent most of the day hanging over the fence talking to Coleridge. When she was quite sure that the Owner wasn't watching she even slipped the occasional Rich Tea biscuit over. A couple for me ensured my silence.

Wednesday, September 23

Molly came over again and sent the Owner to bed while she gave Ella a bath and took us for a walk. She never usually comes over so often and Ella thinks she has a crush on Lolly. The entire time we were out it was stroke, pat, stroke, pat, 'sit', 'down', and then again with the stroking and patting. The last time the Owner paid me that much attention was when I was a fuzzy little puppy, before the now infamous 'hand-stitched Italian leather shoe' incident, an event that made me wonder about our compatibility for the first of many times.

Thursday, September 24

Any day now I think Molly's going to pop the question and Lolly will be led away to a new den. It's a shame really as she won't be able to expect the level of pampering that Coleridge was used to but, whatever issues I may have had with Molly in the past, she's not the type to knock up a chicken-wire cage and has very strong views on corporal punishment. As I've previously noted, Lolly has enough affection for a dozen dogs and Molly is her favourite person in the whole world, along with the Owner, Samantha, the policeman, the postman, and pretty much everyone else she's come in contact with since the rescue.

Friday, September 25

Scottie has been the target of some grumbling. All the dogs that were banished to their sheds by the poo and pee trick are now starting to feel the chill at night, and with no urgent mission to keep them occupied are missing the den. It has dawned on them that they are facing a winter of shivering and are blaming Scottie. He is trying to keep spirits up by planning the Revenge of C.R.A.P., but a number of dogs are demanding he turn his attention to getting them back inside before they freeze. In vain does he remind them of their wolf ancestors and point out the majesty and freedom of chasing prey across moonlit expanses of snow. They have a point though, there's not much in the way of moose in the park, and it can get pretty nippy in the shed.

Saturday, September 26

Constable has been getting to grips with his own problem and has quit the poo-rolling completely. Now he's not being washed every two minutes he smells like a proper dog again and is content with a daily dip in the muddy pond. His Mistress should be pleased, but apparently he's as absorbent as the mop he resembles so much and all that pondy goodness ends up all over the furniture.* He thinks that the dog–Mistress relationship has broken down irreparably. Apparently she was on the phone yesterday afternoon and all morning and has put an advert in a dog magazine listing his achievements.

* She really should have thought that through before getting an Old English sheepdog. With a short, sleek coat like my own the damage is limited to one enthusiastic shake.

'Now I'm not winning dog shows she wants to get rid of me,' he confided gloomily.

'Och, dinnae worry yersel' aboot it. A former celebrity such as yersel' will probably end up stuffed in a museum,' was Scottie's idea of reassurance.

'It was only a couple of paint adverts, I'm not a proper Wonder Dog, like Blake.'

'Aye, ye're right, if any dog deserves tae get stuffed it's Blake the Wonder Dug.'

Scottie ignored my warning growl. 'She's probably just trying to find you more work, Constable,' I added quickly. 'Maybe as one of those rollers they use in car washes . . .'

'It's very kind of you, Blake, but she keeps giving out a price on the phone, I'm sure she's trying to sell me.'

I tried to be positive about it but after he'd been called away I had to agree with Scottie that things are looking bleak for Constable.

Sunday, September 27

Another visit from the policeman today, though this time he wasn't wearing a uniform. The Owner answered the door warily, unleashing a tsunami of fur, with me at the crest displaying my welcome technique to its best advantage. The visitor must have been made of steel. It takes a lot of muscle to withstand a Blake welcome without staggering but he took it in his stride, dispensing an ear tickle here, a chest rub there.

'Don't worry, this isn't an official call,' he replied to the Owner's look of enquiry. 'It's just I'm looking for a dog at the moment and who couldn't help noticing this little girl.' He reached down and patted Lolly, who responded with some excellent tongue action. I couldn't have given a better licking myself. 'That is, if she needs a new home?'

The Owner hummed for a while but let the policeman in and made him coffee. 'I suppose I couldn't talk you into taking Blake instead, could I?' he asked when he returned.

I was mortified – of all the low, base treachery. There was nothing for it but to turn the full glare of the Eyes of Bitter Reproach on him. Thankfully, this seemed to do the trick. He grabbed me by the ears and gave me a rare kiss on the top of my head.

'Only joking, Blake, you're still my Good Boy.'

As a joke this rates alongside his idea of a decent dinner for a dog, and I should have snarled in distain, but my tail betrayed me once more.

'I think the Wonder Dog might be too much of a handful for me,' the policeman interjected. 'But I could give Lolly a good home.'

Lolly herself responded by climbing into his lap and curling up there.

'Well, she does seem to like you, but she's booked for eye surgery tomorrow. Can you wait a couple of weeks until she's recovered?'

So Lolly has a new home to go to and not the one we expected. She is very happy and thinks the policeman and Molly smell equally good, but I suspect she would be happy if she were adopted by a family of hungry-looking Koreans. We're going to miss her though. She hasn't been around for long, but it's given me a swell of pride watching her turn into a proper dog again. When we rescued her she looked like an extra from *Zombies: Dogs of the Dead*, but now she's all sleek coat, wet nose and healthy-smelling anal glands.

Monday, September 28

The Owner took Lolly to the vet's this morning and came back without her. He walked around the house carrying Charlotte for a while and then remembered to tell Samantha about Lolly and the policeman. She was not happy.

'But I promised her to Molly the day before yesterday.'

'Why didn't you tell me? I can't upset him, he'll arrest me for possession of Blake or something.'

I did my best to ignore this comment. He hasn't really grasped how lucky he is to own an actual Wonder Dog yet. I expect it will take a while to sink in. Fortunately, he was eating a sandwich and some tuna dropped on the floor. Licking it up really helped take my mind off the casual disrespect.

Samantha yawned. 'I was going to tell you, but Charlotte started crying and then it was bath time and then an hour to get her to sleep. By then I was so tired it slipped my mind. You'll have to tell him it was a mistake though. After all Molly's done for us we can't let her down.'

'All she's done for us? Like letting Blake make puppies with Ella?'

'That was your fault, if you remember. Besides, we don't know for sure that Ella's pregnant yet.'

'Well, if she's not it will be a miracle,' the Owner replied with some conviction. 'He tries to have sex with Crusty Bob all the time when he thinks no one is looking.'

That's a lie. It was only the once at the height of Ella's season, and I was not responsible for my actions at the time.

Tuesday, September 29

More discussions about the future of us dogs today. With rehoming in the air Ella and I spent all day at their feet, picking up scraps of information and the occasional ear scratch when they weren't otherwise occupied with Charlotte. Why they don't just leave her to cry in a box with a couple of towels to keep her warm is totally beyond me.

The bad news is that Lolly is definitely going to live with Molly. Then the Owner brought up the subject of Coleridge and Miss Meddling, but Samantha was adamant that she couldn't have him.

'That woman is a menace. Coleridge is the size of a zeppelin already. Besides, he's my little puppy.'

'Yes, but he does seem to like her, and so far he seems impervious to any training whatsoever. Even Molly says he might just be dumber than most dogs.'

'He likes cake, and the smell of her knickers, which I suppose does support your theory that he's dumb.' Samantha paused. 'You could always give Blake to the policeman,' she suggested.

'I already tried it, but he's not as stupid as he looks,' the Owner replied, rocking Charlotte in his arms. She was wailing harder than ever and I'm not surprised. If I opened my eyes to find *that* was one of my parents I'd scream the place down too.

Wednesday, September 30

Lolly is back at the den with her eyes fixed. She can see. A simple operation to remove her cataracts was all it took. Her former Owner could have had it done quickly and easily years ago.

The sudden re-introduction of a sense did not have quite the result we'd all been expecting. Instead of wandering about sightseeing, Lolly sat in the corner of the kitchen all day whining and swinging her head about with a big plastic ruff around her neck. Even my jokes about looking like a main course of dog's head failed to make an impression. Only the Owner could calm her down by carrying her around in his arms, showing her the den. After a day of transporting either her or Charlotte around in this manner, he definitely seemed a bit tense. Remembering Lolly's wise words I jumped in his lap to let him work off some stress by stroking me, but on this occasion the old ear-licking and snuffling routine just seemed to increase his blood pressure even more.

OCTOBER

Thursday, October 1

With the Owner gently urging her on, Lolly took a few tentative steps out of her corner and into the garden. She left his side long enough to complete a hasty toilet – with the Owner wincing as she soiled the patio – and to sniff each of us in turn, with me last.

'Blake,' she woofed, 'I've been thinking. When I go to the new den, will I still see Scottie?'

I hadn't anticipated this wrinkle in the grand rehoming of Lolly scheme. The important thing was to get her away from her former Owner, fit, healthy and settle her into the kind of life that any dog has the right to expect a human to provide. None of us had expected love to blossom.

'The park's the only place to walk for miles,' I replied with quiet assurance. 'And Scottie's there all the time. I'm sure Molly will take you there every day.'

You can't keep Lolly down for long and this brought a wag to her tail. What if Molly goes away again though, and takes Lolly with her? The mere thought made me whimper a little, and my own tail sagged.

Friday, October 2

Not a good day for the Owner. Samantha has come down with proper flu as opposed to 'Owner flu'. She is confined to bed and being kept in quarantine while the Owner looks after Charlotte with the aid of a bottle of freshly expressed milk.

If he looked the worse for wear previously, now he resembles an animated corpse. Feeding four dogs while juggling a baby, walking four sprightly dogs with a pushchair and generally having four dogs jumping around his ankles while trying to force a bottle into the mouth of a screaming child was more than he could take. The snapping point came when Charlotte was sick all over him.* Some dribbled to the floor and Coleridge slurped it up enthusiastically. Such was the Owner's fury that even Lolly was banished to the garden, though she just sat by the kitchen door whining and did not join in the Barking-At-Meddling-On-A-Box-Until-She-Gives-You-Biscuits game.

* I'd have given a thumbs up to this, if I had a pair.

Saturday, October 3

Day two of Samantha being bedridden was an even worse experience for the Owner. It was raining, so walks were out of the question, and the garden looks like it has been mined with dog mess. Dinner service, never very polite, has become more perfunctory than usual. Nevertheless, I aim to please, and guarded Charlotte while he passed out on the sofa. Was it my fault if birds approached the window with their dreadful cheeping? Not being human, how was I to know that a little light barking and growling would wake the baby, or that she'd spend the next four hours crying. Too late I found out that this is one of those secret crimes that humans don't tell you about until you're clapped in chokey, or dismissed to the garden in this instance. Obviously, he doesn't watch enough Alfred Hitchcock movies and isn't aware of what those little feathered bastards are capable of.

Sunday, October 4

The Owner called Molly in, telling her to 'just get the damn dogs out of the house for the day'. I haven't seen him looking such a mess since he was dressed as a werewolf and can't help thinking that if he took a little more care of his appearance he might feel better in himself. His coat is a disgrace and is growing out of his face, and his eyes are small and bloodshot. He's started to smell like Constable. At times like this not being able to lick your own balls must be a terrible handicap. As a stress-buster, it's unbeatable. I took pity and tried to do it for him, but he just squealed and jumped away, which woke Charlotte up again. She wailed, and as Molly led us up the garden path I'm sure I heard him start too.

When we got back Molly offered to take Lolly there and then, but the Owner said that she should recover in familiar surroundings for a little while longer, and as she's much less bother than the rest of us he didn't mind. He did try and press her to take me and Coleridge away with her though.

Also, he confessed that he'd promised Lolly to the policeman by mistake. I haven't seen Molly so cross with him since they were dating and he quailed under the onslaught, which I thoroughly enjoyed. Finally she seemed placated – or maybe 'Mollified' – by his grovelling guarantee that he'd rectify the matter and Molly went away, still tutting.

Monday, October 5

Unbeknown to the Owner, Coleridge managed to snaffle a nappy that was sticking out of the bin in the kitchen. He insists it's an acquired taste, but not one that I'm much bothered about familiarising myself with, particularly after smelling the emanations from his backside during the rest of the day. The Owner was too far gone in sleep deprivation to even notice, but for the rest of us it was like spending a hot day on the sewage farm. Samantha even managed to drag herself out of bed to complain about it.

Convinced that such a reek must be due to more than just flatulence the humans tried to find the animal that had died somewhere in the house, but just turned up Coleridge's secret toilet behind the sofa with its dusty stools. Their removal and a thorough scrubbing, however, did nothing to improve the scent of the den, with Coleridge wandering around like the devil's own air freshener.

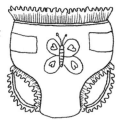

Tuesday, October 6

The Owner discovered shredded nappy all over the garden. Coleridge has obviously been paying attention in class and made the Eyes of Bewildered Innocence almost as well as I could. The concerned but friendly tail thumping was a nice touch too, and one I must remember to incorporate into my own routine. Frankly he looked angelic and I would have bet on him getting away with it if it weren't for a few scraps of stained nappy clinging to his muzzle. The Owner tried aversion therapy by sticking Coleridge's nose in a particularly disgusting remnant, but the puppy interpreted this as permission to start gobbling again.

The Owner should have looked on the bright side. At least it spared him having to clear it up. There's always a silver lining if you look for it, even when your dog is eating your child's soiled nappy before your very eyes.

Wednesday, October 7

Charlotte's crying was audible even in the shed last night so none of us were in the mood for Miss Meddling again today, unless she was being served up with gravy and mashed potatoes.

I gave her the kind of menace I usually reserve for the postman and the Owner growled too. For once we were man and beast working in perfect harmony. Charlotte tried to get in on the act by screaming, and made a good job of it, even going so far as shaking a tiny fist at the old woman.

'Do you know how long I've been awake for?' the Owner snarled.

'No,' Miss Meddling responded, baffled.

'Well neither do I, but it's a very, very long time.'

She paused and then said carefully, 'You're sure you're not on drugs?'

'If only. You've never had a baby, have you?'

'Of course not. I *am* a miss, thank you.'

'Would you like one?' His whisper was conspiratorial.

'What?'

'I'm serious. You can have this one. No one need ever know it's not yours. Take all the dogs too, just let me sleep for half an hour.'

'It's just Bobby . . . Coleridge I wanted.'

'Yes, yes, take him. Take the horrible nappy-chewing, farting mutt out of here.'

And suddenly, just like that, Coleridge is gone. My adopted son off to see the world, or the gnomes on the other side of the fence at least. Ella and I are sunk in depression. I'd be the first to admit that Coleridge is a little tyke, but he's a part of the pack. If the humans can get rid of him that easily what hope is there for us? Added to the 'jokes' about getting rid of me, I'm starting to get the fear. Lolly to Molly, Coleridge to Meddling. Things are looking bleak for Blake the Wonder Dog.

Thursday, October 8

Samantha went through the roof when she found out that the Owner had given Coleridge to Miss Meddling, and he seemed upset when he realised what he'd done as well. In vain did he protest that sleep deprivation had induced temporary insanity and that Coleridge had been making smells all morning that may have had a toxic, mind-altering effect on him. He thinks that Coleridge's eruptions should be banned under the Geneva Convention.

She was all for marching straight round and demanding that he be returned, but the Owner restrained her, pointing out that the house was noticeably calmer and that the persistent nasty smell had disappeared. She couldn't argue with that and they agreed to think about it, but leave the poor abandoned pup where he is for a day or two. They reasoned it would take slightly longer than that for Coleridge to eat himself to death.

Friday, October 9

Molly walked us to the park again. Ella and I wandered at will, playing with Liquorice and Denny and taking some quality scoot time. Lolly preferred to stay by Molly's ankles. Now she can see I'd have thought she would want to explore a bit further, but apparently the vision of Molly is all that a rescue dog needs.

She did, however, run barking to Scottie when he arrived. Given that she has never actually clapped eyes on her beau before I would have expected her to run in the opposite direction; he is, after all, less than half her size, shivers a lot and has discoloured patches of fur. From the way she looked at him though, you would have thought he was Cujo, Dog of Love. There is no accounting for the strange fascination Scottie exerts over the opposite sex. They say that wolf and canine bitches are programmed to mate with the dog that promises the best genetic inheritance for the puppies and the only inheritance Scottie has to offer is a collection of tartan doggie coats and a rather nice food bowl with bones embossed on it.

Saturday, October 10

Samantha is fully recovered, so freed from squalling child the Owner took Ella to the vet's. After carefully palpitating her belly, the man in the white coat confirmed that she is indeed expecting our puppies. Ella says that she knew all along, but it's great to have a professional medic confirm her condition. I celebrated by running around the garden with Lolly barking congratulations. Even Coleridge joined in from over the fence. The humans were less effusive and just came out to tell us to shut up. They seemed even more exasperated than usual. No champagne in my bowl tonight, just the usual meat-flavoured rubbish. Frankly, there's so little actual meat in it I might be an inadvertent vegetarian.

Sunday, October 11

Lolly was deemed ready to leave the den to make her way in the world by Molly's side. The plastic funnel is still attached, but she is a lot more confident now and has been known to leave the Owner or her kitchen corner for seconds at a stretch.

The Owner spent the morning rolling a brightly coloured ball across the kitchen floor and saying 'fetch' to her. He seemed mournful, perhaps because in the true tradition of dogs in this den she has taken exception to this demeaning 'game' already. She was quite happy to walk alongside the ball, watch it carefully, and even push it along with her nose, but actually picking it up and taking it back was out of the question. For some reason I was touched by this more than anything else about her leaving, and had to go and have a lie-down in the shed.

When Molly came, the basket, bowl and lead were formally handed over after lunch and we were all making our last farewells to our new friend as the doorbell rang.

It was the policeman. He had come to check on Lolly's condition and see if she was ready to leave yet. The Owner had forgotten to appraise him of the new circumstances.

Bright red, the Owner invited him in muttering about there being a mix-up and how he's had less than an hour's sleep in the past month. Lolly joined Ella and I in welcoming the policeman to our den and, as usual, he dispensed an abundance of affection, saving most of it for Lolly. Molly, meanwhile, stood in the corner with her arms crossed, looking stern.

Eventually, the policeman straightened up from stroking Lolly and looked at the Owner. His face was stony.

'So, if I understand, sir, you're telling me that having made a promise to let me have the dog, you are now reneging on the aforementioned promise.'

'Umm, yes, I'm afraid so, officer,' the Owner squeaked.

'In direct contravention of the 1967 Verbal Contract Law, article 67, clause b?'

The Owner gave Molly an appealing look, but she shook her head slowly while the Owner continued to shuffle. 'I really am sorry, I'm sure we can work out something. I'll rescue another dog. A black one. You won't even notice the difference.'

'And then there are all those other charges that we dropped, sir. I'd hate to be forced to reopen those files.'

The Owner looked as though he was going to faint. The policeman clapped him on the shoulder. 'If you wouldn't mind accompanying me to the station, sir.'

'Oh no. Please, Molly.'

The policeman broke into a grin and said, 'Only joking.' Samantha sniggered. 'I can't say it's not a disappointment, she's an adorable dog, but these things happen. It would be nice to see her sometimes, though.'

'Of course you can,' Molly interjected. 'Any time you like.' She had started blushing too.

'Oh, that's kind of you. Maybe we could discuss access over dinner?'

Molly's eyes widened. It was her turn to be flustered. 'Ummm, well, that is, yes, I'd like that.'

Meanwhile, the Owner seemed to have rallied. He smiled, and for a moment I thought I saw a hint of cruelty in it. 'But officer,' he said quietly, 'if you can wait a couple of months, Ella here is pregnant and we'll be looking for homes for the puppies.'

'There's no need to call me "officer", I'm not on duty. Jack will do. Well, I had promised myself to help a rescue dog, but if there's a puppy in need of a good home . . . What breed is the father?'

The Owner patted me. 'Well, I don't think the breed name has been invented that would cover Blake's mixed ancestry, but the father is none other than the Wonder Dog here. And a more good-natured, easy-to-manage, intelligent and noble dog you couldn't find anywhere. I'm sure the puppies will be just as special.'

'Well, in that case I'll look forward to taking one home with me. About Christmas time?'

'Yes, we'll give you a call. Say, Jack . . . those are very nice shoes.'

'Hand-stitched Italian leather,' the policeman replied proudly. 'Very comfortable, but a bit expensive.'

The Owner grinned, and said, 'Nice. You are going to *love* this puppy.'

Monday, October 12

Just me and Ella left in the den. For the first time we are outnumbered by humans. I hope they don't start getting ideas above their station; as far as I'm concerned their primary purpose is still operation of the tin opener. Of course, there is the mitigating fact that they won't have too long to get used to the relative peace and quiet. We miss Lolly and Coleridge, but Ella's got a bellyful of Blakes simmering nicely. Since the Owner's glowing commendation yesterday I'm worrying slightly less about rehoming. Not only has he seemed to realise at last that he is the proud Owner of a paid-up Wonder Dog, but that I am 'good-natured, easy-to-manage, intelligent and noble', to boot. What human in their right mind would want to be parted from such an incredible animal?

Tuesday, October 13

Still in shock about impending fatherhood. My genes will be passed down to another generation of Wonder Dogs. I wonder whether they'll be short-coated and patchy like me or long-haired like Ella? Will we have males or females, and in what number? I'm so excited I could fart. So I did; profusely. Charlotte didn't seem to like it, but she doesn't seem to like anything much. She must get her temper from the Owner. Well, he'll see what superior genetics can achieve when my own brood arrives. Doubtless they *will* be as good-natured, easy-to-manage, intelligent and noble as I am. From Ella they will inherit bums that exude a peculiar and mesmerising odour.

Wednesday, October 14

With Samantha fit and well and Charlotte a little more quiet than usual, the Owner was recovered sufficiently to face Meddling over the adoption of Coleridge. Ella and I were in the garden and could hear the conversation over the fence. It went something like this:

'Oh hello, Miss Meddling, I just came to talk about Coleridge.'

'You can't have him back.'

'Oh hello, boy.' There was a couple of seconds during which we just heard Coleridge's excited yapping. He was pleased to see the Owner and obviously giving him a good licking.

'The thing is that I was very tired when I gave him to you, and . . . good God, are those Rich Tea biscuits in his bowl?'

'You can't have him back.'

'Well, I wasn't necessarily going to ask for that, but surely you can see that you can't just feed a dog broken-up Rich Tea biscuits, their stomachs aren't built to cope with refined sugar.'

'He seems to like them fine, thank you very much.'

'Of course he likes them. Dogs will eat anything, and Coleridge is no ordinary dog. He'd scoff a bowl of cat sick if you put it in front of him.'

'There's no need for language, and you can't have him back. You gave him to me fair and square.'

'Yes, but I hadn't slept for forty-eight hours. Besides, I seem to remember you saying that you'd take my advice on what to feed him.'

'There's no need for that. He gets two large tins of best dog food a day, the biscuits are just a snack.'

'Two? Two *large* tins a day? And snacks? Miss Meddling, he shouldn't be getting any more than half a large tin a day with some good-quality dog biscuits. If you're feeling generous a couple of dog treats won't do any harm.'

'He's got a healthy appetite, he eats it all up.'

The Owner seemed to be losing his patience. 'Of course he bloody does. He probably can't believe his luck.' He took a deep breath. 'What about exercise?'

'He runs around in the garden all he wants.'

'But your garden is open to the road.'

'Yes, he can go up and down the street, too.'

'I see. He can go in and out of the traffic as well, can he?'

'We're doing very well together, aren't we, Bobby? And I'll thank you to keep your nose out of it.'

'Miss Meddling, I never thought I'd say this, but unless you give me Coleridge back I'll report you to the police for animal cruelty and neglect.'

There was no answer, just the sound of a door being slammed.

Thursday, October 15

Samantha tried with Miss Meddling today, but had no more luck than the Owner. Coleridge is at the centre of a tug-of-love battle complete with bitter recriminations and legal threats. It's the puppy

I feel sorry for; watching his humans fight over him like this will scar him for life.

Friday, October 16

The weather has taken a turn for the worse and Scottie is governing over an increasingly disorderly pack of dogs. In the park today we heard growled mutterings about the chill and loneliness of shed life and muted calls for Scottie to be replaced with an effective leader who can get them back to their rightful places on sofas, warm baskets and in front of fires. It's the sort of situation that a dog with any political nose could easily turn to their advantage, if – for example – they were intent on becoming Top Dog. As Sir Winston Churchill once said, 'A pessimist sees the difficulty in every opportunity; an optimist sees the opportunity in every difficulty.'

Saturday, October 17

In the garden this afternoon, the Owner came out and put Crusty Bob in a box and took him inside. I don't think he was dead, though it's always difficult to tell with Bob. Perhaps they're going to gift-wrap him for someone, perhaps the pet purge isn't over after all. Perhaps Ella and I are still in danger of being removed.

I calmed myself enough to follow the trail the Owner left with my bloodhound nose and found the box containing poor Crusty Bob had been put on a shelf in a cupboard. This is a new low even for the Owner. The poor little guy is trapped in a tiny box. I've always thought he looks a bit like Rameses II, but actually sealing him up in a tomb is not acceptable. No Wonder Dog could let it pass so I got my feet up on the ledge and tried to release him, but the Owner pulled me off and dragged me out to the garden.

As a playmate, Bob does leave a lot to be desired, but he doesn't deserve to be left to rot in a dark box. Obviously as the defender of the weak, friend to the hopeless, I will have to step in to save the day again.

Sunday, October 18

Samantha came out today and had a long talk with Ella. While dishing out an unprecedented level of stroking, she apologised for not having spent more time with her over the past month or two and told her that Ella was still her favourite dog in the world. With

Ella gently nuzzling her Mistress, Samantha then moved on to say that really she was happy that Ella would be having puppies, it was just that the timing was terrible with Charlotte to look after. It was all very sweet and ended with a long hug, during which Ella gently nibbled Samantha's ear.

Later in the day my own Owner came out, sat on the step, looked at me and said, 'If you ever get another bitch in trouble, I'll cut your balls off.'

First Bob, now my testicles are up for grabs again. The Owner is on a slippery slope that ends in mange and chicken wire.

Monday, October 19

The Owner escaped to the park to avoid the bathing of Charlotte, which she hates.* We were hardly through the gate before we spotted that policeman, Jack, and ran over to say hello and autograph his clothes with muddy paw prints. Behind him, with Lolly at her side, was Molly. It was difficult to know who to welcome first, so I settled for running around the little group barking and giving a bit of nose here and there.

As Ella and I settled down for a more thorough sniff of Lolly, the Owner finally came puffing up. He had a favour to ask the policeman.

Lolly reports that life with Molly is better than she could possibly have imagined just a few months ago. She already has her own place on the sofa, where she can get her head easily into Molly's lap, and the cuisine at her new den is divine. Apparently there are recipes for dog food that are not based on entrails. She spoke eloquently of prime chunks of meat, glistening in a rich gravy with just the right amount of vegetables to ensure health without overwhelming the beefy flavour. This heavenly food apparently comes served on a bed of biscuits that are themselves a taste sensation and are firm enough to provide texture without being so hard as to scrape the enamel off a dog's teeth. She went

* In many ways the baby is almost an honorary dog. She doesn't like baths, howls a lot and seems to want food all the time. It must be why I've taken such a shine to the little cherub. Well, either that or the fact that she's only weeks old and already running rings around the Owner.

on to describe bones so thickly endowed with meat that they should more rightly be called 'joints' and a veritable cornucopia of treats.

To think that I'd been worried about rehoming. Damn my loyalty. I should have been at the front of the queue, throwing myself at Molly whenever she came through the door.

Tuesday, October 20

Samantha has read somewhere that babies sleep better if they have fresh air and sunlight during the day, so in an effort to get a decent sleep she wheeled the baby around the park for hours this afternoon. It must work because Charlotte slept all the way round, no matter how many times Samantha poked her. Ella and I flanked the pushchair like bodyguards around a presidential motorcade, but we did, however, give ourselves a break when we saw Scottie surrounded by ex-C.R.A.P. dogs. We arrived just in time to hear him barking furiously.

'Noo ah'm pack leader ye ken and nae dug gets back inside the den until ah say so. Noo stop yer whinin'.'

'But Scottie –'

'Nay but's, there's still C.R.A.P. afoot.' He stopped when he saw us approaching, then continued. 'Ah, Blake the Wonder Dug an' his trusty sidekick Ella. Jest the dugs tae talk some sense tae ye rabble. Would ye ken, Blake? There's dugs in the park as doesnae want tae avenge Lolly.'

It was a tense moment. The politician inside me sat up, ears twitching with alertness. It was too early to undermine Scottie's authority, but a hint to the poor, suffering animals stuck in their sheds at night that I sympathised with their plight might bear dividends later. Fortunately, I have a gift for eloquence.

'Well, Scottie. While I'm sure we all support your campaign and admire your determination I must say that it's so cold in the shed now that my tongue stuck to my balls last night.'

'That's right. My balls were frozen too.'

Scottie was furious. 'Whut are ye talkin' aboot, Liquorice? Ye wus neutered two years ago.'

'They might have been frozen,' Liquorice muttered. 'For medical science and that. They were good balls. Probably hundreds of scientists want to have a look at them.'

'Ye're mad, dug, I saw thum when ye had thum and they were like a pair o' raisins. Whae'd want tae look at balls like that?'

With the two dogs now growling at each other Ella and I decided that it was a good time to resume guard duty and slunk away. Behind us we could hear the barking becoming louder and more aggressive.

'They were the size of tennis balls. They only took them off because they were so amazing. When all the scientists have finished looking at them they're going to put them back on again.'

'Back oan? Back oan? They're noat detachable! Ye cannae pass thum roond fer iviryone tae admire then screw them back oan agin.'

'Humans can do amazing things these days.'

'But they dinnae tak yer goolies oaf for a game o' marbles an' then give ye thum back, ye stupit dug.'

'They gave Lolly her sight after Blake rescued her.'

Oops, I seem to have started something there. It's the wolf in me, I suppose: utterly ruthless and without any ethics or morals whatsoever.

Wednesday, October 21

After her epic sleep yesterday afternoon, Charlotte was ready for fun last night. We could hear her yelling and the Owner's anguished cries all night long. I don't know why the humans bother keeping us out in the shed now. Even when I'm at my most excited, my bark is as the babbling of a gentle stream next to Charlotte's crying. In terms of decibels she must be up there with jets taking off or the explosion of a small thermonuclear device.

Thursday, October 22

Scottie was looking disconsolate in the wasteland this evening. I gave him a few bars of the theme tune, which usually cheers him up, but today it didn't raise a single wag. After an investigative bum-sniff to make sure he was in good health I asked what the problem was.

'Ah'm losin' the support o' C.R.A.P., Blake. All thum useless mutts want is tae get inside agin. They're a bunch o' mutineers an' deserters ah tell ye.'

This was excellent news. Not only could we avoid a potentially disastrous meeting with Lolly's human, but with revolution already in the air, the time was ripe for a dog to step forward. A Chosen One to lead the dogs out of the cold and onto their comfy sofas. A leader. A hero. A Wonder Dog.

I could hear the cheers already, but as I looked at my best friend I was amazed to find my tail wagging and myself barking, 'I'll come with you, Scottie. You can count on me.'

Damn that loyalty, damn it. It's the humans' fault with their bloody selective breeding.

'Och, I kent that, Blake,' Scottie woofed in reply, and my traitor tail wagged even harder. 'Noo, let's start plannin'.'

Friday, October 23

Jack the policeman was back, and this time wearing full uniform. Our welcome was cut short though. He only stopped for a few words and then left while the Owner hurried out the back door with Ella and me in tow. He stood by the fence and peered over. A few moments later we heard the ringing of the bell and voices. Miss Meddling and Jack.

'Hello, officer, how very lovely to see you again. Do come in for some tea and cake.'

'I'm sorry, ma'am, but this is an official visit,' Jack replied in his most formal voice. 'I'm afraid we've had some complaints.'

'From that dreadful man over the fence? Surely you wouldn't believe the word of that disgusting sex fiend?'

'I should remind you, ma'am, that there is a law about slander. But no, these complaints come from a number of sources.'

'Well, I'm sure I've done nothing wrong.'

'The complaints concern the dog known as Coleridge or Bobby.'

'My little Bobby wouldn't harm a fly.'

'No, ma'am, but he might cause an accident. On several occasions motorists have had to swerve dangerously after he's run into the road, and I also have reports of him overturning rubbish bins and eating the contents.'

'He does have a healthy appetite, bless him.'

'You may not be aware, ma'am, but as the dog's legal owner you are responsible for his actions, and that this constitutes criminal damage. If the dog should cause an accident you are also liable for damages, and in the event of casualties possibly a prison sentence.'

Meddling squealed. The Owner punched the air.

'Oh no, oh no. I couldn't go to prison at my age. Whatever would I do?'

'Knit mail bags possibly, ma'am,' Jack replied gravely. 'I've had a word with Bobby's former owner and he's told me confidentially that he's also worried about the dog's diet.'

'That's no business of his any more.'

'No, ma'am, but you might be interested to know that it is not unheard of for dog owners to be prosecuted for overfeeding their dogs. You are affecting the dog's health and shortening his life span.' Jack paused. 'I personally take a very dim view of animal cruelty. You could call it a mission if you like.'

Meddling's voice now had a note of desperation in it. 'How can it be cruel? He loves his biscuits and cakes.'

'Nevertheless, ma'am, as I believe you've been made aware, they are not good for his health.'

'In trouble with the police, at my age. What will the neighbours think?'

'Well, one neighbour in particular is very willing to help.'

'What? Who?'

'The gentleman over the fence who you persist in referring to as a "disgusting sex fiend" has indicated that he is willing to either take Bobby back or advise you on responsible dog care.'

'Help? From him? I don't think so.'

'That's up to you, ma'am, but I will be monitoring the situation closely and can promise you I will take further steps as necessary.'

'Oh my. Oh my.'

'Quite, ma'am. This visit is just a warning. I'd hate to have to take a nice lady such as yourself down to the station. Good day, ma'am.'

Saturday, October 24

Miss Meddling was on the doorstep when we arrived home from our morning walk. She was carrying a cake and wearing the wig that Coleridge had so liberally sprayed with his own scent. It seemed to have had a rinse, but even from below it smelled like the puppy had marked her head as his territory.

'Hello,' said the Owner with a happy grin. 'Surely the cake isn't for me? Is it Hug-a-Pervert Day again already?'

'I, err, came to say, umm . . . Well, apologise really.'

'Really?'

'Yes, it was wrong of me to say you stole my knickers, but what with you throwing dirty pictures around . . .'

'You mean accidentally letting the wind blow someone else's dirty pictures around?'

'Well, yes, that.'

'And the phone call?'

'Could have been your dog. I'd believe anything of that dog now.'

'So?'

'Well . . . umm, sorry.'

'That's something, I suppose, though being dragged to the police station is an experience I don't want to repeat. Cells – you know – with a bucket in the corner for a toilet. Nothing to eat but stale bread and water, chains on your ankles and just a bit of old straw to sleep on. Crawling with lice, of course.'

Meddling's eyes opened wide in fear as the Owner continued. 'Anyway, we forgot to pay you for the things that Coleridge stole. As his owner I am liable you know?' He was inspecting the cake gleefully and seemed to be enjoying himself.

'Oh, that's all right, keep your money, everything came up fine in the wash. Only . . .'

'Yes?'

'Well, you said you might give me some advice on looking after Bobby.'

'Of course, but you're sure you wouldn't like us to take him back? Dogs are such a handful.'

Miss Meddling muttered something.

'I beg your pardon?'

'I . . . that is . . . well, he's my only company really apart from the cat. I don't get many visitors.'

When the Owner replied his voice was much softer. 'Well, why don't you come in for a cup of tea and help me start this cake off. We can talk about what you need to do.'

For the first time ever, I saw Miss Meddling smile.

Sunday, October 25

Constable is even more worried. His Mistress was on the phone yesterday talking about him. She finished the call with the words, 'Don't worry, Constable will be ready to go.'

'Blake,' he moaned, 'I'm going to be taken away. I'll end up in one of those places for hopeless dogs.'

'Homeless dogs, Constable,' I corrected him, though thinking he might well have been right in the first place.

Scottie is at a loss and my only suggestion was that he make a break for it during the night. With all the Crusty Bob-related cruelty and testicle threats in the den, I'm tempted to join him. However, Constable held his shaggy head high and said that he would take whatever was coming like a dog. Sadly, we made our last farewells to the Old English sheepdog, telling him his name would be remembered throughout the park for years to come.* After the triumph of freeing Lolly, the year is coming to a bad end. Coleridge and Lolly gone, Crusty Bob mummified on a shelf, Scottie with a crazy plan that will see us all in a dangerous-dogs pound, and now Constable taken from us.

Monday, October 26

The Owner left with his tool kit this morning, and for most of the day we could hear sounds of drilling and sawing from Miss Meddling's garden. Late in the afternoon the fence itself came under attack. Ella and I barked at the end of a saw as it made a small square in the wooden fence. Finally this fell out and Coleridge rushed through to greet us. Then the Owner's head popped through, grinning at his handiwork. Obviously it was at exactly the right level to be covered in spit, so Ella and I slathered him in it. The cunning human has made his hole too small for Ella and I, but Coleridge can now come and go from garden to garden at will. I managed to get my head through and noticed that Miss Meddling now has a side gate, so I suppose if we can't use it as a route to freedom then access to her garden is pointless anyway. There's only so many times you can marvel at her gnome collection.

Tuesday, October 27

It was a surprise to see Constable in the park this morning, and in fine fettle too. I've never seen a dog jump in and out of a pond with such elation. Scottie, Lolly, Ella and I sauntered over to find out how he had managed this reprieve from certain rehoming.

'Oh, I never was going to be taken away, I just didn't hear the Mistress properly. She was arranging dogs to come to me.'

* Probably as an adjective, as in 'Look that dog's covered in shit. He's gone completely Constable.'

'Whitiver would she dae that fer?' Scottie woofed.

'So I could mate with them.'

There was a stunned silence, disturbed by a duck landing on the pond.

'What?' I whined eventually.

Ella panted, 'You're a stud, Constable.'

'Thanks, Ella, that's just what Princess said after our third time yesterday.'

'Princess? Third time?' I managed to bark, aghast.

'Oh yes, and I found the right end after only sixteen attempts, with some help from the Mistress.'

'And you did it three times? That's not bad is it, Scottie?' Lolly barked innocently.

'Nae, n-noat bad,' Scottie stammered. Even on a good day with the wind behind him, Scottie can only manage once. Twice if he's had his arthritis medicine and a six-hour sleep in between.

'And then,' Constable continued, 'Princess's Mistress gave my Mistress some money and went away. Today is for recovery, and tomorrow I have another booking. Angel, I think her name is.'

My jaw dropped, my tongue lolled. I noticed that Scottie's had done the same. Constable is a prostitute, a gigolo, a street-walker. Not so much a 'Good Boy' as a 'Rent Boy'.

'It's quite fun, isn't it? The mating?' Constable continued happily. 'Much more fun than standing on a podium.'

Once, perhaps twice a year. That's how often I get to have real live sex with a bitch in season, and then only by sheer luck and chance. And Constable's Mistress is serving them up on a conveyor belt, a different backside every day. Not that I'd swap Ella for an endless stream of willing bitches, all on heat and begging for my attentions. Oh no. Nevertheless, with Lolly enjoying food that I can only dream about, Constable looking forward to life as a sex object and even Coleridge having his own frilly cushion, I'm wondering – and not for the first time – if it's possible to return your human and ask for one that works properly.

Wednesday, October 28

The little Blakes inside Ella must be growing, she's looking distinctly Coleridge around the middle. It's a pointless exercise because the Owner and Samantha are bound to overrule us, but we lay on the lawn and picked out names anyway. Dog knows, neither of us have a pedigree, but I don't see why just the purebred dogs – and human celebrities – should have all the fun with unusual names, so top of our list was 'Red Fang Tin Opener II, son of Blake the Wonder Dog' for a boy and 'Princess Ploppy Smelly Bum, daughter of Blake the Wonder Dog' for a girl. When I say 'our' list, Ella had a few objections – particularly with the surnames. She wants something simple and traditional (probably the awful Rex or Sparky). Doubtless the Owner will continue with his ridiculous habit of naming dogs after human poets, so the poor pups will be stuck with pathetic names like 'Poe' or 'Longfellow'.

Thursday, October 29
Another check-up for Ella at the vet's today. By his calculations the puppies should be due in a fortnight or so and he thinks there might be quite a number. According to Ella the Owner went slightly green when he found out, but refused the offer of an x-ray to confirm the size of the litter, saying he'd rather not know.

Friday, October 30
With puppy-time approaching, I'm starting to understand how the Owner felt when Charlotte was coming and Ella is getting fed up with me snuffling around her all the time. The humans have made few concessions to her condition, but then they don't really have to. We dogs are made of sturdy stuff and aside from a slight thickening and a less bouncy approach to walks you'd hardly know that Ella was expecting. Tonight though, they let her inside the den to sleep and consequently were forced to let me back in too after she sat by the back door and whined.

With his usual lack of tact the Owner warned me that I am strictly on trial. One bark, just one instance of waking the baby, will see me back in the shed again, almost certainly without my balls.

Saturday, October 31
Oh, the bliss of lying in front of a dying fire curled up around my mate and knowing the rest of the pack are near. The fulfilment of keeping an ear cocked for the approach of an intruder, the responsibility of knowing that the nocturnal safety of the den rests in just my paws. I had forgotten how much I missed it. Even half asleep I could hear the humans stir. Samantha's gentle snoring, the Owner's occasional fart, Charlotte's sudden, deafening wails. It was good to know all was well.

NOVEMBER

Sunday, November 1
Just one alert last night. The Owner had left the front gate open and the breeze made it squeak on its hinges. I've lost none of my old prowess and had my paws on the windowsill ready to sound the alarm in less than two seconds. Not bad considering I'm as rusty as the gate. I was about to start barking when Ella pounced on me and woofed me into silence. It goes against everything I've ever believed about guarding, but at her insistence, I'm now trying the silent and invisible routine. It does make sense not to give my presence away until my jaws are around the actual throat, I suppose. It's what a wolf would do.

Monday, November 2
Scottie pointed out that my being back in the den at night will make it impossible for me to join him in a raid on Lolly's ex-Owner. In all the excitement about the puppies and moving back into the den, I'd almost forgotten all about Scottie's potentially disastrous expedition.

'Ye'll jest huv tae get oot agin,' he yapped sternly.

'But Scottie,' I remonstrated. 'Ella. The puppies. Guarding . . .'

'Och, all right, ye kin huv until the wee 'uns come, but aftir that, C.R.A.P. strikes back.'

I tried to argue that I was on a strict assessment period and one instance of bad behaviour would end my den privileges for all time, but my protests fell upon deaf ears. It's probably his age.

'Ye know the drill, Blake,' he barked. 'Poo and pee, poo and pee.'

Tuesday, November 3
I have to admit Scottie's plan is elegant in its simplicity, though the possible consequences of attacking a human still make me go weak at the sphincter. All of the old C.R.A.P. pack has sullenly agreed to join the effort, much to Scottie's relief. Although they're on the verge of mutiny the authority of the Top Dog is not easy to refuse. Obedience is ingrained into a dog's very soul and even Scottie with his wobbly legs and underpants breath commands respect.

C.R.A.P. dogs will enter by the back gate and once in place Razor and I will remain hidden from sight while Scottie attracts attention by barking. Unable to resist an opportunity for cruelty, Lolly's ex-Owner will rush out into the yard to give Scottie a kicking, whereupon Razor will cut off any possible retreat through the back door. With Scottie then leading the way, I, with Liquorice, Claude, Constable and Rudy, will chase the human up the alley to a suitable tree. Cornered here, he will attempt to climb it, presenting his posterior for the ultimate in canine revenge – the seat of the pants rip.

After that, who knows? Probably the van with the wire mesh on the back will come to collect us.

Wednesday, November 4

Ran into Liquorice during a short walk today, causing an impressive triple-roll dog pile-up that ended in a bush.

'Do you have to do that, Blake?' he barked, getting back on his feet.

'Sorry, Licky,' I woofed, 'just excited to see you.'

'Well cut it out. As if I haven't got enough to worry about with freezing in the shed every night.'

I thought for a moment. It wouldn't necessarily be disloyal to help the other C.R.A.P. dogs, would it? After all, I'd pledged my own assistance to the cause. If it just happened that there were no other dogs available when the time came, wouldn't Scottie be forced to cancel his attack, even though his trusty lieutenant was still keen for action? Plus, I'd still have the gratitude of all those now happily dozing on their favourite sofa. All in all I'd come out smelling of faeces and in an excellent position to slip back into the Top Dog role, should it become available.

I was deeply ashamed of these dark, treacherous thoughts, but only so long as it took to sniff Liquorice's bum. You don't get to be Top Dog by being a Good Boy and thwarting Scottie's scheme might just save us all.

Thursday, November 5

I have a plan to tackle the re-admittance of C.R.A.P. dogs to their dens. Once again it's based on careful analysis and psychological profiling of humans, taking Charlotte as my test subject and formulated with the help of my trusted lab assistant Ella, who added her own notes on Human Whimpering.*

We have observed that should we dogs start barking too loudly it ends with us being ejected into the garden, whereas if Charlotte starts wailing, it guarantees the humans' instant attention and expressions of concern and affection. Why the disparity? Our hypothesis is that the human response to a child is a conditioned reaction brought on by an array of body-language signals. After careful study all afternoon the Blake–Ella team has concluded that Charlotte effectively controls her parents with the following tactics:

1. Attracting attention with pitiful crying.
2. Creating and maintaining eye contact.
3. Appearing helpless.
4. Attempting to maintain body contact with them.

By adapting these signals for dogs, we will attempt to tap into the same instincts that Charlotte exploits and thus exert greater control over the humans, in this instance manipulating them into letting their dogs back inside the den. Obviously this cutting-edge research is in its early stages, but if all goes to plan, surely a Nobel Prize awaits.

Friday, November 6
Completely worn out after yesterday's mental exertions so after pawing at the door to Crusty Bob's final resting place in a last attempt to save the poor little guy, I spent the day sprawled across the sofa dozing. To the untrained eye my twitching feet and occasional tiny woof may have looked like deep sleep, but as ever I was ready to spring into action at the drop of a leaf, or at least that's the impression I tried to give whenever a human came into the room. I'd hate for them to think I was slacking on the guard front.

Saturday, November 7
Coleridge popped through the fence today soon after the morning handful of concrete chunks and the Owner took us round to Miss

* She's only actually one eighth Lab, but that's enough to qualify her as an assistant.

Meddling's to ask if he could join us on our walk. It was a mistake, of course. Although it was nice to have Coleridge's company in the park, by the time we had returned Meddling had rounded up a carload of senior citizens for a shopping expedition and also negotiated the Owner taking Coleridge for a walk twice a week to spare her knees.

As always the idiot human fell for it and as usual expects to be taken seriously as a pack leader. It's a shame that Human Whimpering doesn't yet allow me to communicate on a complex level or I could advise him to chase her off into some cave where she could scratch out a meagre living by dining on moles and suchlike. Having said that, I don't see why I should even attempt to pass on my wisdom to the tortoise-boxing, testicle-threatening potential rehomer.

Sunday, November 8

Liquorice was in the park again today and after a strenuous work-out that involved crashing into each other a lot, I mentioned mine and Ella's scientific research. While being careful to make no suggestions about how our findings might be used, I outlined the Human Whimpering technique for him.

'So, by whimpering at the back door, looking the Master in the eyes with a look of – how did you put it? – Great Pleading, trying to appear small and helpless and snuffling him, you believe I should be able to bend him to my will?'

'That's what our findings suggest, Licky. Why don't you give it a go?'

'You mean I might be able to get back in the den?'

'That would be totally against Scottie's orders. I make no recommendations for the purposes for which my research is used, but be sure to pass it on.'

Monday, November 9

A *rapprochement* with the Owner today after an Olympic stroking session and general love-in this evening. There was no mention of a new home or of my public parts. I'm still wary after his cruel incarceration of Crusty Bob, but perhaps there is a good reason for it after all. For all I know there might be a human tradition calling for the sacrifice of a tortoise after the birth of the first-born, or maybe tortoises like a few weeks in an isolation chamber every now and then. Maybe he's just tired out having moved three whole feet all year and needs a nice long rest.

Anyway, I have decided to give the Owner the benefit of the doubt. He has noticed how much care I have been taking of Charlotte and repaid his debt to her trusty guardian with an all-over body massage and by doing that thing with my ears where he grabs them and waggles them about. I'd prefer he stuck to the stroking, but I suppose you can't look a gift cat up the bum.

Tuesday, November 10
Puppy-time is getting closer. Ella is now officially enormous, bigger even than Coleridge. Despite being more sleepy than usual there's not been much of a change in her during her pregnancy, but now she's getting restless at night, scratching the floor and walking around in circles. She's also started taking cushions from the sofa to make a nest in the corner. It's all very peculiar and I don't pretend to understand. Like every mammalian father all I can do is watch and woof at her. It's not much, but I've tried humping her and apparently this is not considered such a great expression of sympathy and compassion as I thought it might be.

Wednesday, November 11
Ella has been excused walks save for a three-times-daily lead around the garden, with the Owner following her around with the handy pooper-scooper. As always, the sight of him scurrying around with a load of dog mess was thoroughly enjoyable. It's the funny little faces he makes while carrying the funny little faeces that really do it for me.

Just for good measure I left an extra one on the patio for him while he wasn't watching. Was rewarded with the gnashing of teeth and muttered swearing.

Thursday, November 12
The humans have helped Ella make a nest in the closet under the stairs, which is warm and dim. My mate contributed by insisting that

Samantha's favourite cushion go in the large, towel-lined bed they have made for her. I've never understood humans who smoke, but for some reason I feel the need to pace the floor of the den with a pipe in my mouth. As there isn't one in the house, I've had to make do with one of the Owner's slippers.

Samantha has started taking Ella's temperature. When I try for a quiet and gentle hump I get Ella's teeth at my throat, but Samantha is allowed to stick stuff up her bum with impunity. I just don't get it.

Friday, November 13

Liquorice is back in the den. Human Whimpering works like a charm. After just ten minutes of looking pitiful and whining softly his Owner succumbed to the inevitable and the Lab spent a warm and cosy night in the kitchen. He has vowed neither to poo nor to pee inside again. As a result he also thinks I'm some kind of canine Sigmund Freud, though his actual words were, 'Blake, I'm starting to think you're not quite so dim after all.'

Saturday, November 14

A new harmony seems to have descended on the den. Charlotte has stopped wailing quite so much and the humans seem more relaxed. They have started allowing me to guard Charlotte alone for a few moments at a time while they make coffee. At times like these I lie quietly next to her and watch for any possible threat while breathing in her delicious smell. Being useful is its own reward, but the Owner and Samantha are impressed at how attentive I am and the rate of strokes and pats has increased threefold. They seem particularly pleased when Charlotte's little hand emerged from her sleep chair and grabbed my ear. Anyone else would have received a stern warning, but the little human just got the Eyes of Total Adoration. Apparently, I am turning into a Very Good Boy.

Ella is still restless, but still no sign of the puppies.

Sunday, November 15

Word has been passed along and other dogs have proven the efficacy of Human Whimpering. Even Barney, who usually likes sleeping outside in his kennel, has given it a try and is a late convert to a warm sofa. None of them has found the courage to tell Scottie, but I am enjoying a new respect across the park. It looks like the Westie's plan for waging war on Lolly's ex-Owner is all but over, and next to crumble will be his tenure as Top Dog. I'm not the sort of dog who cackles in maniacal glee, but can't help enjoying the quietly gruffed 'Thanks, Blake', whenever we go to the park now.

Monday, November 16

For some reason I can't help thinking about Scottie's little bearded face, when he finds out his plan is at an end and his authority as a Top Dog fatally torpedoed. I keep telling myself it's for his own good. He might be disappointed in the short term, but when he's had the chance to reflect he'll realise what a burden being Top Dog is, plus someone has to stop him attacking the human. Even so, the inbred loyalty is difficult to shift and I can't help feeling like a cur. I'll make it up to him by promoting him to beta again, so he can spend his retirement thinking up a cool nickname for himself. Perhaps after his urinating-up-the-leg trick, he could be 'Pee-Me-Up Scottie'.

Tuesday, November 17

This evening Ella is more restless than usual. She has retired to her new bed and is busy licking herself, which should be my job really, but I am *canine non grata* in her dim little space. Just before they went to bed, Samantha took Ella's temperature once more, then looked at the Owner.

'Looks like we could be in for a busy night,' she said.

Wednesday, November 18

They are here! Five little furry bundles of sweetness, suckling Ella with all the enthusiasm of Coleridge in a pie shop. We have three females and two males, all patchy like me.

The Owner and Samantha were alerted by Ella's howling about midnight and Samantha came down to sit with her dog while the Owner took over Charlotte duties. With me pacing the lounge and hallway and occasionally looking over Samantha's shoulder, Ella did just fine. She'd squat, push one out and lick them clean, then have a rest while Samantha carefully cut the umbilical cord, sterilised it and tied it off with dental floss. Then another would come and the process would start all over again. It was like a puppy production line.

The last one was half the size of the rest, but had my markings exactly. He struggled to get between the others lined up on Ella's teats, but with a little help from Samantha finally made it and by about three in the morning it was all over. Samantha cleaned Ella up, made sure that all the towels were new and that Ella had something to eat (prime stuff, none of the normal rubbish) as well as a bowl of water nearby, though not so close that the puppies could crawl into it. After that they sat with us and watched the puppies feed and wriggle close into their mother for warmth in the dim light for a while, their faces wreathed in smiles.

Thursday, November 19
I know that male dogs aren't supposed to care much for their offspring, but I stayed with Ella for most of the day, looking at the five little dogs we'd made with my mate-for-life curled around them. Occasionally I'd lean over and sniff them. Brand new and soft as feathers.

Friday, November 20
The Owner and Samantha have named the puppies. As I feared, Monkey Boy is set in his ways and out came his compendium of great poets again. He thinks having dogs named after wordsmiths makes him sound intellectual, though anyone who's ever spent more than thirty seconds with him knows he's got the intellectual capacity of the average toaster. The fact that even Coleridge outwitted him for six months speaks volumes.

The females are called Shelley, Aphra and Maya. One of the males is called Eliot and the little one with my markings is Marvell. The last one isn't too bad actually. Marvell, son of Blake the Wonder Dog, has a good ring to it.

Ella was taken to the vet's for a check to make sure there wasn't anything left inside and has been pronounced fit and well, but otherwise hasn't left the pups all day. All they do is suckle and sleep though, and the fascination wore off for me after looking at them for twelve hours straight. I woofed at them a bit to let them know that

I was their dad and therefore to be obeyed at all times, but they didn't take much notice and Ella eventually told me to leave them alone. Frankly, it was a relief to work off some energy with my twiggy pal in the garden.

Saturday, November 21
Scottie was in the wasteland this evening and got all misty-eyed when I told him about the pups, but not for long.

'Noo we're all ready fer tae teach yon human a lesson he willnae forgit.'

I tried one last time to reason with him. 'Scottie,' I woofed, 'are you sure about this? Attacking a human is a serious crime, we could all be exterminated.'

'Och, it willnae come tae that, an' ah cannae rest until ah see that bastid treed.'

I farted quietly, then said, 'OK, Scottie, you round up C.R.A.P. and tell me when to be ready.'

'Aye, ah will do, and gi' Ella a sniff fer me.'

All too soon, he's going to find out there's no C.R.A.P. left. Suddenly I don't feel so clever after all.

Sunday, November 22
I am a traitor, the worst of all possible feelings for a dog. Scottie showed up in the wasteland again tonight, looking listless and broken, his tail drooping.

'C.R.A.P. is nae more, Blake,' he whined. 'An' they tell me 'twas your idea tae get thum back in the den.'

For a moment I considered denying it, but couldn't find it in me. 'Yes, Scottie,' I woofed. 'I was trying to save us all from the pound.'

'An' become Top Dog agin in the process, eh?'

I should have realised it would take him like this. My own tail was now between my legs and I was on my belly. 'Sorry Scottie, I just wanted to . . .'

'Och, dinnae bother, Blake. Scottie's too aild tae be Top Dug. I ken whut ye're doin'. I ken ye didnae really lose that scrap we hud, jest made it look like it. Kent all along ah wasnae really Top Dug.'

'No, Scottie, it's not like that.'

'Ah, yes it is, Blake. Ah've bin a foolish aild dug. Thinkin' Lolly might love a stupid aild mutt like me. Tryin' tae feel young wi' all them bitches. Ye take ye're place at the top o' the pack agin, an' ah'll get oot yer way.'

I tried to stop him, but Scottie shuffled off with his Owner, the two of them suddenly looking as ancient as each other.

As they left he looked back at me and barked, 'Ah can feel mah doom, Blake. Look aftir Lolly fer me when ah'm gone, and Coleridge.'

Monday, November 23

Tried to shake the horrible feeling of betrayal by being extra assiduous in my guarding of Charlotte today and spending lots of time with the puppies, but nothing I could do would shift it. Looked so miserable that even the Owner noticed and, as noted previously, he's not renowned for his powers of observation.

The ear scratch and 'Cheer up, boy', didn't make me feel any better at all, my balls had lost their sedative power, even Ella's backside didn't console.

Tuesday, November 24

A crispy, frosty day. Charlotte was wrapped up warm and the humans took me to the park where we joined Jack, Molly and Lolly for a walk. Ella stayed at home with the pups. It was the kind of day I love; sunny and cold enough to make a dog look like a steam engine streaking across the white grass, but I stayed by Charlotte's pushchair. No sign of Scottie, though plenty of other dogs were there.

'What's the matter, Blake?' Lolly woofed at me after a while. 'You're not yourself.'

'No,' I whined. 'I'm a traitor, a turncoat.'

And I told her the whole story, from throwing the fight with Scottie to making sure that C.R.A.P. deserted him. When it was over Lolly looked at me and said, 'You did all that for me, Blake? You *are* a Wonder Dog. You were quite right though, no dog should put their life in jeopardy again on my account, so I'm glad you stopped it, but you are a bit dim.'

For some reason, being called dim made me feel ever so slightly better, but I couldn't help asking her why. 'Because all you had to do was tell me and I'd have made sure that Scottie didn't go anywhere near that brute of a human.'

'But what about trying to become Top Dog again?'

Lolly looked at me, her newly working eyes shining. 'I'm no

expert on wolf behaviour, Blake, but as I understand it scheming and fighting for the alpha position is part of our inherited nature.'

She's right, of course. I just hope Scottie learns to see it that way.

Wednesday, November 25
Molly and Lolly came over to see the puppies and sat with them for hours. Being Molly she couldn't help dishing out advice that no one really needed. Both Samantha and the Owner can, in fact, read and had already acquainted themselves with a working knowledge of the optimum temperature for a newborn puppy, how to tell if it was dehydrated, signs of sickness, etc. Nevertheless they let her prattle on about trimming the pups' toenails so that they didn't hurt Ella while suckling, wiping their bottoms with damp cotton wool to induce urinating and a load of other stuff that was of very little interest to me. Basically, so long as they're warm, seem to be feeding happily and aren't puking all over the place then there's not a lot anyone can do but watch entranced as the little fluffballs wriggle around.

Thursday, November 26
Ella has her own food at the moment and is eating three or four times a day. Her stuff looks and smells like the fare that Lolly describes getting all the time. I can smell wafts of it from time to time and it has me salivating like that Pavlov man. Who would have thought that humans were capable of such culinary heights. I've tasted the Owner's attempts at lasagne once or twice and, frankly, would rather stick to the lips-and-arseholes diet. I might have guessed that I wouldn't be invited to sample Ella's decent dinners, though. Same old muck for the proud father.

Friday, November 27
Looking at Ella to make sure it was OK, Samantha picked little Marvell up and put him in the palm of her hand where his head bobbed and weaved. 'Isn't he adorable?' she said.

'Yes, that's why we're keeping him,' the Owner replied.

'We are? That's news to me.'

'But look, he's just like Blake.'

'And perhaps you could explain why that's a recommendation.'

At that point Samantha's finger must have gently brushed Marvell's bottom. He peed over her hand liberally.

The Owner's right, he is just like me.

'You seriously want another puppy after all we've been through this year?' Samantha asked.

'So long as it's that one, yes.' The Owner picked him gently out of Samantha's palm and held him to his face. 'Who's a widdle cutie den?' he lisped. Marvell peed again, baptising the Owner in puppy urine and thus sealing the Owner–puppy contract in time-honoured fashion. He *is* a widdle cutie. Samantha too had succumbed to his charms, even while wiping her hand on the Owner's shirt.

'Oh, all right then. I just hope there's more of Ella in him than this idiot,' she said, scratching my head.

Saturday, November 28

Haven't seen anything of Scottie or his Owner recently, and neither has Lolly. She's getting worried, as usually her and Molly get to the park around the same time as him every day. He hasn't been at the wasteland either and his scent markings are old and weak. Felt another pang of guilt. When I see him again, I'm going to make sure that as far as I'm concerned he's Top Dog for life.

After a particularly trying week of ferrying them to the shops, the Owner has drawn up a rota for shopping with the local elderly. No longer is he to be disturbed at any time of the day or night with their constant demand for biscuits and incontinence items. From now on the Supermarket Express leaves promptly at 6 p.m. on a Tuesday, after my walk, and all purchases must be made within ninety minutes. Any stragglers will be left to shuffle home under their own steam.

Sunday, November 29

Jack was in the park again with Molly and Lolly today and this time the two humans were clutching hands. Lolly reports that the policeman has been spending a lot of time at Molly's den. I hope he knows what he's getting into. Although I will always be grateful to Molly for the part she played in bringing the pups into the world, she's still got her 'views' about neutering, and I'd hate for poor Jack to find himself being wheeled along to the vet's for the operation.

Monday, November 30

Still no sign of Scottie and meanwhile the humans are taking all the fun out of being a father. As mentioned previously, your wolf dad plays a very active role in bringing up his offspring, and I tried to get involved by regurgitating some food into the corner of their bed. Ella appreciated my trying, even if they are a bit too young for solids yet, but the Owner and Samantha kicked up an enormous fuss about my old-fashioned parenting techniques.

In high dudgeon I had to content myself with guarding Charlotte. At least she rewarded me with giggles and pulling my ear all afternoon.

DECEMBER

Tuesday, December 1

I have declared a state of emergency. It has been over a week since Scottie was last seen and there's not been a whiff of fresh urine since then either. As his beta I have been unanimously appointed Acting Top Dog with all necessary powers for search and – if necessary – rescue. Top Dog again, just as I planned. It's a hollow victory and I'd happily sacrifice all my executive power for one sniff of the little Westie, no matter what he'd been eating.

Wednesday, December 2

My first act as Top Dog was to form the Scottie Hunt and Investigation Team from the dogs of Canine Rescue And Protection and give them a bloodhound mission to find him. Razor is heading the squad. I was surprised when he volunteered. The pit bull said it was because he has come to like and respect Scottie. 'He's got balls,' he barked, with just a note of wistfulness.

Thursday, December 3

The Scottie Hunt and Investigation Team has nothing to report. We need to widen the search, but now most dogs are inside at night our resources are spread whippet-thin. However, Razor and Constable still have access to the outside world at night using the Red technique. I have ordered them to begin searching at Scottie's den and report back as soon as possible.

Friday, December 4

Still no scent of Scottie. Razor and Constable visited his den under cover of darkness and while they found plenty of evidence of the two puppies Edina and Jock, there was nothing to suggest Scottie lived there but a few tattered 'Lost Dog' posters along the street. Lolly is beside herself with worry.

'Blake,' she whined, 'I've got to find him. What was that plan for getting out of the den? Something about ruining the furniture . . .'

'Don't even think about it, Lolly. This is my fault, and I'll find Scottie,' I woofed in reply.

'But how?'

I looked at her sternly. 'Who should you whistle for when things go astray?' I asked.

Saturday, December 5

Wonder Dog or not, I have no idea where Scottie could be or how to find him. Fortunately, I do have a trusty sidekick, even if she is currently being suckled half to death. At the rate little Marvell is going, I'll be lucky if there's anything left of my mate by the end of the week but a dry husk with five puppies hanging off it.

I hadn't wanted to worry her while she has her paws full of pups, but the situation has become so serious that after the humans had gone to bed I confided in Ella. When I'd finished, she looked up at me with her soulful eyes and said, 'I bet I know where he is.'

I nearly peed when she told me her suspicions, but there's only one way to find out if she's right, and only one dog to undertake such a mission. I have to get to Lolly's old yard. Ella thinks that Scottie tried to avenge her on his own, and is either being held there against his will or has met an untimely end at Lolly's ex-Owner's hands.

Whether it's to be rescue or revenge the consequences may be dire, but I feel the hand of destiny tugging at my lead and shouting 'heel'. Obedience may not be my strongest suit, but when destiny whistles, the Wonder Dog leaps into action.

Sunday, December 6

There's been no opportunity to raise the forces of the Scottie Hunt and Investigation Team and there's no time to spare. Scottie is in danger and it's my job to rescue him. All my attempts to slip away today came to naught. It's been raining and I've been stuck inside. Since Charlotte was born Samantha and the Owner have stepped up security and the door is now usually locked. As I write this I am preparing to resort to desperate measures. This may be my last diary entry so before I launch what could be my last plan I am going to snuffle the puppies and take a final sniff of Ella.

Monday, December 7

Success. Scottie is saved, though even now my Photofit picture may be hanging in every police station in the country.

I said my goodbyes to Ella, then, steeling myself, I took position in the middle of the Owner's favourite rug, looked at him with the Eyes of I Really Don't Want to Be Doing This, squatted, raised my tail and squeezed out the biggest poo I could manage while Samantha and the Owner looked on in stunned silence. Looking round anxiously at the results I was quite proud despite the circumstances. You'd have needed to establish a base camp or two before making an assault on the peak.

The humans continued to stare at me, their mouths hanging open for what felt like an eon, so for good measure I cocked my leg and peed on the coffee table. I hadn't got halfway through before the Owner leaped into action, shouting, 'Blake, you disgusting hound' and grabbing me by the collar. I was dragged through the entrance hall and into the kitchen, leaving a trail of urine behind me, and unceremoniously dumped outside.

In the wet dusk I walked to the end of the garden, turned and ran for the side gate. Beneath my coat, muscles of steel coiled and sent me scrambling over the gate to freedom. It took less than five minutes to reach the alley and woof gently by the fence where once C.R.A.P. gathered nightly. Ella's guess proved to be right. There came an answering groan with an unmistakable accent.

'Blake, is that ye?'

'Scottie? Are you all right?'

His bark was weak, but all Scottie. 'Aye, Blake, havin' the time o' mah life. Remind me tae spend mah holidays in a chicken-wire cage iviry year frae noo oan.'

My nose found the hole in the fence, but it was still blocked. I reared up and put a paw on the handle to the gate. It opened and I was through. My relief evaporated completely and was replaced by a cold hard fury as I spied my old friend lying in Lolly's old cage. Even through his matted fur I could see his ribs, and they were rising and falling with difficulty. Straining, he lifted his head and peered at me.

I've often considered what it must be like to be a proper wolf and at that moment I think I experienced it. All the memories of Lolly returned, her dreadful mange, her being kept caged on a bed of faeces; the poison her Owner had put out without a care for which animal ate it; his kicking of Scottie. And now my best friend in the same cage and looking like death. Thought vanished to be replaced by a primitive killer instinct.

'Och, the shame,' Scottie whimpered. 'Rescued by a bluidy Wonder Dog.'

I just managed to bark back, 'Hold on Scottie,' and then I was on the cage in a flurry of teeth and claws. Never have I been possessed of such violence. Not even in those old fights with Razor. Gripping chicken wire between my teeth I tore the cage from side to side while Scottie bounced around inside. He was singing my theme tune in what I considered a sardonic manner. Wood cracked beneath my jaws and wire tore under my shredding claws. In fact, Lolly's ex-Owner, the dog torturer, chose exactly the wrong moment to rush out of the door and swing a boot at me. I turned and he stepped back, stopped in his tracks at the sight of my dripping fangs, hackles like coat hangers and flattened ears. There was a moment of stillness as he stared into my crazed eyes and then he made for the door. Unfortunately for him, four legs are quicker than two and I leaped past him and turned again, snarling savagely.

Distantly I could hear barking, Scottie yapping, 'Nae, dinnae do it, Blake. Get away wi' ye,' but I paid no attention, just began slowly, stiffly, stalking my prey, which began walking backwards towards the gate, holding his hands out in front of him and whining pitifully, 'Good boy, nice dog.' I was way beyond Good Boy now, though. Ten thousand years of ingrained respect of humans evaporated in the face of this monster who abuses dogs.

He turned to run and I pounced in pursuit, jumping forward as he approached the gate and sinking my teeth into the fleshiest part I could reach. Fabric tore, he howled and stepped up the pace, dragging me behind him. There was nowhere for him to run to but a tree at the end of the alley and he made for it at top speed with me close behind, jumping into it as once again my teeth fastened and ripped another great hole.

Gibbering with fear he climbed into the branches as I rested my paws on the trunk and snarled after him. As he started calling for help I heard a tired yapping beside me.

'Ah think that'll dae, Blake, calm doon noo.' I looked down and saw Scottie beside me. Still in a blaze of rage I snarled again.

'Noo that's whut ah call revenge, an' look, ye were right. Spotty underpants.'

I glared at him, still barking a savage war cry, but gradually sense returned. 'Such a cliché,' I growled.

'Aye,' woofed Scottie, 'ye should bite him fae crimes against originality.'

I agreed wholeheartedly and turned my head to bark furiously up the tree again.

'Blake, ah wus jestin'. Shut up noo, we huv tae get oot o' here.'

The red mist was clearing. I dropped my paws from the trunk of the tree and under the lights that were coming on along the alley I slowly walked Scottie away from his prison. To keep his spirits up I led him in another rousing chorus of the theme tune, this time sung as it ought to be.

Our progress was slow but he finally made it back to his den and collapsed gratefully on to the front step. Pausing only to alert Edina and Jock with a bark I slipped away into the night and back to my cold shed.

Tuesday, December 8

Stuck in the shed most of the day apart from two walks. It's probably the best place for me, the desperate fugitive. My sphincter goes every time I hear a siren, which will not please the Owner when he comes to clear the garden again. I'm wondering if I can perform plastic surgery on myself with a trowel. Unfortunately, I seem to be incapable of growing a moustache. I have, however, managed to disguise my patchy coat by rolling in the muddy flowerbeds.

Wednesday, December 9

Still in disgrace. In vain did I deploy Human Whimpering, and Ella sat by the door staring at me shivering outside to no avail. The penalty for Rug Soiling is banishment for life with no chance of parole and an extra sentence has been added on for ruining the flowerbeds. Meanwhile Charlotte goes unguarded and the puppies are growing up fast without their father. As I watched through the glass, Shelley, Eliot and Marvell heard the call of the wild and made their own first break for freedom. They got as far as the kitchen before realising that it wasn't the wild calling, but nature. Pretty soon the kitchen floor was swimming in pee and poo, and all they got was a gentle scolding and a lift back to their bed. Poor Blake, sitting out in the rain and staring in mournfully, got a stern look and another 'Bad Dog'.

Thursday, December 10
No park again and just an icy hose down to report. Scottie wasn't on the wasteland so I still don't even know if he's all right. Not feeling much like a Wonder Dog at the moment. Lying by the back door in the rain with muzzle on paws is not the kind of reward that I anticipated when I started the job. By rights I should have my own TV show by now, more trips to the grooming parlour than Constable, a jewelled collar and a genuine catskin doggie coat. I'm beginning to wonder if being a plain old 'dog' isn't a better alternative. Right now I'd definitely trade a life-size bronze statue for a warm sofa by the fire and a scratch behind the ears.

Friday, December 11
Thank Dog the Owner finally relented and took us to the park. Mainly because Miss Meddling was on the doorstep at the break of dawn with Coleridge on his lead. Even Ella was dragged away from the puppies for an hour. The first thing I did was check the gatepost and it was a joy to sniff the somewhat malodorous scent of elderly West Highland Scots terrier. As soon as the lead was snapped off I bounded into the park to find Scottie, with Coleridge and Ella close behind me.

We found him escorting Lolly on a walk around the pond. The two of them spotted us and for a while there was just a scrum of happy noses and bums. Scottie is still looking the worse for wear after his ordeal, but only has a few bruises and a touch of malnourishment. His Owner is giving him the special dog food on an hourly basis, which means of course that I am now the only dog in the park still on the by-product diet.

Lolly jumped me like a cat on steroids, barking out my theme tune, and even Scottie growled his thanks. When we were alone for a couple of seconds he yapped softly, 'Ye should huv seen yersel', Blake. Like some kind o' wild animal ye were. Almost . . .'

'Lupine?' I suggested.

'Loopy, aye that's it. Like a mad ferret.'

I shook my head, but I'm used to Scottie now, and this was high praise indeed. 'It was my fault you were there in the first place.'

Lolly trotted up and sniffed the Westie happily. 'No it wasn't, Blake, Scottie is an idiot and you rescued him from a fate worse than death. Did you say thank you to Blake the Wonder Dog properly, Scottie?'

Scottie hung his head and mumbled something.

Lolly barked, 'What was that?'

'Thank ye, Blake the Wonder Dug,' Scottie yapped querulously.

My tongue unfurled happily. 'That's all right, bounding to the rescue with a hip-hip-hurray is second nature.'

'Aye hip bluidy hurray,' Scottie whuffed.

We made our way back to the Owner and I found him in conversation with Scottie's. Mr McCormick was telling my human that Scottie had miraculously returned during the evening a couple of days previously after an absence of two weeks and that he was sure he spotted me disappearing down the street when he opened the door. The Owner gave me a funny look.

Saturday, December 12

I was let back inside the den for a few minutes today while Jack came round to pick out a puppy. He has to wait two more weeks until they are fully weaned, but instantly fell in love with Maya. While he sat and played with her on his lap he told the Owner a story that almost made me soil the rug again. A few nights previously a man had come into the police station with the seat of his trousers ripped out, demanding that a police marksman shoot a mad dog that was loose in town. Jack had recognised the address that the Owner had given him after rescuing Lolly and had taken a look around the next day. In the backyard he had come across the mangled remains of a chicken-wire cage and a box of rat poison.

'The funny thing was,' Jack finished, 'he described the dog that attacked him and it sounded exactly like Blake here.'

Any moment now, I thought. The muzzle is going to come out and I'll be led away to death row. Meanwhile the Owner sat deep in thought for a moment, then said slowly, 'That's impossible. Blake hasn't left the house in weeks except for walks.'

'That's what I thought,' said Jack. He reached over and stroked me. 'You wouldn't hurt anyone, would you, Wonder Dog?'

I could have licked the pair of them, so I did, spreading best drool liberally over their precious monkey heads. After Jack had gone the

Owner checked in my mouth and found my gums scratched and torn where I'd bitten through the chicken wire. 'No,' he whispered. 'It's just not possible. You're as dumb as a brick.'

Nevertheless, that night I was back on the sofa. As I settled down, I gave praise to Dog for my deliverance and swore that if destiny ever whistled again, it would find me running in the opposite direction. To your own nature be true and all of that.

Sunday, December 13

Everything is back to normal in the den, though the Owner keeps looking at me strangely and muttering, 'If you're Lassie I'm an orang-utan.' He's not far out, except of course orang-utans are considered to be the most intelligent of primates. He'd be more a chimpanzee.

Monday, December 14

Another blissful day on the sofa with my legs splayed and twitching while puppies scampered around me. Now they have started eating solid food as well as their mother's milk they are a lot more mobile and are also learning the basics of life, which means scrapping for dominance with each other, bless their little hearts. Had an unpleasant dream about being caught by the tail by a maniacal postman and started awake to find Marvell hanging from it by his teeth. In her chair opposite Charlotte gurgled happily as I fell off the sofa in the confusion.

Tuesday, December 15

With pure-breed dogs it's possible to some extent to judge what sort of personality it will develop as it grows older. Great Danes are known for being placid, West Highland Scots terriers for being smelly little tyrants, Old English sheepdogs for operating on two or three brain cells, and so on and so forth. With the mixed breed it's more difficult to tell what part of their genetic inheritance is going to float to the surface, but now the puppies are getting a little older it's becoming possible to make out their emerging characters. Maya is a fighting, chewing, peeing little thug while Shelley errs towards being a peeing, chewing, fighting little vandal. Eliot and Aphra share common traits in that they are both hooligans with a talent for chewing, peeing and fighting. Marvell, on the other paw, is much more like me.

Wednesday, December 16

The Owner is slowing down work for Christmas and took Ella and me to the park where I received my second hero's welcome of the year. The assembled dogs of C.R.A.P. and the Scottie Hunt and Investigation Team gambolled around me barking the theme tune. It was all a bit embarrassing really, especially when Scottie walked forward. He looked a bit reluctant, but Lolly pushed him with her nose while he yelped, 'All right, ah'm daein' it, ah'm daein' it.'

He turned to face me and then barked imperiously, 'Blake, it hus recently come tae mah attention that ah owe ye . . .' He trailed off.

'My life,' yipped Lolly happily.

'Aye, that. And Lolly tae. Plus, ye took a well-deserved nip oot o' a known dug abuser. In recognition o' ye services tae dugs ah'm formally makin' ye Top Dug o' the park agin.'

'And?' Lolly yapped again.

'And pronouncin' ye official . . .' There followed some unintelligible low growling.

'Go on, Scottie,' Lolly cut in again encouragingly.

'Och, tae howl wi' it. Pronouncin' ye official Wonder Dug. There, ah said it. Are ye happy noo, Lolly?'

In answer she just banged her tail on the ground.

Overwhelmed, I sat in the middle of the sea of dogs all barking congratulations. After a while I woofed for silence. When the reception committee had come to order I looked around and at my little Scottish friend.

'Thanks and all that,' I woofed, 'but I respectfully decline.'

There was a shocked silence. A dog near the back cut in, barking, 'Brilliant, can I have a go then? I like being on top.' It was Constable.

'No, Constable. Though you are stout of heart, solid of head and indefatigable of loins, I had another dog in mind.'

Every dog looked at me expectantly. I walked forward and lay at Scottie's feet in submission. 'Can anyone think of a better dog than Scottie to lead the pack?' I barked.

There was an enthusiastic chorus of barking around me, and Scottie was unanimously re-elected. He looked at me and softly barked, 'Thank ye, Blake, but ah'll chew mah oan balls oaf afore ah call ye "Wonder Dug" agin.'

'That's all right, I'm giving up the Wonder Dog business. The hours are terrible and frankly the quality of rescuees has dropped sharply recently.'

'Ye dinnae say? There's sich a word as "rescuees" then is there?'

Thursday, December 17

The Owner put an advert in the local newspaper last week and today a couple of humans came to see the puppies. Ella tried her hardest to make them behave but they spent the entire time rolling over each other, attacking and yipping, and didn't take a bit of notice of their prospective new Owners, which bodes well for the future.

The Owner was quite stern, making sure the humans weren't just looking for a Christmas present and asking them to donate money to a dog charity for each dog to ensure that they were serious. He also asked a lot of questions about their experience with dogs, their lifestyles and the quality of life the puppies could expect. Coming from someone whose idea of a decent meal is minced roadkill I found his interrogation faintly hypocritical. Nevertheless, he eventually seemed satisfied and Shelley and Eliot now have a home to go to in a couple of weeks. In the meantime, I am getting a little fed up of scrapping puppies underpaw, attacking my ears and climbing over me while I try to sleep.

Friday, December 18

Curiously Scottie hasn't disbanded the Scottie Hunt and Investigation Team. I pointed out to him that he wasn't that difficult to find now, all too easy in fact, but this hasn't put him off.

'There could be a parcel o' dugs oot there that need rescuin' frae bad humans ye ken, Blake, there's always a place fae S.H.I.T. in the park. An' if needs be C.R.A.P will follow.'

He paused for a moment, his little head to one side. 'O' course, noo we'll be needin' a new Wonder Dug.'

'Any ideas?'

'Aye,' he yapped. 'Ah always fancied a statue, somethin' classy in bronze, ye ken. An' ah huv mah wee collection o' tartan coats whut'll make grand capes. Scottie the Wonder Dug hus a good ring tae it, de ye noat ken?'

For once eloquence failed me.

Saturday, December 19

The Owner spent the day putting up decorations as a surprise for Samantha who had taken Charlotte on a visit. It would have been an easier task if puppies had not been climbing all over bags and boxes and pulling at Christmas tree branches with their teeth. Also if the Owner hadn't taken the opportunity of being Charlotte-free to help himself to the stock of Christmas wine that Samantha had bought. After he had been buried in the tree for the fourth time (twice puppies, twice his own drunken ineptitude) the youngsters were banished to the kitchen, which is much the best place for them. Preferably inside the oven. I'm beginning to see the point in Koreans. Even Ella was relieved that they had to continue their yapping and scrapping elsewhere. It may be a valuable part of their socialisation, but it's a complete pain in the backside.

As yuletide peace descended the gate squeaked and I was instantly at the door, warning off the intruder. Unfortunately, it was Miss Meddling, who appears to be deaf to ferocious barking as well as everything else. No one is immune to a nose in the groin though, and I stuck it in with vigour until the Owner pulled me off.

He opened his mouth to speak, but Meddling got there before him. Handing over a large bag she said, 'I noticed you were putting up your decorations so I brought you these to put under your tree. They're from all of us you've been taking to the shops.'

'What a surprise, thank you. And what are you doing for Christmas, Miss Meddling?'

'Fanny.'

'You're doing what?'

'You may call me Fanny.'

'Oh, yes. How could I forget. So will you be having Christmas Fanny, funny? I mean funny, Fanny?' The Owner took a deep breath. 'Will you be having fun this Christmas, Fanny?'

'Are you drunk?'

'No, no, just practising with a glass of wine.'

'Well, in answer to your question, it will just be me and Bobby this year. My sister is going away.'

'I see.'

'And in answer to your other question, yes I will join you for a small glass of wine. It is Christmas, after all.'

Sunday, December 20

Who would have thought an old lady could drink so much. By the time they had finished the Owner virtually had to crawl to the door to let her out. He also had some news for Samantha when she returned.

'You did what?' she shouted for the fifth time.

'Please stop shouting,' he replied, clutching his head. 'I invited Miss Meddling . . . Fanny . . . for Christmas.'

'After all she's done this year? How drunk were you? And Jack and Molly are already coming.'

'I couldn't help it, she's going to be all alone and she kept pouring wine into me. And her wig kept slipping over to one side. It confused me.'

'A likely story.'

'Ask Blake, she was drinking like a drain.'

'Well, I suppose if she's going to be on her own . . . but you could have asked me first.' Samantha paused. 'We'll have to buy her a present, too.'

The humans looked at each other and as one said, 'Knickers.'

Monday, December 21

Constable had a busy autumn and his Mistress has had twelve telephone calls confirming pregnancies. At a conservative average of five puppies per litter this means there will soon be sixty more Constables in the world, enough to lower the canine intelligence average by a small but significant amount. I put this to him, and he looked at me seriously for a moment, before replying, 'I had a sausage last Tuesday.' Then he ran off to jump in the pond again.

Tuesday, December 22

Found Scottie alone in the park today and fell in next to him, shortening my graceful lope to suit his asthmatic pace. After the nasal preliminaries I looked down at him. There was a question that had been bothering me for some time now.

'Scottie, just how did you get banished from the den so quickly when we were forming C.R.A.P.? It took the other dogs at least a week of pooing and peeing.'

'Och, ye dinnae wunt tae ken, Blake.'

'But I do, and seeing as how I saved your life I figure you owe me.'

Scottie sighed and stopped. 'Ye huv a point, but it's no' a moment o' which ah'm prood.'

'You can trust me to keep it under my tail.'

He looked at me sharply, 'Aye, like ah can trust ye noat tae try fae Top Dug as soon as mah back is turned.'

'You said you knew all along I threw that fight.'

'Aye, but if ye're stupit enough tae gie it away, wull whut's an aild dug tae do?'

'I prefer to think of it as a noble gesture and one that guaranteed you'd help Lolly.'

'Aye, ah figured as much. Ah'd huv come tae help her eventually, ye ken?'

'At the time we were desperate,' I gruffed. 'You can't blame me for trying for Top Dog again when she was free.'

'Ah knew ye'd gie it straight back though: "Ooooh, Blake, ah'm a puir geriatric dug, mah doom is comin".'

'You were making that up?'

'O' course. Ah played ye like a wee dug-sized violin.'

'Talking about stupid, you went after that human on your own.'

'Aye,' Scottie growled. 'I admit ah let mah thirst fae revenge get the better o' me oan that one. Ye did well wi' the pants an' the tree there, Blake. Ah might even gie ye one o' thum wee beta nicknames.'

Before I could stop it my tail started wagging. I stopped it immediately but the damage was already done.

'Ah kent ye'd like that, ye big haggis.'

'Anyway,' I said stiffly. 'The exit strategy, if you please.'

'Och, all right. So there ah wus oan the sofa as usual tryin' tae think o' the most effective place tae defecate. Mah aild Master wus havin' a plate o' curry an' a glass o' beer, when the phone rang. Noo ah'm a trustworthy dug an' Edina an' Jock were oot the back, so he jist put the plate o' curry an' the glass o' beer oan the floor while he went tae answer it.' Scottie stopped.

'Then what?'

'It wus a plate o' curry an' a glass o' beer. Dae ah huv tae draw ye a picture?'

I thought about it. 'You ate the curry and drank the beer?'

'Aye, that's right, Blake.' His Master began whistling and Scottie turned to go. Looking back over his shoulder he barked, 'Ye really are dim, ye ken.'

Wednesday, December 23

The last puppy has been chosen. Aphra is going to live with a female human along the street so we will still see plenty of her. In the meantime Samantha took them all to the vet's for a check-up and some injections. Her reward for watching over their health? An afternoon scrubbing out the back of the car. As a new mother herself I'm surprised she hasn't seen the sense in fitting them all with their own nappies.

The rest of the day was a mess of torn wrapping paper and puppies and Samantha getting confused about whose present was whose as the Owner had just aimlessly thrown all the boxes onto the shelf in the cupboard under the stairs.

Thursday, December 24

'Twas the night before Christmas and all through the house, not a creature was stirring except for five puppies causing total bedlam, Charlotte screaming and the Owner cursing as he tried to wrap last-minute presents. As I tried to dislodge Marvell's teeth from my ear for the eighth time, I found myself getting nostalgic for the old days in the shed with just the sound of Coleridge humping Miss Meddling's girdle to soothe us to sleep.

Friday, December 25

Christmas Day started well with a frosty walk to the park with the Owner. Samantha's dinner was a masterpiece and my bowl was filled with succulent white meat, stuffing, gravy and sprouts. Afterwards, Miss Meddling began farting quietly, so I slipped in a few of my own and was gratified when she apologised for the smell on my behalf.

The real fun came after lunch though with present giving. It took about an hour to get through just Charlotte's, during which she fell asleep, then Samantha presented Jack, Molly and Miss Meddling with gift-wrapped boxes. The latter opened hers with an expression of delight, but she was nonplussed when she opened the lid.

'Is it a hat?' she asked.

The Owner looked over her shoulder while filling her glass. 'No, that would be a sleeping tortoise,' he slurred. 'More wine?'

'Yes, please. What am I supposed to do with a tortoise?'

'I have no idea,' he replied owlishly. 'Samantha, why did we buy Miss Meddling a sleeping tortoise? I thought we said knickers.'

'Oh, for crying out loud, it's Crusty Bob. I just got the boxes mixed up. It's your fault for throwing them in the cupboard like that.'

'So these aren't for me then?' asked Jack, holding up a pair of knickers that could have doubled as a parachute.

The *pièce de résistance*, however, came when Miss Meddling distributed the gifts from the Owner's senior shopping group.

'And this one's for you from Delia Ramsay,' said Miss Meddling, handing the Owner a long slim package, which he blithely unwrapped while trying to drink more wine.

As the paper fell away Samantha gasped, Molly giggled and the Owner spat wine over his precious rug.

'Oh, what a beauty,' said Miss Meddling.

In the Owner's hand was my dream chew toy. A replica of my old friend Mr Wobbly, which I stole from our ex-neighbour last year. The same neighbour who left the magazines and treats in the shed. If anything though this model came with even more knobs and buttons and gizmos.

The Owner was aghast. 'Do you know what this is, Miss Meddling?'

'Of course. It's a chew toy. Bobby has lots, but none as big as that. It would keep him going for weeks.'

The Owner got the same wicked look in his eyes as when he saw Jack's hand-stitched Italian leather shoes. 'I tell you what,' he said. 'I'll swap it for your tortoise.'

It was sad for me to see it leave the house, but I know that Coleridge will appreciate it.

Saturday, December 26

A long pack walk in the park, this time accompanied by Miss Meddling and Coleridge, as well as Jack, Molly and Lolly. After a strained year, the humans all seem to be getting on better. If they'd just spent some time sniffing each other's anal glands to begin with I'm betting that a lot of this year's problems would have been avoided. As a way of really getting to know someone it's second to none.

Miss Meddling received some strange looks having brought Coleridge's new toy along to play fetch with. For some reason the sight of an old woman with a foot-long, whirring and wriggling rubber thingy was the subject of raised eyebrows and shocked gasps. You'd have thought no one had ever seen a chew toy before.

Sunday, December 27

In view of Scottie's pretensions of Wonder Dogginess, as a final apology for my betrayal I've been working on a little surprise for him, and premiered it at the wasteland this evening. It's a catchy little number, which really needs a marching band of pipers to do it justice, but having Ella, Edina, Jock and Coleridge as my backing barkers was almost as good. It goes:

> Who should ye whistle for when thing's go astray?
> Not Scottie the Wonder Dog,
> If he finds ye at all, it'll take him all day,
> Scottie, the Ger-i-a-tric Wonder Dog . . .

> Who's that . . .
> Smelly old rag?
> Who's so close to death?
> Trembly legs, and terrible breath?
> Yes, it's Scottie, the Ger-i-a-tric Wonder Dog.

> As Heroic Dogs go he's not Blake or even Lassie,
> Scottie the Wonder Dog,
> But he's old and infirm and he's very, very gassy,
> Laird Scotland McIvor of Strathpeffer the Wonder Dog.

And then there's a lengthy farting solo. And repeat chorus to fade.

I have to admit that he didn't enjoy the tribute as much as I'd hoped, but it will probably grow on him when he's heard it around the park a few times.

Monday, December 28

At six weeks the puppies were deemed old enough to leave the den and their respective new Owners came to pick them up today. It was difficult watching them go, their little tails wagging as they were carried away to make their way as trusty guards and valued companions in their own dens. Ella whined and moped in her box, but Samantha cheered her up with some Olympic-level affection and reassured her that all the new Owners lived in town so we should see the puppies in the park. The way Shelley and Eliot were fighting as they left, I wouldn't be at all surprised if they were returned as faulty within a few days. I feel sorry for the new Owners, it's going to be like living with a WWF championship taking place in the den.

At least we've still got Marvell, who is more than enough puppy for anyone. He has already discovered the joy of shoes, but his technique is amateurish. Fortunately, his father is an expert so I could teach him the best way to extract an insole while maximising damage, and – most importantly – the art of hiding the evidence beneath the sofa.

Tuesday, December 29

The den is quiet and peaceful again, at least when Charlotte and Marvell are sleeping, and after all we have been through this year all threat of rehoming seems to have evaporated. I am even allowed to sleep under the Owner's desk again during the day. In appreciation I have gallantly refrained from biting his feet off when he rests them on me.

Ella joined us and lay down next to us. Looking from me to him, she woofed eventually, 'You know, it's true humans do come to resemble their dogs.'

'I'll try and forget you said that,' I replied. I don't like taking my mate-for-life to task, but some insults cannot be ignored.

'No, really. Dumb as a box of toenail clippings, but would help anyone and very affectionate when not rushing about causing mayhem.'

'I suppose that's true, but I don't see what it's got to do with me.'

'I was talking about you, moron.'

Looking up between those two gorgeous legs into his cavernous nostrils I was struck with a wave of love. Perhaps we are alike, and perhaps it's no bad thing. Then I farted. It was just wind after all.

Wednesday, December 30

Hardly through the park gates this morning before Scottie summoned us to a pack meeting. It was another sunny, frosty day so almost all the dogs were there – Razor, Liquorice, Lolly, Barney, Constable, Claude, Fabienne, Choo Choo, Trixie and Ginger. It took a while to work our way through so many bums, but when order had been restored, Scottie barked for attention.

'As ye ken, Blake, it is customary for exceptional betas tae be honoured with a nickname.'

I let my tongue loll in acknowledgement. I liked the sound of 'honoured'.

''Tis a name by which they will be remembered wheriver dugs meet tae discuss the great deeds o' the past.'

My tail wagged. I'm all about 'great deeds'.

Scottie continued. 'Aftir much discussion wi' members o' S.H.I.T. an' C.R.A.P. an' in view o' ye contribution tae rescuin' Lolly an' mahsel' as wull as pioneerin' both the poo-and-pee plan an' the Red technique, we huv decided tae so honour ye.'

At last fame beckoned – my name would live on in the annals of dog history.

Solemnly, Scottie pronounced, 'Frae noo oan, ye wull be known as "Not-Quite-So-Dim-As-Ye-Might-Huv-Thought Blake".'

My jaw dropped, tail stilled.

'Realising that yer full nickname is a wee bit long we huv also agreed oan an abbreviated version. Henceforth ye shall be called "Quite Dim Blake". Long may ye live up tae sich an illustrious title.'

As the pack barked congratulations I somehow got my legs working and chased Scottie all the way into the pond.

Thursday, December 31

The end of another year and a time for looking back and weighing up its successes and failures. On the plus side I have been officially recognised as a Wonder Dog and awarded a beta nickname that will never die. I've also been responsible for rescuing a dog in distress, fathered a litter of puppies, and menaced postmen, old women and sticks more than could be reasonably expected. On the negative the nickname is rubbish (demanding some kind of revenge), the regular steak dinners never materialised as promised, and by some weird mind-control process I seem to have become distressingly obedient, though not to the extent where I've lowered myself to 'fetch'.

All in all it could have been a worse year. Not only did rehoming never happen but, as I reflected, I was lying by the fire with my nose almost inserted in Ella, with Marvell, a tiny version of me, asleep between us. On the sofa the Owner and Samantha were chatting with Charlotte asleep between them. Steak may not be on the menu but the Christmas leftovers have lasted well and it looks like there's at least another few days in the fridge before I'm returned to ground hooves in jelly.

In fact, contentment was so high on the agenda that I had to get up and give the humans a little nuzzle of affection. Samantha stroked my head and said, 'Now Ella's had a litter I suppose we ought to think about getting the dogs neutered.'